BOURDIEU IN ALGERIA

FRANCE OVERSEAS
Studies in Empire and Decolonization

SERIES EDITORS
Philip Boucher, A. J. B. Johnston,
James D. Le Sueur, and Tyler Stovall

BOURDIEU IN ALGERIA

COLONIAL POLITICS,

ETHNOGRAPHIC PRACTICES,

THEORETICAL DEVELOPMENTS

Edited and with an introduction by

Jane E. Goodman and

Paul A. Silverstein

University of Nebraska Press   Lincoln & London

Acknowledgment for previously
published material appears on p. 269,
which constitutes an extension of
the copyright page.

∞

Library of Congress Cataloging-
in-Publication Data
Bourdieu in Algeria : colonial politics,
ethnographic practices, theoretical
developments / edited by Jane E. Goodman
and Paul A. Silverstein.
p. cm.—(France overseas: studies in
empire and decolonization)
Includes bibliographical references and index.
ISBN 978-0-8032-1362-3 (pbk. : alk. paper)
1. Bourdieu, Pierre, 1930–2002—Criticism
and interpretation. 2. Ethnologists—Algeria—
Kabylia—Biography. 3. Ethnology—Algeria—
Kabylia—Fieldwork. 4. Kabyles—Algeria—Social
life and customs. 5. Kabylia (Algeria)—Social life
and customs. I. Goodman, Jane E., 1956–
II. Silverstein, Paul A., 1970–
GN21.B617B68 2009
305.800965—dc22
2009002372

Set in Sabon by Bob Reitz.

CONTENTS

TABLE

ACKNOWLEDGMENTS

This book has been a long time in the making. It originated in 2002 as a panel at the American Anthropological Association's annual meeting titled "Bringing Habitus Home: Reappraising Bourdieu's Studies of Kabylia." Since then, many individuals have contributed to its success. Dale Eickelman believed in the book from the beginning; we are grateful for his vision and guidance. Michael Herzfeld and Stefania Pandolfo offered invaluable comments and strong encouragement. Jeremy Lane provided a critical reading of the entire manuscript; we thank him along with anonymous press reviewers. Heather Lundine and Bridget Barry, our editors at the University of Nebraska Press, have been models of efficiency and a great pleasure to work with. Our series editor, James Le Sueur, infused the project with fresh energy; we thank Jim for including this book in the *France Overseas* series. Finally, we are most grateful to our contributors for their patience as well as for the unique perspective that each brings to bear on Bourdieu's Algerian ethnography.

Earlier versions of several of these chapters appeared elsewhere. We thank the publishers for permission to reprint.

Introduction

Bourdieu in Algeria

PAUL A. SILVERSTEIN AND JANE E. GOODMAN

For over thirty years Pierre Bourdieu's *Esquisse d'une théorie de la pratique* (1972) has been "good to think with," to invoke the famous phrase of Claude Lévi-Strauss. Translated into English and heavily revised, the *Outline of a Theory of Practice* (1977a) remains an anthropological standard, often overshadowing Bourdieu's own subsequent rewritings of the text in *The Logic of Practice* (1990) and *Pascalian Meditations* (2000). The theoretical constructs that Bourdieu developed in this work—most notably, *habitus*, misrecognition, and symbolic domination—have had a long and productive history in social theory and political philosophy. Yet these notions have entered the mainstream of social thought independently of the North African and French political and social contexts in which they were initially developed. Almost independently, that is. For the ethnographic exemplars of Bourdieu's concepts—the Kabyle Berbers of northern Algeria, distantly shadowed by the Béarnais peasants of southwestern France—have tended to accompany the theory that they supposedly incarnate: sometimes persistently reinvoked alongside the constructs that they help to illuminate, other times mere traces of their original embodiment as the ethnographic representatives of Bourdieu's theories. Bourdieu himself would continue to draw on his Kabyle and Béarnais ethnography as the empirical base for his theoretical refinements throughout his career, even to his last publications before his untimely death on January 23, 2002 (see Bourdieu 2001, 2002).

At the same time that *habitus* has made the theoretical rounds, circulating widely across disciplines and geographies to illuminate new contexts and concerns, the politics of scholarship and the poetics of scholarly representation have come under increasing and well-deserved scrutiny (e.g., Clifford and Marcus 1986; Said 1978). Within this substantial literature, the representation of ethnic or indigenous Others as well as the colonial location of much ethnographic research have been subjected to special attention (Asad 1973; see also Cooper and Stoler 1997; Dirks 1992; among others). Bourdieu himself has been lauded for the way in which he "has taught us to ask in what field of power, and in what position in that field, any given author writes" (Rabinow 1986: 252). Yet the colonial location of Bourdieu's work is nearly impossible to discern from the *Outline*, the primary ethnographic study in which the notion of *habitus* was brought to maturity.[1] Bourdieu himself began to speak and write about it only during the final years of his life in publications that by and large appeared posthumously (see Bourdieu 2003a, 2003b, 2004a, 2004b, 2008; Bourdieu et al. 2002; Honneth et al. 1986). While Bourdieu's portrayals of Algerian Kabyles have received some critical attention, such critiques have largely been articulated in theoretical rather than ethnographic terms. For instance, his Kabyle ethnography has been variously evaluated as "occidentalizing" (Reed-Danahay 1995); as underwritten by untenable "dualistic typologies" (Free 1996: 412; cf. Lane 2000: 112); as overly Durkheimian in its presumption of a stark dichotomy between supposedly homogenous and differentiated

2

societies (Herzfeld 1987: 83–86; Free 1996; Lane 2000: 13–16); or as inattentive to national, regional, or colonial contexts (Herzfeld 1987: 7–8; Free 1996). Yet few scholars, to our knowledge, have revisited the ethnographic, historical, and political terrains within which Bourdieu developed his Kabyle corpus.

In this volume scholars of North Africa and France come together to critically reexamine some of Bourdieu's foundational concepts in relation to the ethnographic, intellectual, and political contexts out of which they developed and in which they continue to circulate. Bourdieu's Algerian oeuvre is predicated, we contend, on the colonial setting in which he carried out his research. This context led him to portray Algeria in terms of a profound cleavage: what Bourdieu understood to be an "originary" or precolonial Algerian society is set against a "destructured," ruptured, and fragmented society that 130 years of colonial occupation had irrevocably destabilized. This fault line traverses nearly every aspect of Bourdieu's Algerian ethnography. His books themselves line up along it: whereas the *Outline of a Theory of Practice, The Logic of Practice,* "The Kabyle House," and companion studies portray a traditional Algerian Berber society seemingly untouched by colonial relations, emigration, or capitalism, a corollary set of writings—among them, *Travail et travailleurs en Algérie* (Work and Workers in Algeria, 1963) and *Le Déracinement* (The Uprooting, 1964)—depict an ethnically mixed (Berber and Arab) society fractured by colonial practices of land expropriation, capitalist regimes of labor, and large-scale population "resettlements" that were a key form of control throughout the colonial period, and particularly during the Algerian revolution. The methodologies that drive the two kinds of studies also diverge: whereas the latter set of works are supported by lengthy statistical analyses and extended interviews with named, situated informants,

3

the former are informed by structuralist and symbolic approaches to social behavior, albeit recalibrated to Bourdieu's practice-based theoretical framework. Informants themselves are disjunctively cast. They are quoted at length and highly individualized in the sociological studies, while they remain largely silent in the *Outline* and related works, where they are collapsed into timeless and nameless ethnic figures. The same kind of bifocal lens—focused through the angle of the rupture and fragmentation brought about by modernity—informs Bourdieu's analysis of both his natal province of Béarn (1962a, 1962b, 2002) and his more recent study of neoliberalism in contemporary France, *La Misère du monde* (Bourdieu et al. 1993), which explicitly follows from the earlier *Travail et travailleurs* project (Addi 2002: 38 n. 3; Sayad 2002: 71; Wacquant 2004: 407 n. 16; but see Colonna, this volume).

Our volume begins from this cleavage. In placing Bourdieu's "two Algerias" in productive tension with each other and with his work in Béarn, we seek to unsettle what Loïc Wacquant (1993) has rightly described as a tendency in American scholarship to import discrete aspects of Bourdieu's work while divorcing them from the larger intellectual and political projects in which Bourdieu was engaged. This results, Wacquant contends, in "partial and fractured understandings" and even "systematic misconstrual of [Bourdieu's] thought" (Wacquant 1993: 238–39). While we do not pretend to engage Bourdieu's lifetime scholarly trajectory, we seek to gesture toward the kind of inclusive reading Wacquant calls for by reconnecting the *Outline* and related works to the earlier and little-known set of sociological studies that Bourdieu carried out during the Algerian war as well as in his natal region.

Bourdieu's theories have been productively analyzed elsewhere with regards to their embeddedness in a European philosophical tradition extending from Sartre, Merleau-Ponty, Bachelard, Panofsky, Lévi-Strauss, Canguilhem, and Althusser back to Marx, Durkheim, Mauss, Weber, Sombart, Husserl, and beyond (e.g., Addi 2002; Héran 1987; Lahire 2001; Lane 2000; Pinto 1998; Shusterman 1999; Vandenberghe 1999), as well as in relation to Anglo-American social theory (Calhoun, LiPuma, and Postone 1993). While not neglecting these important trajectories, our primary focus lies with the relationship between theory and ethnography in Bourdieu's work. Bourdieu himself later narrated his development of practice theory as much as an outcome of his academic studies of phenomenology (and particularly his engagement with Husserl and Merleau-Ponty—see Hammoudi, this volume) and his eventual philosophical break with the objectivist approach of anthropological structuralism, as a particular response to the specific problems encountered in the course of his Algerian field research (Honneth et al. 1986: 38–45; Wacquant 2004: 390–91). The authors in this volume are thus specifically concerned with the development of Bourdieu's theoretical project as it relates to at least five specific ethnographic contexts: first, the French-Algerian war,[2] in which Bourdieu himself was directly implicated initially as a member of the French military, and later as an engaged critic of both French colonialism and revolutionary utopianism; second, the ethnolinguistic and religious dimensions of the Kabyle region at the time of Bourdieu's research; third, Bourdieu's involvement with a particular constellation of Berber intellectuals during and after the war—most notably, novelists Mouloud Mammeri and Mouloud Feraoun and sociologist Abdelmalek Sayad; fourth, the transnational Berber Cultural Movement, with which Bourdieu was in dialogue at various points throughout his career; and finally, the resonances between Bourdieu's own upbringing in rural Béarn, his wartime research in Algeria, and his later intellectual life in Paris—including the twin lenses of equilibrium and disjuncture through which he approached socio-spatial oppositions of rural/urban and colony/metropole.

It is easy, with some four decades of hindsight (decades that also witnessed the burgeoning of the field of postcolonial studies), to be critical of Bourdieu's Algerian ethnography. A self-taught ethnographer (Honneth et al. 1986: 38), Bourdieu was learning to do ethnographic research on the fly, at times with machine guns firing around him (Bourdieu 2004: 423). Conducting ethnography of and during wartime conditions,[3] he worked in dangerous and unsettling situations that would discourage most researchers. Bourdieu's strong anticolonial stance and his unswerving advocacy of Algerian independence earned him the confidence of many of those Muslim Algerians he interviewed in Algiers and across the war-torn countryside. It also earned him a place on a Far Right assassination list and led to his precipitated departure from the country under cover of darkness during the final months of the war (Yacine 2004: 491). His work was principled and politically engaged at a time when colonialism was barely in the purview of most anthropologists. Yet our admiration for the intellectual, political, and personal risks Bourdieu took should not preclude critical engagement with his Algerian research. Indeed, such an engagement is long overdue.

Wartime Ethnographer

Writing on Bourdieu's life is a complicated task for, as his longtime translator Richard Nice has remarked, there exist "two versions of Bourdieu's past. One is the mythical one in which he is the peasant boy confronting urban civilization, and the other, which he actually thought more seriously, is what it's like to be a petit bourgeois and a success story" (Mahar 1990, quoted in Reed Danahay 2005: 34). In the case of his wartime years, the retrospective gaze of Bourdieu and his students tends to promote a heroic image of an engaged intellectual battling the twinned distortions of colonialism and nationalist utopianism, risking his personal well-being for ethnographic truth and scientific valorization of Kabylia, and altering his academic trajectory according to a larger "civic impulse" (Bourdieu 2003b: 85; see Yacine 2004).

A more critical reading would underline Bourdieu's professional ambition and intellectual continuity across his Algerian experience, emphasizing Bourdieu's approach to Algeria as a "living laboratory" in which to conduct an "epistemological experiment" (Bourdieu 1972: 222; see Addi 2002: 42; Sayad 2002: 66; Wacquant 2004: 389; Yacine 2004: 498) into the continuity and rupture of social practices and cultural *doxa* in contexts of extreme upheaval. Such a reading would connect Bourdieu's Algerian research to his ongoing philosophical interests in phenomenal fields (Hammoudi, this volume) and relations of domination and resistance (Colonna, this volume). It would further emphasize his metropolitan academic pedigree from the École Normale Supérieure, the support received from his family's regional connections, and the later patronage offered by Raymond Aron—elements of class reproduction that Bourdieu himself would later examine in a variety of sociological and reflexive studies (Bourdieu 1988 [1984], 1996 [1989], 2004a; Bourdieu and Passeron 1970). This social and educational capital made possible a number of research and professional opportunities for Bourdieu in Algeria and later upon his return to Paris—opportunities unavailable to his indigenous Algerian collaborators like Mouloud Mammeri and Abdelmalek Sayad, who would later come to rely on Bourdieu's own patronage during the postwar years. In the end, both "versions of Bourdieu's past" obviously reflect important conditions in the production of Bourdieu's Algerian ethnographic work and his elaboration of specific ethnographic practices, and in what follows we attempt to demonstrate how they both are encapsulated within it.

Bourdieu's introduction to Algeria, like many colonial ethnographers before him, was mediated by his military service. In general, the ethnology of Algeria—and of Kabylia in particular—had been closely tied to military interests since the mid-nineteenth century, with most of the foundational ethnographies and linguistic studies written by military personnel (Lorcin 1995; Lucas and Vatin 1975). However, Bourdieu's relationship to the imperial project was quite different from the military ethnographers before him; he was deployed to Algeria, paradoxically, because he already opposed the military actions being taken to preserve French Algeria from the nationalist movement for independence. In spite of being a graduate of the École Normale, when Bourdieu was drafted into military service he refused to follow his peers into the Reserve Officers' College, to which elite young men were typically assigned. In his later narration of events, Bourdieu points to his upbringing in a petit bourgeois family in the rural French province of Béarn—where his father had been a postal worker and his grandfather a sharecropper—which made him ill at ease with class-based privilege and reluctant to separate himself from the "rank and file" (2004b: 416).[4]

Sent instead to serve with the Army Psychological Services in Versailles, he soon found himself at odds with his superiors over the Algerian question. As he describes it, "heated arguments" over whether Algeria should remain French or be granted independence led to his deployment to the French colony in October 1955 at the age of 25 (2004b: 416; see Yacine 2004: 490–91, 2008: 30). Once in Algeria, Bourdieu was initially part of a unit charged with guarding air bases and other strategic sites (including, at one point, a large munitions dump in the Chellif Valley) (Bourdieu 2004b: 416; Yacine 2004: 491,

2008:30). He appears to have become progressively disillusioned with what he characterized as his fellow soldiers' blind submission to authority, and increasingly interested in the dynamics of Algerian society (Bourdieu 2004b: 418). In 1956 during the final months of his tour of duty, Bourdieu was reassigned to clerical work in the documentation and information service of the French administration in Algeria, following his parents' intervention through Colonel Ducourneau, a member of the Algerian government who happened to be from Bourdieu's natal region of Béarn (Bourdieu 2004b: 419; Yacine 2004: 491, 2008: 30). There he had the opportunity to meet leading scholars of Algeria, among them Emile Dermenghem, archivist of the government's well-stocked Algerian library and author of key works on the Maghreb, as well as the young historian André Nouschi.[5] Under Dermenghem's guidance and with Nouschi and other fellow-travelers as interlocutors, Bourdieu began to read "everything written about Algeria" (Yacine 2004: 490) and particularly about Kabyle culture, which had been deployed as a central ethnographic case in the emerging social sciences since Durkheim (Hammoudi, this volume).[6]

Like most wars the French-Algerian war was characterized as much by ideological struggles as by what transpired on the battlefield. In this case the opposing camps can be roughly grouped into proponents of a "French Algeria" (*Algérie française*) and an "Algerian Algeria" (*Algérie algérienne*). At the war's start many French and Algerian intellectuals associated with the "Ecole d'Alger"—including such respected figures as Albert Camus, the French sociologist and ethnographer Germaine Tillion, and the Algerian novelist and educator Mouloud Feraoun—favored a "reconciliation" between France and Algeria that would ensure a continued economic and political relationship between the metropole and the settler colony, albeit one premised on the civic, political, and social equality of all subjects/citizens. Termed "integrationism," this approach was increasingly adopted as state policy in the years following World War II and became enshrined in the 1958 Constitution of the Fifth Republic that simultaneously defended the territorial indivisibility of France, reaffirmed categories of legal subjectivity based on religious or geographic origin, and established policies of social promotion to ensure the future equality of all citizens.[7] In contrast, from the earliest moments of the war, Bourdieu endorsed an "Algerian Algeria" that would be fully independent from the French state.

Yet Bourdieu sharply demarcated himself from other leading intellectual proponents of "Algerian Algeria"—most notably, Jean-Paul Sartre and Frantz Fanon. In Bourdieu's view, Sartre, Fanon, and others aligned with the Communist Left were blind to the socioeconomic realities of the Algerian population. If the Far Right Orientalists, who dominated the University of Algiers during the war, were mired in a form of "colonial ethnology" fueled by studies of Arabic language and literature (Adnani and Yacine 2003: 232; Bourdieu 2003b: 6; Sprecher 2003: 297–300), the leftists sought to locate in the Algerian peasantry a nascent revolutionary consciousness that would align them with an emerging transnational proletariat (Le Sueur 2005: 253–54). For Bourdieu, as he later recalled, proponents of both positions were equally blind to the complex realities of Algerian society under colonial domination. He found the Left's utopianism "misleading and dangerous" (Honneth et al. 1986: 40; see Addi 2002: 61–66; Lane 2000: 19–20) and even "irresponsible" (cited in LeSueur 2005: 252). The Left's views were motivated, Bourdieu contended, by "Parisian" ideas (Le Sueur 2005: 252) that fed "a mythical conception of Algerian society" (Honneth et al. 1986: 38) but paid little heed to the "objective situation" of colonial Algeria.

While Bourdieu shared the Left's interest in the conditions of possibility for the development of revolutionary consciousness, he wrote that Algerians' support for the war did not necessarily make them—sociologically speaking—"revolutionaries" (Bourdieu 1961, 1962c). Instead he approached the Algerian peasant as caught up in a "millenarian utopianism" (Bourdieu 1958: 125) that was motivated by "an incoherent resentment" against the colonial situation rather than "a true revolutionary consciousness" (Bourdieu et al. 2002: 32). To gain critical purchase on their condition would require "a certain distance as well as the instruments of thought inseparable from education" (Bourdieu et al. 2002: 32). In these writings from within the wartime context, we see early formulations of Bourdieu's theorization of a divide between prereflexive and reflexive consciousness that runs through his later practice-oriented theoretical work (see Hammoudi, this volume), as well as initial intimations that literacy and education provided the only gateways to critical reflexivity (Goodman, this volume; Lane 2000: chapter 4).

As he was formulating these sociopolitical arguments, Bourdieu began working on a book for the popular French series "Que Sais-Je?"[8] titled *Sociologie de l'Algérie* (Sociology of Algeria) based on the library research undertaken while finishing his military service. Tassadit Yacine (2004: 497) has averred that this early work establishes an "umbilical connection between politics and social science," and Loïc Wacquant has underlined the book's political engagement, noting that the 1962 English translation featured on its cover the flag of the revolutionary National Liberation Front (FLN) prior to the independence of Algeria (Wacquant 2002: 551). Bourdieu himself, well after the fact, narrated his motivation somewhat differently, referring to the project as arising from a civic, more than political impulse. I believe that the French of this period, whether they were for or against independence, converged in their lack of knowledge of the country, and they had poor reasons for being for or against independence. It was thus very important to provide the bases for a judgment, for an adequate understanding, not only for the French of the period, but also for educated Algerians who, for historical reasons, were ignorant of their own society. (Bourdieu 2003b: 85)

Sociologie de l'Algérie is the only work in which Bourdieu's "two Algerias" appear side by side, albeit fleetingly. The majority of the book is a study of the "objective structures" (economy and social organization) of traditional Algerian society. The first four chapters are devoted to discrete Algerian populations: three Berber groups (the Kabyles, the Shawiya, and the Ibadites) and "the Arab speakers." A fifth chapter ("A Common Stock") is concerned with the social, economic, and religious[9] structures that Bourdieu thought united these various groups as "variations on a single theme" (1958: 80). The colonial project makes a brief appearance only in the final chapter ("Alienation") where it is portrayed in terms of profound disaggregation and de-culturation wrought on "traditional" Algerian society.[10] The theme of rupture would subsequently come to dominate Bourdieu's writing on Algeria until after the war's end.

An Ethnography of Rupture

In 1958, the year *Sociologie de l'Algérie* appeared, Bourdieu took a position as assistant professor at the University of Algiers (1958–61) and began conducting research during the academic breaks as part of a team sponsored by ARDES (Association for Demographic, Economic, and Social Research), the Algerian branch of the French INSEE (the

National Institute for Statistics and Economic Studies). Issues of rupture, alienation, de-culturation, disaggregation, and uprooting characterize the two major studies that he carried out under the auspices of ARDES: an analysis of the "resettlement" centers established by the French army (Bourdieu and Sayad 1964) and a study of the impact of capitalist labor practices in Algerian cities and towns (Bourdieu et al. 1963). The projects were funded by the Algerian Development Fund and derived from the French "integrationist" policy of social service reforms designed to reduce economic inequality and through which the government sought to maintain control of the colony in the face of the burgeoning nationalist movement. An unanticipated result of such efforts was the arrival of many young functionaries and military recruits like Bourdieu who were not inclined to the same political conservatism of the colonial *ancien régime*. In the countryside they occupied the ranks of the Specialized Administrative Sections, army units deployed to gather intelligence and maintain local order while providing social, economic, educational, and medical aid (Bourdieu and Sayad 2004 [1964]: 479 n. 5). Likewise, in urban areas, such development initiatives resulted in the creation of a number of educational and social centers and services that brought young French and Algerian functionaries into close working relations.

The ARDES was one such organization that was established under Alain Darbel to provide the first comprehensive statistical survey of the Algerian populace—a project of both military and development interest. Upon the recommendation of Jacques Breil, a Catholic statistician who had previously worked with Bourdieu on an underdevelopment study (Yacine 2004: 503 n. 13), Darbel solicited Bourdieu in 1958–59 to provide sociological interpretation of the statistics gathered. A true "scientific entrepreneur," Bourdieu accepted but expanded the project to include a full ethnographic study of housing and work conditions, with teams of researchers headed by Bourdieu conducting fieldwork across the urban terrains of Algeria (Sayad 2002: 70–71). In the midst of this project, which would result in the *Travail et travailleurs* volume, the ARDES was similarly commissioned by the government to conduct a scientific investigation of conditions in the "resettlement centers" (*centres de regroupement*). These camps had been constructed and administered by the French army for resettled villagers from areas that the army had declared "forbidden zones" in an effort to dismantle the supply chains for the National Liberation Army (ALN). The metropolitan press had quickly denounced these centers as veritable concentration camps, an accusation the government sought to counter with the ARDES study (Sayad 2002: 72). Darbel opted to focus the investigation on some of the most war-torn areas (including Collo, the Ouarsenis, and Kabylia [Djemaa-Saharidj and Barbacha/Soummam]) and seconded the project to Bourdieu, who organized a research/interview team from among several of his liberal French and Algerian students from the University of Algiers—including Abdelmalek Sayad, with whom he later coauthored the resulting *Déracinement* study—and pursued a series of site visits in 1960. In spite of the limited government commission, the suspicion among interviewees that the research teams surely generated (and about which the researchers were self-reflexive), and the dangerous conditions under which the research was effectuated, the resulting studies masterfully melded statistical data, ethnographic description, and sociological analysis into the most comprehensive picture to date of the socioeconomic underdevelopment and dislocation of late-colonial Algeria. Because of the implicit (and sometimes explicit) political critique embedded in the two studies, neither saw publication until after the war ended (Yacine 2004: 501).

Both *Travail et travailleurs* and *Déracinement* are predicated on a "clash of civilizations" (*choc des civilizations*) model that Bourdieu

14

had initially outlined in an article of that title that appeared in the volume *Under-Development in Algeria* published by the Secrétariat Social, a Catholic development association based in Algiers (Bourdieu 1959).[11] In this article, Bourdieu took up key premises put forth by the sociologist Germaine Tillion, who had recently published an influential work outlining the political and economic conditions under which Algeria could viably remain part of France (Tillion 1958 [1957]).[12] Whereas Tillion refused to attribute the economic decline of Algeria's Aurès (Shawiya Berber) region entirely or even primarily to colonialism ("There is not and never has been a French settler living nearer than sixty miles," she would say [Tillion 1958: 17]), Bourdieu argued that almost from the moment the French set foot in Algeria, they had profoundly and irremediably disrupted the traditional socioeconomic organization.

Invoking Redfield, Linton, and Herskovits' acculturation model (1936), Bourdieu contended that this was no mere "contact of civilizations" in which the "receiving culture" could assimilate aspects of the new system into its own structure. As early as the *Sociologie de l'Algérie*, Bourdieu had invoked the pioneering work of Georges Balandier (1951) to insist that such "contact" occurred within an asymmetrical "colonial situation" of domination characterized by "cultural upheavals that were deliberately and knowingly provoked" (1958: 118, cited in Yacine 2004: 496–97). As he later elaborated, the resulting "shock" of colonialism altered the very foundations of the "original culture": "This society, . . . which was constituted through a totality of indissociable elements that were all expressions of the same original 'style,' suffered [*a subi*] the shock of another civilization that did not make itself felt in a piecemeal or targeted fashion but *in totality*, rupturing not only the economic order but also the social, psychological, moral, and ideological [spheres]" (1959: 57).

The initial moment of rupture for Bourdieu came with the Senatus Consultus decision of 1863 (reinforced by the Warnier law of 1873) to divide and privatize property that had formerly been tribally owned and conceived as "indivisible." These laws constituted for Bourdieu a "master key" (*clé de voûte*, 1959: 59) that would set in motion the irrevocable crumbling of Algerian culture and society. In his view, Algerian peasants were not psychologically equipped to adjust to a new form of property organization: "It was dangerous to attribute private property to individuals lacking the psychological structures and 'virtues' that are not only its foundation but its condition of possibility" (1959: 59–60). In Bourdieu's implicit equilibrium model of traditional Algerian society, to alter such a significant element was to produce a domino effect in which the entire social and cultural edifice would come crumbling down.

Bourdieu's emphasis on colonial asymmetry and social rupture put him additionally at odds with the integrationist reforms that Tillion outlined, which ranged from massive investments in Algerian education and worker training to housing subsidies to modern social legislation (Tillion 1958). Such reforms missed the key point that the colonial system had already taken from the Algerians something they could never recover: their cultural unity, and in particular, the one-to-one mapping of objective and subjective structures that lent their former world its *doxic*, unquestionable character. *Travail et travailleurs* (1963) and *Le Déracinement* (1964), as well as the essays later collected in *Algérie 60* (1977), document Bourdieu's ethnographic description and sociological analysis of this conundrum. In these works Bourdieu elaborated Algerian peasants' encounters with a rationalized economic system in which labor, salary, time, and value are conjoined very differently than they were in the traditional "good faith" economy. Through this encounter, a new spirit of calculation and a "diabolical ambition" came to negate "all the old wisdom": "The growth of monetary circulation, together with the concomitant spread of an accompanying spirit, ate away at the enchanted naïveté of former times" (Bourdieu and Sayad 1964: 93). Patrilineal family structure; fraternal spirit; the values of honor and modesty; and the "mythical" connections between place, time, activity, and personhood were sundered.

Moreover, for Bourdieu and Sayad, such colonial capitalist processes disrupted peasants' intimate connections with—their rooting in—the land they cultivated, which, in their reading, served as the site of their genealogical memory, the source of their symbolic economy, and the objectification of their moral values. As they maintained, "The peasant can only but live rooted in the land on which he was born and to which his habits and memories attach themselves. Uprooted, there is a good chance he will die as a peasant, in that the passion which makes him a peasant dies within him" (Bourdieu and Sayad 1964: 115).[13] With the commodification of property and the forcible resettlement of villagers, Algerian peasants were transformed in Bourdieu's view into veritable cultural monsters, betwixt and between traditional and modern *habitus*, in a permanent state of social liminality, or what he called a *habitus clivé* ("split *habitus*").[14] What remained was "a new kind of men . . . who let themselves be defined negatively, by what they are no longer and are not yet, de-peasanted peasants, self-destructive, who carry in themselves all the opposites" (1964: 161).

Bourdieu simultaneously applied this same model of civilizational clash and de-peasantization to describe the social transformations his natal region of Béarn was undergoing, where the "rural exodus" to urban areas and the resulting high rate of bachelorhood challenged the ability of the cultural system to reproduce itself (Bourdieu 1962b).

Indeed Bourdieu pursued ethnographic research in Béarn in 1961 as he and Sayad were finishing the writing of *Le Déracinement* (Adnani and Yacine 2003: 240), and it is clear that the two fieldwork situations, although markedly different in terms of context of domination, became conjoined in Bourdieu's intervention into the Weber-Sombart debate. As Deborah Reed-Danahay discusses, Béarn and Kabylia became reflective lenses through which Bourdieu formulated his nostalgic construction of *tristes paysans* (Reed-Danahay 2005: 73–78, this volume).[15]

In Kabylia, Bourdieu and Sayad's deployment of a trope of rooting and uprooting functioned within the wartime context of their research as a critique of colonialism; yet, Bourdieu's application of it within the larger Mediterranean context presupposes a projection of "traditional," peasant culture as a unified—if not ahistorical—whole, with elements of dissonance or change emerging exogenously. Such a model of historical transformation as exogenous rupture would later inform his theories of practice, *doxa*, and *habitus* as they were formulated in *Outline of a Theory of Practice* (1977 [1972]), a work principally based on his Kabyle ethnographic data gathered under the ARDES project, and whose French edition was prefaced by three ethnological essays on Kabylia (including a reprint of his structuralist nod to Lévi-Strauss, "The Kabyle House, or the World Reversed" [1970]). While Bourdieu would later revise his theoretical model to recognize the internal symbolic flexibility, cultural dissonance, and possibility for endogenous transformation within social systems (see Bourdieu 1990 [1980], 2000 [1997]), his continued reliance on arboreal tropes of rooting and uprooting for depicting cultural contact/clash (Silverstein, this volume) weighted his avowedly dialectical formulations of *habitus* in the *Outline* to epistemological circularity and social reproduction, as a number of critics have commented (see Comaroff 1985: 5; de Certeau 1984: 57–59; Eickelman 1977: 40; Herzfeld 1987: 84).

In commenting on this limitation of Bourdieu's early culture concept, we of course do not wish to imply that the private property laws and resettlement policies that Bourdieu identifies were not pivotal and deeply problematic moments in Algerian history. Nor do we wish to suggest that the colonial project was not destructive of much of the Algerian social fabric; clearly it was. Yet to focus solely on moments of rupture and dislocation risks both neglecting the accommodations Algerians may have made to colonialism and obscuring from our analytical purview those areas of society that may have been less dramatically impacted by colonial relations.[16] The "clash of civilizations" model that Bourdieu adopted as early as 1958 allowed Algerians minimal room for creative maneuvering or selective accommodation. It also neglected the specific ways that the "traditional" property order may have functioned to ensure individual land use even as it was ideologically grounded in principles of indivision. Instead Bourdieu's model placed colonial Algerians in the untenable position of being "between two worlds," of suffering from a *habitus clivé*, condemning them to the painful realization that the world that they had previously taken to be axiomatic (or *doxic*) was merely contingent, one of many possible configurations. At the same time, in his view Algerians lacked the reflexive and critical capacities to navigate successfully between and across these worlds. Their only possible condition was one of alienation.

What impact, if any, might Bourdieu's thesis of de-peasantization have had in Algeria itself?[17] In the preface to *The Logic of Practice*, he wrote that a "desired reconciliation of the practical and the scientific intention" had animated some of his early works, and suggested that he had made "predictions, or rather warnings" at the conclusion of his "two empirical studies of Algerian society" (i.e., *Travail et travailleurs* and *Le Déracinement*). Yet these warnings, he went on to say, "were subsequently used to justify some of the probable deviations which they strove in advance to prevent" (Bourdieu 1980: 2). It is admittedly difficult to ascertain the degree to which Algerian officials were cognizant of Bourdieu's work, but the two "empirical studies"—unlike his more philosophically elaborated works—would have been accessible to educated lay readers. Yet it is undeniable that Algeria's "Agrarian Revolution"[18] was predicated on a model of the Algerian peasantry that was remarkably similar to Bourdieu's dispossession model. Raffinot and Jaquemot, in a 1977 study of state capitalism in Algeria, make this clear: "The analysis of Pierre Bourdieu permits us to explain why we are witnessing the regression of the influence [of peasants] at the level of the governing authorities of the FLN when it started, beginning in 1965, to develop a structure and to define its nationalist project" (Raffinot and Jaquemot 1977: 47, also cited in Colonna 1987: 78).

The countryside, as Colonna has noted, was construed in both scientific and state discourse as a "sad object": a "non-society," a "non-culture" (Colonna 1987: 68; see also Colonna 1995). Yet if Bourdieu's view of a broken and marginalized peasantry that could be characterized only in terms of loss became a cornerstone of independent Algeria's Agrarian Revolution, this figure was continuously haunted by its opposite: the idealized "empeasanted peasant." It is through Bourdieu's reliance on this latter trope—a reliance that runs throughout his oeuvre—that we can perhaps understand Bourdieu as perpetuating a "mythical" view of Kabyle society.

Bourdieu's Kabyle Myth

The war arguably overdetermined Bourdieu's approach to Algerian society, furnishing a lens of rupture through which he viewed the entire 130-year colonial project. Yet although Bourdieu criticized the French Left for its utopian view of the revolutionary potential of Algerian peasants, his ethnography of rupture is predicated on an equally untenable myth: that a precolonial Algerian society had existed in relative equilibrium prior to the imposition of colonialism. As Goodman (this volume) notes, it was among the "de-peasanted peasants" of the French army's resettlement villages that Bourdieu's theories of *habitus* and *doxa*, as formulated in the *Outline*, were born. Both during his initial wartime fieldwork and in his later revisiting of the ethnographic data collected, Bourdieu was clearly well aware that the traditional Kabylia he was writing about had long ago ceased to exist. In that sense, the "outline" can perhaps be understood to refer not only to a sketch of Bourdieu's theory of practice; it was also his attempt to recover the nearly obliterated outlines of precolonial Kabylia, to resurrect a precontact traditional society from the ruins of resettlement camps and the detritus of war.

There was a clear political side to this recovery process, of which Bourdieu was aware at the time, and which he retrospectively acknowledged in his reflections on his Algerian research. In the first place, he viewed the larger descriptive enterprise as a vital contribution to finding a just solution to the question of Algerian independence. As he detailed in a 1986 interview:

> I couldn't be content with just reading books and visiting libraries. In a historical situation in which every moment, every political statement, every discussion, every petition, the whole reality was at stake, it was absolutely necessary to be at the heart of the events and to form one's own opinion, however dangerous it might have been—and dangerous it was. To see, to record, to photograph. (Honneth et al. 1986: 39)

So pressing was the need that Bourdieu rushed into the ARDES research with no formal training in qualitative field methods or Berber language (only later taking Berber classes at the Institut des Langues et Cultures Orientales [INALCO] in Paris), absorbing most of his knowledge of anthropology through his readings while working in the Algerian government library. He was particularly enthralled with the work of Margaret Mead, who more than anyone else linked ethnographic praxis to cultural critique and worked to position the anthropologist as a public intellectual with popular relevance (Nouschi 2003: 31; Sanson 2003: 284).

The pressing nature of Bourdieu's project was furthered by his distinct sense that "traditional" Kabyle culture was in danger of disappearing. Retrospectively, he understood his research and writing project as one of rehabilitation: "My goal was to provide information which was not at all accessible, and, bit by bit, I hoped for a recovery (*réhabilitation*). Dominant colonial society is not happy with simply exploiting; it destroys the dominated, it destroys them symbolically across time, through an entire operation. . . . It destroys them culturally" (Adnani and Yacine 2003: 232–33). He spoke of an "extreme sadness and anxiety" that drove him to "collect a game, to see such and such an artifact (a wedding lamp, an ancient coffer, or the inside of a well-preserved house, for instance)" (Bourdieu 2004b: 424), even at the risk of personal harm. What Marie-France Garcia-Parpet (2003: 146) has characterized as a "work of reconstitution of a traditional universe" thus amounted to an anthropological salvage operation, not for the purpose of merely archiving a series of disappearing practices, folklore, or technology, but with the goal of restoring a degree of dignity to the victims of colonization and abetting a larger public recognition of Algerians (and Kabyles in particular) as possessors of an integral (national) culture.[19] "What one must rigorously demand of an ethnologist of the colonial situation is that he endeavor to restore (*restituer*) to these other men a sense of the behaviors of which the colonial system has, among other things, dispossessed them," Bourdieu would say (Bourdieu et al. 1963: 259). As Tassadit Yacine (2004: 498–99) has maintained, Bourdieu's configuration of ethnosociology as an "instrument for rehabilitating peasant cultures"—for restoring a lost or endangered wholeness—thus emerged from the larger ethic of cultural relativism and egalitarianism prevalent in the late-Boasian anthropology of Mead and others.

Such a political ethic of restitution and cultural recognition has certain consequences.[20] In our experience, Kabyles today do talk about the loss of traditional lifeways much in the way Bourdieu describes, although they typically locate the "before" prior to the war rather than prior to colonial occupation (see Goodman 2005: chapter 3). Yet in taking people's talk about "bygone days" (Briggs 1988) as evidence for how things once were, rather than as a form of "structural nostalgia" (Herzfeld 1997: 109), Bourdieu may have participated in the reification of a "time before time" in which a particular set of practices, institutions, or discourses stand in as a synecdoche for a Kabyle cultural integrality defined in contrast to the Algerian (post)colonial present (Goodman 2005; Silverstein, this volume). Such a "romanticizing nostalgia" (Reed-Danahay 2005: 75)—no doubt mediated by Bourdieu's own rural upbringing—led him to regard ritual practices as well as oral sayings as "survivals" of an earlier era, as present windows into a lost past (Goodman, this volume). Even more explicitly, he viewed Kabylia itself as a survival of an originary, pan-Mediterranean society, preserving the symbolic oppositions and legal codes of ancient Greece or nineteenth-century France: "Kabylia preserved in a more durable manner—because there were rituals that kept them alive—many things that had been common across the Mediterranean, universals (*des invariants*)" (Adnani and Yacine 2003: 239–40). Bourdieu returned to such Mediterranean universals in one of his last publications, *Masculine Domination*, which drew on his Kabyle ethnographic data as primary evidence of "the 'phallonarcissistic' vision and the androcentric cosmology that are common to all Mediterranean societies and that survive even today, but in a partial, as it were, exploded state, in our own cognitive structures and social structures" (2001: 6, cited in Reed-Danahay 2005: 89).

The presentation of Kabyle ritual forms and social institutions as survivals of an integral Kabyle cultural, if not ur-Mediterranean, past in many ways recapitulates a *leitmotif* of the very colonial ethnography from which Bourdieu was at pains to distinguish his work. French military ethnographers consistently projected Berber-speakers in general—and Kabyles in particular—as the original inhabitants of North Africa who had preserved more than any other people their Mediterranean identity. General Edouard Brémond was perhaps the most outspoken in this regard: "If the Maghreb received nothing from Arabia, little from the Sudan, and almost everything from the Mediterranean, it has also many traits in common with our Middle Ages, traits which we have since forgotten" (1942: 362).[21] Moreover, for colonial scholars Kabyles constituted the prime example of an *homme frontière* ("border man"), racially embodying the cultural heterogeneity marking the "genius" of the region, and thus positioning themselves as the perfect middleman between the Orient and the Occident, Europe and Africa.[22]

These projected origins and racial affiliations bolstered parallel colonial presentations of Kabyles as sedentary, hard-working laborers who were less fanatically attached to Islam than their Arab neighbors and thus more obvious targets of the French "civilizing mission" (*mission civilisatrice*). Such representations—which date to the eve

24

of the conquest of Algiers, were particularly prevalent during the 1840–70 period, but continued to impact the later French colonial imaginary—have since been characterized as amounting to a "Kabyle Myth," which, like the myths Roland Barthes (1957) examined, served to justify and naturalize the French imperial presence in Algeria (see Ageron 1961; Guilhaume 1992: 236–41; Lorcin 1995; Lucas and Vatin 1975: 45; Sayad 1992; Silverstein 2004: 52–67). While Kabyles never became the colonial toadies that later Algerian nationalists accused them of being—and indeed Kabylia was repeatedly the center of anticolonial resistance from the early period of conquest through the French-Algerian War—the myth of Kabyle autochthony, hybridity, and assimilability did have several concrete effects in colonial Algeria. It directed subsequent scientific study to the region, with ethnologists, folklorists, and archaeologists scouring the region for material artifacts, proverbs, and social institutions (particularly legal codes [qanoun] and political forms [such as the village assembly, or tajmaat]) that bespoke of a classical (Roman) heritage or even a neolithic Mediterranean past.[23] Further, the myth underwrote the preference for Kabylia as a space of colonial social experimentation in village planning and education, including the placing of some of the earliest Algerian teacher training schools in the region (Colonna 1975). It was precisely from these schools that many of Bourdieu's own Kabyle interlocutors and collaborators emerged.

Thus, in spite of Bourdieu's explicit rejection of the Orientalism, primitivism, imperial apologism, and material effects of this earlier research (see Bourdieu and Eribon 1980), the prominent place that Kabylia occupied in the colonial ethnographic and administrative imagination nonetheless influenced his own ethnosociological project of cultural recovery. His choice to devote his analytical energies to Kabylia rather than to the other field sites visited during his ARDES research was no doubt shaped by his prior familiarity with the region gained through the wealth of earlier studies read in the government library at the end of his military service, by the centrality of Kabylia in the development of the French social scientific field (particularly in the work of Durkheim and his followers), and by the disproportion-ate number of Kabyle student-scholars with whom he had been in intellectual dialogue. He sustained colonial ethnography's reliance on material artifacts (particularly domestic architecture), proverbs, and legal codes—citing earlier observations and recorded sayings alongside those he himself collected (see Goodman, this volume)— even as he read these politically against the grain as embodiments of a threatened symbolic unity and materializations of vulnerable generative schemes of strategizing and practice (i.e., *habitus*) rather than as evidence of Kabyle autochthony or savage republicanism. While he criticized the earlier studies' disproportionate focus on magic and religion as "the racist arm used by colonial ethnology to discredit and thus claim that [the Kabyles] are primitive" (Adnani and Yacine 2003: 233), his own later salvaging of Kabyle myth and ritual and bracketing of Islamic religious or colonial educa-tion institutions (particularly in works published after 1966, see De Certeau 1984: 52; Lane 2000: 111; and Reed-Danahay 1995) arguably reinscribed the fantasy of primordial cultural unity that underwrote the Kabyle Myth. And his temporal and epistemological linking of Kabyle and Béarn peasant societies recapitulated earlier efforts to ascertain an ur-Mediterranean shared patrimony. In these ways anthropology's colonial legacy remained marked in Bourdieu's anticolonial ethnography and, indeed, in the ways in which his work has been appropriated into contemporary academic theorizing and postcolonial Kabyle identity projects.

Between Two Worlds

As much an inheritance from earlier colonial scholarship that emphasized the frontier or borderlands character of the Kabyle personality (the *homme frontière*), Bourdieu's description of a late-colonial
habitus clivé also derived from the positioning of Bourdieu and his
main informants as subjects self-consciously "between two worlds."
Reed-Danahay (2005 and this volume) has discussed at some length
Bourdieu's own awareness of himself as a child of a minor rural
functionary and grandchild of a sharecropper whose academic success brought him into rarefied Parisian intellectual circles, and how
such an identity of being betwixt and between different social worlds
provided a unique perspective from which to examine the processes of
social reproduction in both locales—a perspective of self-distancing
he later termed "participant objectivation" (Bourdieu 2003c).[24] What
is particularly interesting for the purposes of this volume is how he
brought such a perspective to his research and writing concerning
Algeria as well.

Beyond the influence of Bourdieu's Béarn upbringing on his military
career (his refusal to join the officer ranks, his reassignment to the
clerical position) already discussed, such identification with a peasant
society furnished the basis for an imagined solidarity with his Kabyle
informants. The romanticizing "structural nostalgia" (Herzfeld 1987)
that Bourdieu's studies both drew on and reinforced did not simply
derive from an anticolonial political project of cultural restitution
but was also linked to an affective bind that Bourdieu deeply felt
with Kabylia. As he later recounted,

> I was crazy about the [Kabyle] country. I was really in love with
> the country. When I saw a Kabyle with his mustache, I found it
> amazing. I found these people wise, magnificent, intelligent, etc.

I was really moved to see these so unhappy people hurry towards us to tell us about their problems. . . . They wanted us to go report, witness them. At the same time, I had my own problems with ancient cultural traditions. That was my madness. (Adnani and Yacine 2003: 235)

In this sense, his Kabyle romanticism was less the urban pastoralism so present in the work of earlier colonial ethnologists as a nostalgia for a timeless, premodern Béarn, which he certainly never directly experienced, but which he had intimated in the stories and proverbs told by southwestern France's own mustachioed "men of honor." But, intimately familiar with the genre of peasant storytelling, he also questioned it as a window to any present empirical reality. "When I was in Kabylia, I distrusted those old Kabyles, while at the same time admiring them. . . . I said to myself: if that was an old Béarnais peasant who was telling me that, what would I think? I would take some, and I would leave some" (Adnani and Yacine 2003: 240). This skepticism was further bolstered by Bourdieu's ongoing statistical research, which demonstrated that certain elements that were orally represented (and anthropologically inscribed) as "rules"—such as Kabyle patrilateral parallel cousin (FBD–FBS) marriage, which in Bourdieu's empirical reckoning made up only 3–5 percent of village unions (Bourdieu 1977: 210n85; Honneth et al. 1986: 40)—were often rarely practiced. It directed Bourdieu's attention to the strategic interests and states of misrecognition manifested in his informants' speech acts, as well as the "officializing" and strategy-generating mechanism (*habitus*) that inspired them. It also motivated him to pursue simultaneous research in Béarn, so as to "gauge [the] instrument" of his own participant objectification (Adnani and Yacine 2003: 240).

Bourdieu's own position "between two worlds"—Béarn and Paris,

Béarn and Kabylia, rural and urban, petit bourgeois and academic elite—suggests that he may have experienced himself as the "de-peasanted peasant" (*paysan dépaysanné*) that he so eloquently described as inhabiting the Algerian resettlement camps and working in Algerian factories (Reed-Danahay, this volume). In contrast to the "em-peasanted peasant" (*paysan empaysanné*), a hapless creature whom Bourdieu saw as unable to adapt as the world changed around him, he thought that the de-peasanted peasant—although a tragic figure in his own right—was more easily able to move from one world to the other precisely because he was fully at home in neither. In describing his own experience of moving between seemingly incongruous social realities, Bourdieu found a parallel in the upbringing and experiences of his key Kabyle informants and interlocutors, most notably the sociologist Abdelmalek Sayad, the novelist and teacher Mouloud Feraoun, and later, the novelist, poetry specialist, and Berber cultural icon Mouloud Mammeri. Each of these figures was in his own way a "de-peasanted peasant": like Bourdieu, each man was raised in a rural village from which he later separated; each was among a handful of indigenous Algerians to attend schools that catered primarily to the children of European settlers. Each moved between the worlds of school and home, city and village, colonizer and colonized.

As native intellectuals, Sayad, Feraoun, and Mammeri were all the kind of informant/interlocutor of whom Bourdieu should have been wary given his own theoretical proclivities: already outside the *doxa*, they could no longer speak of social practices from within the normative *habitus* but only from a *habitus clivé*. From this hybrid position, Kabylia could only appear as divided: on the far side was the precontact, quasi-mythical Kabyle culture, seemingly integral and intact; on the near side was war, emigration, and more than a century of colonial occupation that had sundered traditional bonds and destroyed the social fabric. Whereas Sayad foregrounded the latter position in most of his writings, Feraoun and Mammeri wrote from both sides of the divide but—like Bourdieu—rarely bridged it in the same work.

Abdelmalek Sayad (1933–98), Bourdieu's closest collaborator for his wartime studies, was a member of the ARDES team and coauthor of *Le Déracinement* as well as of one of Bourdieu's later essays on Kabyle marriage practices (Bourdieu and Sayad 1972) and subsequently a formidable scholar of the Algerian emigrant/immigrant experience as seen from within (see Sayad 2004 [1999]). Sayad was the third child of a modest Kabyle family from the village of Aghbala, which later became one of the key resettlement villages in the ARDES study. Sayad's minor notable (*qa'id*) great grandfather had built a school on his property for the education of his children and those of successive generations.[25] While initially schooled in the village setting, Sayad was quickly pushed by his father into classes normally reserved for the children of French settlers, and he later traveled to the provincial capital of Bougie (Bejaïa) and then on to Algiers for his secondary and university education.

Initially trained as a teacher and assigned to an elementary school in the Algiers Casbah during the early days of the war, Sayad later pursued graduate studies in philosophy and psychology at the University of Algiers, where he encountered Bourdieu. In the midst of a war-torn campus, Sayad became heavily involved in nationalist protests and student strikes, while maintaining his independence from the formal organization of the FLN, as one of the very few Muslim students on a mostly European campus dominated by student associations in favor of "French Algeria" (Sayad 2002: 50–59). Such involvement brought him into direct conversation and alliance with the "Liberal" groups of European students—and particularly the Student Committee for Laïc and Democratic Action (CELAD)—and the few sympathetic professors, including Bourdieu (Sprecher 2003: 298–302).

In Bourdieu (who was but four years older than him), Sayad found a mentor, colleague, and friend, from whom he discovered that his academic education could be connected with his political aspirations for his country, and that sociology, by approaching society itself as an object of study, "a laboratory for experimentation and observation," could serve as an "instrument for the construction and invention of [social] reality" (Sayad 2002: 59–60, 66–67). Employed in the ARDES studies and accompanying Bourdieu and his other European and Algerian students across the landscape of resettlement camps, Sayad rediscovered his country in a state of upheaval, which he saw anew with some analytical distance through the lens of "participant objectivation" and his assigned role as a cultural mediator/translator for Bourdieu. Through this experience he became a witness and—as Bourdieu (1991) later called him—a "public scribe" (*écrivain publique*) for a Kabylia in turmoil and subsequently for those displaced persons (resettled peasants, emigrants/immigrants) who could not write their own history.[26]

If Sayad thus developed a role as an engaged and organic intellectual, such training and research experiences did not necessarily translate into a stable position at the war's end, unlike for Bourdieu, who was able to transition seamlessly—thanks in part to Raymond Aron's support—from Algeria to university positions at the Sorbonne, Lille, and later at the Ecole des Hautes Etudes en Sciences Sociales and, eventually, the Collège de France. Rather, Sayad emerged from the war in a state of utter disenchantment and personal depression (Saint-Martin 1999: 36–37). Returning from France where he had worked with Bourdieu on the latter's Béarn research and the writing of *Le Déracinement*, Sayad found independent Algeria to be in a state of "complete disorder" (*désordre intégral*), a perception that was doubled by the death of his father: "Everything was disoriented, in the literal sense of having 'lost its orientation': the system of references had foundered" (Sayad 2002: 83). Shortly after, in 1963, Sayad, with Bourdieu's help, left again for France and enrolled in doctoral studies in sociology with Aron. In spite of his failing health and frequent hospitalizations, Sayad pursued extended field research among Algerian immigrant workers and eventually found positions in Bourdieu's Center for European Studies, and, only after 1977, as a permanent member of the National Center for Scientific Research (CNRS). And yet, Sayad never fully joined the ranks of French intellectuals as Bourdieu did, refused French citizenship, and remained until his untimely death in 1998 on the margins of French academic society, an *homme frontière* until the end (Temime 1999).[27] Like the "de-peasanted" Kabyle peasants or the immigrant workers whose many qualities, sufferings, and struggles he viscerally embodied, Sayad was an "*atopos*, a quaint hybrid devoid of place, displaced, in the twofold sense of incongruous and inopportune, trapped in that 'mongrel' sector of social space betwixt and between social being and nonbeing" (Bourdieu and Wacquant 2000: 178).[28] In this way, his own *habitus clivé* was as much a scientific instrument for field research as a cardinal example through which he and Bourdieu could build a theory of societal rupture and its attendant cultural effects.

Bourdieu had a very different relationship with Mouloud Feraoun (1913–62), who is perhaps best known today for his ethnographic novels and in particular, *Le Fils du pauvre* (Son of a Pauper, 1992 [1950]), which portrays traditional Kabyle lifeways with a textured detail and local specificity largely absent from Bourdieu's ethnography.

A semi-autobiographical work, *Le Fils du pauvre* provides a first-hand account of growing up in a Kabyle village that culminates with the protagonist's departure for the regional capital Tizi-Ouzou as a scholarship student. In effect the book narrates Feraoun's own trajectory from an "em-peasanted" to a "de-peasanted" peasant, a trajectory accessible only to a privileged few *indigènes* (Feraoun was one of just twenty Algerians out of a total 318 students who entered the Ecole Normale of Bouzaréa in 1932, the same school Sayad would later attend). Following his studies, Feraoun was employed as a school teacher, first in the Kabyle region and, from 1957 on, in Algiers, where he was tapped in October of 1960 to work as an inspector for the Service des Centres Sociaux[29]—a French liberal reformist educational organization designed to foster Franco-Muslim solidarity by providing educational opportunities, economic services, and medical care (Le Sueur 2000: xviii, 2005: chapter 3). Like Bourdieu's corpus, Feraoun's work lines up along a divide: whereas his early novels and essays afford an arguably idealized portrayal of Kabyle social institutions and traditions (cf. *Jours de Kabylie* [1992/1954]), he later wrote a compelling and graphic diary-style account of the French-Algerian war as he experienced it (Feraoun 2000 [1962]) over an eight-year period. The war would lead to his own tragic demise: he was assassinated by an ultra-Right paramilitary squad operated by dissident French military officers opposed to any accommodation (the Organization of the Secret Army or OAS) on March 15, 1962, mere days before a cease-fire agreement was reached.

If Feraoun's ethnographic novels foreground a kind of timeless Kabyle tradition, this was not only out of a nostalgic desire to resurrect what had already been lost. Rather, as for Bourdieu, it was also in response to what Feraoun viewed as the dangerous revolutionary ideology espoused by the French Left and embodied in Fanon and

Sartre. As Feraoun saw it, the revolution would not create a tabula rasa on which a "new man" could emerge, free from the yoke of patriarchal traditionalism and religious authority (Le Sueur 2000: xxviii). In contrast he saw the war as wreaking havoc, destroying what remained of the fabric of Algerian society while proposing only more violence in its place. Yet although committed in principle to the revolutionary cause, Feraoun was not ready to relinquish some of the benefits that accompanied colonization—in particular, education. He remained ultimately committed to the goals espoused by the Centres Sociaux even as he recognized that they came too late (Le Sueur 2000: xxxviii). As he would eloquently characterize his own duality: "The French are inside me, and the Kabyles are inside me" (Feraoun 2000 [1962]: 90).

Bourdieu appears to have discovered Mouloud Feraoun's work early during his stay in Algeria; fellow Normalien Lucien Bianco, who followed Bourdieu into military service, recalled that Bourdieu had advised him to read Feraoun's books before Bianco's own deployment in 1958 (Bianco and Yacine 2003: 269). Feraoun was among the informants Bourdieu consulted in Algiers (Goodman, this volume); indeed, Bourdieu's "ethnography" of Feraoun's natal village Tizi Hibel, especially prominent in the 1966 essay "The Sentiment of Honour in Kabyle Society," derived largely from those conversations (Bourdieu 1966: 233). Bourdieu would carry this ethnography into his later works; there, however, the village name dropped out and the ethnographic passages that had originally been linked to Tizi Hibel were integrated into what became Bourdieu's larger, regional ethnography, joining the idealized precontact narratives that Bourdieu elicited from the "uprooted" Kabyles in the resettlement camps. Some of this ethnography may even have been drafted by Feraoun himself; Bourdieu noted at a 1997 conference that Feraoun had read and annotated Bourdieu's earliest works on Algeria (Bourdieu 2003b: 7).

Bourdieu's encounters with Mouloud Mammeri (1917–89) were of yet a different nature. The two did not meet until well after Bourdieu had left Algeria, as Mammeri's subversive role in the anticolonial resistance during the early years of the war had forced him into hiding in Morocco beginning in 1957, following the arrest, imprisonment, and torture of his close collaborator Tahar Oussedik (Yacine 1990b). By the time Bourdieu and Mammeri met well after the war, Mammeri had already published several novels, had been appointed the first Algerian director of the Center for Archeological, Prehistoric, and Ethnological Research (CRAPE), and was a key figure in the burgeoning Berber cultural revival. Unlike Feraoun and Sayad, who hailed from modest backgrounds, Mammeri was born to privilege: he was the eldest son of a wealthy and highly respected family of metal workers in the village of Taourirt Mimoun (At Yenni). His father was the local *amin* (village leader) and had been among the first generation of Algerians to attend French schools; previous generations of Mammeris had been appointed to the status of *qa'id*, serving as liaisons between the French and the local populace (Arkoun 1990). Mammeri's own uprooting came at an early age: when he was eleven years old, he left his village to live with his uncle in Rabat, Morocco, where—like Sayad and Feraoun—he was one of the few *indigènes* to attend the French *lycée* (high school), returning home to his Kabyle village each summer. Mammeri would later narrate the first train trip to Rabat in terms of a fall from grace, recounting the experience as one of "banish[ment] from a lost paradise" (Yacine 1990a: 69) or as being abruptly torn from the cherished culture he had until then never called into question (Mammeri 1991 [1938]: 17).

At the same time, Mammeri acknowledged the many benefits

of the broad classical education he acquired; while studying Greek and Latin in school he simultaneously immersed himself at home in traditional Kabyle poetry, in which his father and uncle were both considered among the last remaining specialists (*imusnawen*). Subsequently, he would claim that it was in Rabat that he learned to situate his own cultural traditions on a par with the classics: "I felt that writing Berber verse was like Homer, who had composed the *Iliad* and the *Odyssey*" (Yacine 1990a: 76). Mammeri went on to university study in Algiers and then Paris, although his studies were interrupted by World War II, during which he was drafted into the French army.[30] After completing his studies he taught secondary school in Algeria while editing the underground anticolonial publication *Espoir-Algérie* and composing eloquent letters and reports on behalf of Algerian independence, including a report for the FLN delegation to the United Nations.[31]

By turns a novelist, essayist, linguist, ethnographer, and ardent collector of Berber poetry, Mammeri became a central—indeed, a venerated—figure in the nascent Berber Cultural Movement during the 1970s and 1980s. Yet although Mammeri became an almost iconic representative of Kabyle tradition, Bourdieu—writing for *Le Monde* five days after Mammeri was killed in a car accident in February 1989—also acknowledged the ways in which he was "a doubled figure, divided against himself" (Bourdieu 1989: 1). From within his own *habitus clivé*, Mammeri (like myriad other postcolonial intellectuals) would seek to recover the culture and in particular the rich oral traditions of his people. As he would later put it, his work was intended as "an affirmation of something I saw dying out among the men who surrounded me" (Yacine 1990a: 71).

It was with regard to Berber oral traditions that Bourdieu and Mammeri engaged in their first published "dialogue" (Mammeri and

Bourdieu 2004 [1978]). Although perhaps intended as a conversation, this "dialogue" reads more like an interview, with Mammeri cast as the informant. Bourdieu was seeking to understand the figure of the *amusnaw*, or the highly respected sage who blends poetic language with political critique and local savvy, wielding *tamusni* (traditional wisdom) as art and social practice simultaneously. Bourdieu repeatedly pressed Mammeri to articulate how it was that poetry could be simultaneously "oral" and "*savant*," reiterating that in the western tradition these qualities were rarely conjoined. Read retrospectively, Bourdieu's position clearly betrays his own folk belief that oral traditions constitute unreflexive manifestations of *habitus* (Goodman, this volume).

Yet as Colonna (this volume) notes, Mammeri clearly established in this conversation the existence of a long and deep tradition of endogenous critique, thus calling into question Bourdieu's positing of a "divide" between prereflexive and reflexive consciousness. Mammeri likewise obliquely criticized Bourdieu's lack of ethnographic attention to the specificities of both regional history and Kabyle oral traditions. By furnishing a wealth of situated detail about both particular named poets and the social contexts in which oral poetry was produced, Mammeri demonstrated that Kabyle oral poetry did not emerge as a collective cultural product but was created by specific individuals responding to emergent sociopolitical concerns (see Goodman, this volume). However, Bourdieu never took up these challenges in his subsequent writings. Instead, he dubbed Mammeri a reinvented or resurrected *amusnaw*, able to "mobilize his people in mobilizing the words in which [his people] could recognize itself" (Bourdieu 1989: 2).

Bourdieu and Mammeri's second dialogue, published in 1985 and titled "On the good use of ethnology," was somewhat more reciprocal, with both scholars discussing the implications and challenges of doing fieldwork in their own societies (Bourdieu and Mammeri 2003 [1985]). For Mammeri, "good" ethnology had to be useful not only in scientific terms but also—and perhaps primarily—as a vehicle for promoting the survival and flourishing of a people (see also Mammeri 1980, 1989). In "recovering" vanishing traditions, ethnology, Mammeri thought, was valuable in that it countered the standardization and homogenization of cultural difference promoted by a globalizing world of nation-states. Similarly, for Bourdieu, ethnology, even if admittedly a "phantasmic reconstruction," "could be utilized as an ideological instrument of idealization" in ways that were both potentially dangerous and politically strategic: "the fact of developing representations, even if they are a bit delirious and contain a bit of mythic millenarianism, can have political utility" (Bourdieu and Mammeri 2003: 17).

In this second encounter, Mammeri was at times more directly critical of the kind of reconstructive scholarship to which Bourdieu had subjected Kabylia. For instance he questioned the way Bourdieu had drawn analogies between Béarn and Kabylia as "small autonomous republics that had their own customs . . . , the same masculine values, the same values of honor, democratic assemblies," asking whether such a reconstructive portrayal was not "complicated by the fact that these societies . . . were in a state of total crisis?" (Bourdieu and Mammeri 2003: 15 16). This critique notwithstanding, in the context of 1970s and 1980s postcolonial Algeria, in which a strongly Jacobin government sought to "Arabize" the population and to actively suppress and even eradicate the Berber language and culture, an ethnography of a precontact Berber society—even if idealized—appeared politically necessary to both Bourdieu and Mammeri. For such an ethnographic myth could help establish Berber claims to authenticity, thus providing symbolic capital that could be marshaled to legitimate Berber rights in the new nation-state. Mammeri admitted as much: "It remains obvious that in practice, for concrete reasons (political, social, and cultural), a Kabyle intellectual today is too often called upon to construct an ideal re-creation of his own society, particularly in reaction to the devalorizing image that those who would deny this society tend to offer" (Bourdieu and Mammeri 2003: 15).

Despite their shared engagement in Berber cultural politics, the relationship between Bourdieu and Mammeri would unavoidably bear the legacy of the colonial situation. Alongside the relative nonreciprocity of the "dialogues" (it would have been fascinating, for instance, to hear Mammeri ask Bourdieu about his own Kabyle ethnography), Bourdieu—as he did with Sayad—was the one to facilitate important institutional connections for Mammeri in the metropole, including sponsoring the publication of the journal *Awal* in which the second interview appeared. Given that Mammeri relied on this patronage relationship, he was not on equal footing; in such a context, he would have been hard pressed to engage directly in a critique of Bourdieu's Kabyle ethography.[32]

Berber Cultural Movement

Today both Bourdieu and Mammeri have been almost mythologized in Berber cultural circles, where both seem to have achieved posthumously the status of *imusnawen*, sages who speak from a deep knowledge of Berber tradition and history, despite the fact that they could only imagine an integral Berber culture from their position of already existing between two worlds. Or perhaps because of this fact; indeed, avowals of in-betweenness generally chart the politics of the contemporary, transnational Berber Cultural Movement. Present-day Kabyle activists re-present organic intellectuals like Feraoun and Mammeri as their forebears—if not martyrs—in the struggle to promote Tamazight (Berber language and culture) as the core of North Africa's cultural particularity and as a middle ground between Islamic and Western civilizations. Bourdieu's affinity with Mammeri as reflective *imusnawen* underwrote Bourdieu's support for Berber studies in France—including his help in the foundation of the Groupe d'Etudes Berbères at the Université de Paris–Vincennes and later the Centre de Recherches et Etudes Amazigh at the Maison de Science de l'Homme—and the native anthropology that largely comprises it.[33] These centers and their respective publications (including Mammeri and Yacine's journal *Awal*) have provided the intellectual basis and institutional support for Kabyle men and women (both in Kabylia and in the diaspora) to objectify their culture as a set of values to be learned, preserved, and fought for. The terms of this objectification and avowal largely follow from Bourdieu's example, and share in a similar structural nostalgia for a "time before time" of colonial rupture and postindependence Arab national imposition.

As much as Bourdieu sought to restore dignity and modern value to Kabyle culture, the independent FLN government—ideologically uniting Islamic reformism, Arab nationalism, and state socialism— largely devalued it as a feudal survival and imperial construction, pointing to the colonial politics of the Kabyle Myth as evidence of its incompatibility with a new, decolonized Algeria.[34] Such a confla- tion of Berber identity and sectarianism was reinforced in September 1963 during a ten-month armed confrontation between the Algerian national army and fighters of the Kabyle leader Hocine Aït-Ahmed's Socialist Forces Front (FFS), which sought greater autonomy for Kabylia. Aït-Ahmed's arrest and flight to Europe shifted the locus of Berber political claims to the community of Kabyle emigrants and expatriates living in France, many of whom had been politicized during the French-Algerian war by the FLN and its various antecedent and rival organizations. Drawing on this earlier history, in March 1967, a group of scholars (including Mammeri), artists (including singer Taos Amrouche), and FFS activists (including Bessaoud Mohand Arab) founded the Berber Academy for Cultural Exchange and Research (renamed in 1969 as Agraw Imazighen) in Paris.[35] While originally dedicated to the "universal" and "harmonious cooperation between all humanity," the Agraw's goals became increasingly irredentist—"to introduce the larger public to the history and civilisation of Berbers, including the promotion of the language and culture" as stated in the second article of its 1969 statutes. Adopting the appellation *Imazighen* ("free men"), members of the Academy worked to standardise Berber (Tamazight) and develop a neo-Tifinagh orthographic script; it pushed its ideology of a "Berber nation" through the medium of "Arab cafés" and the variety of village assemblies (*tajmaat*s) transposed onto the French urban landscape (Chaker 1998: 44).

The Agraw's efforts were carried over in the 1973 formation of the Groupe d'Études Berbères, which—with the aid of Bourdieu and other scholars of Berber societies like Ernest Gellner—dedicated itself to teaching Berber language and culture. In 1978 the organization spun off the Ateliers Imedyazen, a publication cooperative in Paris created to diffuse such intellectual debates to a wider audience. Over the course of the next several years, the cooperative published works on linguistics, theatre, poetry and other Berber fiction (including translations into Tamazight of the work of Brecht, among others), grammar manuals, *dossiers de presse* that followed events in Algeria, and political communiqués (including the 1979 FFS party platform). These publications were paralleled by the growth of a Kabyle recording industry in France, in which performers like Idir, Lounis Aït-Menguellet, Ferhat M'henni, and Lounès Matoub adapted traditional poetry and folktales into "revolutionary songs of struggle" (to cite an early Ferhat album), and eventually came to play direct political roles in the struggle for Berber language rights.

In March–April 1980, the locus of Berber politics shifted back to Kabylia when—following the cancellation by the governor of the *wilaya* of Tizi-Ouzou of a lecture on ancient Berber poetry, which was to have been given at the University of Tizi Ouzou on March 10 by Mammeri—students occupied the university. When security forces arrived, violent confrontations broke out that would last for two weeks, culminating in widespread student demonstrations, a general strike throughout the region, and eventually a large number of arrests and beatings of many strikers when the newly-installed president Chadli Benjedid called in the military. These events, collectively known as the "Berber Spring," concretized the previously amorphous Berber Cultural Movement (MCB) and initiated Berber identity politics as a force in postcolonial Algeria and the diaspora (see Chaker 1998; Goodman 2005: chapter 2; Maddy-Weitzman 2001; Roberts 1980; Silverstein 2003).[36] Successive waves of contestation to state authority in October 1988, the autumn of 1994, July 1998, and April 2001 have drawn directly on this early moment of confrontation for their spatial and ideological dimensions. Moreover, the 1980 events politicized the various Kabyle cultural organizations and artistic groups that formed across the French urban landscape after the legalization of immigrant associations in 1981. These associations became sites for political speeches and electioneering of the various factions of the MCB—as well as the FFS and Rally for Culture and Democracy (RCD), Kabyle parties legalized after 1989—which sought (in their different ways) the officialization of Tamazight as a national language of Algeria and for greater cultural and economic autonomy of Kabylia within a potentially federal state.

42

As we have argued elsewhere (see Goodman 2005: chapter 3; Silverstein, this volume), what has united these various manifestations of Kabyle cultural politics has been their reference to a timeless—but continually threatened if not partially submerged—Berber culture in dire need of preservation and rehabilitation. Cultural associations on both sides of the Mediterranean archive material artifacts and recorded poetry, songs, and rituals; sponsor lectures and conferences on Berber history and culture; teach courses in standard, written Tamazight; and stage public celebrations of seasonal festivals. These celebrations often include dance demonstrations and musical performances, actively seeking to transmit forms of cultural knowledge not taught in state educational systems. The symbolic repertoire mobilized in these performances closely parallels that highlighted by Bourdieu in his ethnography, drawing on gendered images of village or domestic settings (including the architectural features highlighted in his famous essay on the "Kabyle House" [1970]) while bracketing the "Islamic" or "modern" dimensions of Kabyle history or contemporary life (see Scheele 2007). Moreover, in their political discourse, Berber activists emphasize—like Bourdieu—the Mediterranean dimensions of Kabyle culture, distinguishing themselves from the peoples of the Middle East with whom Orientalist scholars and Arab nationalist ideologues had allied them. Like Bourdieu these activists draw on rooted tropes of Kabyle authenticity and autochthony.

More than simply sharing a similar structural nostalgia, Bourdieu and contemporary Berber activists are further linked by a politics of ethnography. Bourdieu explicitly prided himself on recuperating ethnology from a colonial science of racial domination to a modern instrument of cultural renewal or "liberation" for Kabylia (Adnani and Yacine 2003: 243). Bourdieu's response to Mammeri's subtle critique in their second dialogue is revealing:

I believe that ethnology, when it is done well, is a very important instrument of self-knowledge, a kind of social psychoanalysis which allows one to grasp the cultural unconscious which all who are born in that society have in their heads . . . and one must include in that cultural unconscious all the traces of colonization, the humiliating effects. . . . Claiming that ethnology is a colonial science, thus worthless, is a great stupidity. (Bourdieu and Mammeri 2003 [1985]: 15)

Bourdieu later summed up the dialogue by pointing to his role in "making ethnology acceptable for Kabyles": "[The dialogue] attests to the fact that there is no antinomy between the intention of rehabilitation which animated Mammeri's research on ancient Berber poetry of Kabylia, and the ethnological intention of interpretation. Ethnology opens one of the necessary paths to a true reflexivity, condition of self-knowledge as exploration of the historical unconscious" (Bourdieu 2003b: 87).

Kabyle intellectuals have followed in Bourdieu's path by engaging in an archaeology of the Berber cultural "unconscious." From the associations' museological practices, to the compiling of a "Berber Encyclopedia," to autodidact ethnography and folklore collection, to the enrollment of activists in degree programs in anthropology and linguistics, the Berber cultural movement has appropriated ethnology as an instrument of identity politics. This has included a rehabilitation of colonial studies—and particularly the work of the Pères Blancs Jesuit missionary educators like Devulder and Sanson with whom Bourdieu had been in close contact (cf. Adnani and Yacine 2003: 243; Sanson 2003)—which have been mined for evidence of precolonial Berber culture. Indeed, as contemporary ethnographers in North Africa, we have had the repeated experience of visiting

Berber associations and being presented with weathered copies of colonial military texts as the definitive sources on local tradition. And recently Bourdieu's works themselves have entered into this folk anthropological canon, not only as promoted by his Kabyle students (and students of students), but also by self-taught scholars on the North African periphery who can now access some of his texts via the Internet. Moreover, activists increasingly recognize Bourdieu's contributions to the Berber Cultural Movement even if they are less familiar with his theoretical work. Upon Bourdieu's death in January 2002, the president of the World Amazigh Congress, Mabrouk Ferkal, issued a communiqué rendering homage to the scholar as "one of the Kabyles' dearest friends" (cited in Silverstein, this volume). In this way, although Bourdieu remains best known for his contributions to a social theory of practice, symbolic violence, and social capital, the legacy of his early Algerian ethnography lives on in the contemporary cultural politics of the region.

Outline of the Volume

The chapters that comprise this volume explore these various aspects of Bourdieu's research and writing on Algeria, from the circumstances and politics of his early field studies, to their influence on his later theoretical development, to their legacies in later scholarship and social movements in and of Algeria. Although taking slightly different slices of Bourdieu's oeuvre as their objects of investigation and critique, each of the contributors emphasizes the symbiotic relationship between his fieldwork, ethnography, and theory, and the way in which all three of these practices evolved in concert with the changing political and material conditions under which he was operating. Overall, the chapters present a picture of a deeply engaged scholar whose work—in both its contributions and shortcomings—serves

45

as a model of self-reflexivity and intellectual and ethical commitment. Exploring Bourdieu's Algerian research gives us a window into larger, enduring issues surrounding the politics of ethnography in a changing world.

Fanny Colonna takes up what she characterizes as an agonistic social vision that runs through Bourdieu's corpus, from his earliest writings on Algeria (e.g., Bourdieu 1958; Bourdieu and Sayad 1964) to his 1993 landmark study *The Weight of the World* (1993) via *The Logic of Practice* (1980) and related works. She interrogates how the premise of radical deprivation repeatedly functions as the condition of possibility for a theory of domination, which constituted for Bourdieu the keystone of social relations. The implications of this theory of deprivation/domination for Bourdieu's ethnography of peasant societies in Algeria are dramatic: his description, and especially his theorization of the consequences of the social and spatial exclusion produced by colonization, take place at the expense of recognizing the peasants' own cultural resources in the form of written traditions or a meticulously preserved scriptural religion, both of which serve as endogenous reflections on their historical experience. Moving widely across Bourdieu's oeuvre, Colonna shows how the frame of his deprivation model repeatedly oversimplifies and obscures what was a far more complex social reality. For instance, drawing on Bourdieu's dialogues with Kabyle poetry expert and novelist Mouloud Mammeri (Mammeri and Bourdieu 2004 [1978]), Colonna contends that Mammeri's discussion of the historical reflexivity exercised by the Kabyle sages (*imusnawen*) was at odds with Bourdieu's "logic of practice" model, which would have denied them the capacity for critical reflection. If Colonna is critical of the ways in which Bourdieu's theory came at the expense of the ethnographic and historical record, she also acknowledges that Bourdieu's own praxis—in his dual capacity as a teacher and as an engaged intellectual—was in many ways more complex, nuanced, and "variegated" (Corcuff 1995) than his theoretical model would have allowed for. In setting the trajectories of deprivation and domination in Bourdieu's discourse against his own political commitments, Colonna shows how the latter worked to temper Bourdieu's contention that domination alone constitutes the essence of the social—as was apparent in Bourdieu's sustained engagement with the 1995 public worker strikes and demonstrations that sunk the austerity reforms proposed by then–Prime Minister Alain Juppé.

Jane Goodman makes the related point that Bourdieu's portrayals of Algeria appear to be more a function of his theoretical proclivities than of indigenous practice. She begins from what she characterizes as a Manichean divide that underwrites Bourdieu's representations of Algerian Kabyles: whereas those of the *Outline*, *The Logic of Practice*, and related works are made to represent a kind of enchanted precolonial order, the Kabyles of *Travail et travailleurs* and *Le Déracinement* appear solely in terms of dispossession and loss. As Goodman shows, Bourdieu constitutes this divide in part through representations of language: whereas the Kabyles in the latter works speak in eloquent, extended prose about the difficulties of their "uprooted" condition, those of the former speak in proverbs and sayings when they speak at all. Here Bourdieu was implicitly drawing on the Herderian tenet that oral lore provides a timeless conduit to a people's identity, without heed for the pragmatics of contemporary proverb use. Moreover, Bourdieu intermingled texts elicited in war-torn Kabylia with those he found in colonial ethnographies and missionary publications, thus molding the particular products of historically positioned individuals into evidence for a shared *habitus*.

For Goodman, Bourdieu's dualistic approach to language poses a number of problems. Since Bourdieu maintains that informants cannot articulate the logic of their own practice, endogenous reflexivity is all but foreclosed: Kabyles can never exercise critical purchase on the conditions of their own social life. Instead they are either made to endlessly reproduce an enchanted universe (as exemplars of a western fantasy of precolonial Others) or are condemned as victims of war and outcasts of capitalist modernity. For Bourdieu literacy constituted a key pivot on which this dualism rested: he believed that literacy fostered a critical consciousness that orality precluded. Yet as Goodman notes, Bourdieu neglected historical evidence of literacy in Kabylia—a region that had long included literate scribes, *marabouts* (religious specialists), and calendrical experts. In locating the region on the far side of an unwarranted dichotomy between literate and illiterate societies, Bourdieu reinforced a view of Kabyle society as primarily oral that was ethnographically unsustainable and politically problematic. Theory, then, came at the expense of both methodological rigor and ethnographic evidence.

Deborah Reed-Danahay similarly emphasizes the split in Bourdieu's thinking between the "em-peasanted peasant" (*paysan empaysanné*) who fully embodies his *habitus* and the "de-peasanted peasant" (*paysan dépaysanné*), a tragic figure unable to adapt to urbanizing or modernizing influences. Placing Bourdieu's work in rural France (specifically, in his natal province of Béarn) into dialogue with his research in Algeria, she finds versions of both figures in each place, suggesting that Bourdieu "was seeing French peasants in the faces and bodies of Algerians and perhaps vice versa" (this volume). Like Colonna, Reed-Danahay points to the discourse of dispossession that underwrites Bourdieu's theory, as several sets of victims are made to parallel each other: in Algeria, unemployed youth and dislocated peasants; in France, perpetual rural bachelors who lacked the symbolic capital to attract a wife in a rapidly urbanizing society. Both figures, for Bourdieu, were portrayed as "locked in their *habitus*" (Goodman, this volume), unable to adapt to a changing world.

Bourdieu's theory of *habitus*, Reed-Danahay further notes, was formulated in the 1960s (inspired by earlier work by Marcel Mauss and Norbert Elias) in the dual contexts of peasant studies and Mediterranean studies, both informed by a presumed dichotomy between urban and rural societies that itself was predicated on an equilibrium model of a premodern world subject to rupture and dislocation. Yet if Algeria and rural France constituted for Bourdieu "parallel worlds" in which he developed similar themes, they were also his own personal worlds. With Bourdieu's upbringing in rural France and his subsequent entry into the environment of the École Normale and the French university system, perhaps Bourdieu himself, Reed-Danahay suggests, embodied or at least could identify with the "de-peasanted peasant." In that sense Bourdieu's own autobiography may have furnished a model for the figure of the "man between two worlds" that would become a key leitmotif of his early ethnography.

Paul Silverstein follows Reed-Danahay's discussion of societal rupture with an exploration of the arboreal tropes of rooting and uprooting that underwrote Bourdieu's discussion of social transformation as exogenous crisis. Focusing on Bourdieu's essay on the Kabyle house (*akham*) and the later reappropriations of domestic architecture by the Berber cultural movement, Silverstein examines discourses of authenticity and autochthony embedded within a "structural nostalgia" (Herzfeld 1995) for a precolonial Kabylia shared by scholars and activists. In nostalgic practice, domesticity becomes a salient synecdoche for a rooted cultural tradition relatively untouched by a disruptive colonial and state-national modernity, and as such it is not surprising to find the *akham* (as described by Bourdieu) the object of contemporary archiving, restoration, and rebuilding projects by organic Kabyle intellectuals.

At issue is the politics of ethnography—and ethnic representation more broadly—in an era where culture has become an object of human rights discourse. As overseas Kabyles incorporate aspects of idealized village public and domestic structures into their urbane everyday lives, they objectify their culture as a scarce and endangered resource to be preserved if not revivified. Bourdieu's early writings, based largely on interviews with displaced villagers engaged in their own forms of structural nostalgia, participate in a similar ethic of recovery and rehabilitation, and thus find themselves open to later appropriation. The essay thus furthers Bourdieu's own interest in objectification and "objectivation," as it explores a particular case of how both academic and local synoptic representations of Kabyle social practice—of history-as-uprooting—are mutually determined.

Abdellah Hammoudi takes the volume full-circle, connecting Bourdieu's development of a theory of *habitus* in his Kabyle research to his earlier philosophical investigations of phenomenology. He discusses how *habitus*, in Bourdieu's later usage, retained many of the presumptions of the category of prerational, prereflexive "tradition" or "custom" found in earlier, colonial ethnological writings on Kabylia, as well as Bourdieu's initial publications. In elaborating and extending a theory of embodiment and the "feel for the game" (*le sens du jeu*) from Merleau-Ponty, Bourdieu actually emphasized the tendencies towards social reproduction and the limits placed on the improvisation—on the facts of practical and lived creativity—which Merleau-Ponty had seen as continuous and structurally effectual. In this respect, Bourdieu perfectly occupied the intellectual juncture between phenomenology and an emerging structuralism that marked the state of French social theory in the mid-1960s.

50

In like manner Hammoudi argues that such a model of *habitus* as a phenomenological field of reproduction recapitulates a division of labor between anthropology (as the study of peasant *habitus*) and Orientalism (as the study of more explicit, institutionalized cultural norms of language and religion). Hammoudi explores the ethnographic choices Bourdieu made to limit his scope of research to that of a "deep culture" (*culture profonde*) which bracketed dimensions of institutionalized Islam or an earlier history of social adaptations to the exigencies of Ottoman governance. Bourdieu's relegation of these latter elements to a superficial "level" of cultural influence points to the continuity of his work with the colonial ethnology on which he drew.

Throughout all of the chapters, the authors engage with Bourdieu's theoretical formulations in the various contexts in which they were developed. In pointing to the various shortcomings of his theories and descriptions, the authors are well aware that all ethnography is necessarily partial. We are convinced that critical engagement is the highest form of recognition and gratitude we can offer to a scholar as inspiring to our own projects and intellectual development as has been Pierre Bourdieu. We offer this volume in his memory.

Notes

1. In the wake of Bourdieu's death, special issues of several academic journals—including *Actes de la Recherche en Sciences Sociales* (2003), *Awal* (2003), and *Ethnography* (2004)—and a published collection (Bourdieu 2008, which appeared as this volume was going to press) focusing on Bourdieu's Algerian fieldwork experiences were edited by his former students and colleagues. These include republications of Bourdieu's own earlier writings, interviews with Bourdieu and a number of his Algerian research collaborators, photographs taken by Bourdieu while in the field, and some of Bourdieu's later thoughts on his earlier research, written just prior to his death. See also Addi (2002: 37–77); Lane (2000: 9–33); Reed-Danahay (2005: 69–98); Sayad (2002: 45–74); and

Yacine (2008) for further discussions of the colonial conditions of Bourdieu's ethnographic research and early theorization. Earlier discussions include De Certeau (1984: 50–60); Eickelman (1977); Lacoste-Dujardin (1976); and Reed-Danahay (1995).

2. Following Le Sueur (2005), we opt for the appellation "French-Algerian war" to underline the fact that the struggle constituted as much a civil war within France (insofar as the Algerian departments had been integrated into the juridical structure of the French state, and insofar as many of the events of the war were sited within metropolitan France) as a revolutionary war for independence. As Todd Shepard (2006: 1) emphasizes, "the Algerian Revolution was at the same time a French revolution." Indeed, it was only in the final days of the struggle that "France" and "Algeria" emerged as separate legal categories.

3. Other anthropologists—from French colonial ethnologists of North Africa (e.g., Adolphe Hanoteau and Robert Montagne) through early British social anthropologists like E. E. Evans-Pritchard—had conducted ethnographic fieldwork as part of (or alongside) military ventures, but Bourdieu was among the first to engage in an anthropological project under wartime conditions that was separate from—if not in opposition to—military logistics. See Greenhouse, Mertz, and Warren (2002) and Nordstrom and Robben (1995) on conducting ethnography under conditions of war.

4. On how Bourdieu's rural upbringing may have helped to shape his scholarly interests, see Reed-Danahay (2005).

5. See Dermenghem (1954) and Nouschi (1961). Other scholars working in the government around that time included Germaine Tillion, Robert Lacoste, Jaques Soustelle, Vincent Monteil, and Louis Massignon (Yacine 2004: 490).

6. Bourdieu describes this period of research in several posthumously published essays (2003, 2004a, 2004b), and in a televised interview (Adnani and Yacine 2003). For well-documented accounts of the intellectual and political conditions of this formative moment in Bourdieu's work, see also Garcia-Parpet (2003); Nouschi (2003); Sanson (2003); Sayad (2002); Wacquant (2004); and Yacine (2004, 2008).

7. On "integration" as a political solution during the closing years of the war, see Le Sueur (2005: 23–24) and Shepard (2006: 45–53).

8. *Que Sais-Je?* (What Do I Know?) is a series of reference works on historical and contemporary issues geared to an educated general populace.

9. This is one of the few places in Bourdieu's oeuvre that he devotes sustained attention to Islam (Bourdieu 1958: 107–18). See Hammoudi (2000, this volume) and Reed-Danahay (2005: 18) for a discussion of the religious aporia in Bourdieu's work on Algeria.

10. The English translation (1962d) also includes an extended version of Bourdieu's essay "Revolution in the Revolution," initially published in 1961.

11. Bourdieu's "clash of civilizations" is obviously quite distinct from Bernard Lewis and Samuel Huntington's later use of the term to describe a post–Cold War conflict between Islamic and Western societies, or to encapsulate the "rage" experienced by "Muslims" when confronted with an imperializing, Christian-secular modernity (Lewis 1990; Huntington 1996). As is discussed below, Bourdieu's highlighting of the asymmetrical relations built into colonial situations is not predicated on a primordial Orient/Occident, Islam/West distinction, and indeed he explicitly rejected the Orientalist tendency of colonial ethnography to approach Algerians as principally Muslim subjects.

12. See Lane (2000: 12–15); Nouschi (2003: 31–32); Wacquant (2004: 393); and Yacine (2004: 496–98) for further discussions of Bourdieu's "clash of civilizations" model as a response to acculturation theory and modernization theory, and to the earlier work of Germaine Tillion in particular. Bourdieu's engagement with Tillion is further evidenced in his later collection of scholarly essays based on his ARDES research, *Algérie 60* (1977b), the title of which is calqued on Tillion's earlier *L'Algérie en 1957* (1957, later translated as *Algeria: The Realities* [1958]).

13. For a discussion of arboreal tropes of rooting and uprooting, see Silverstein, this volume.

14. See Turner (1967) on ritual liminality as a situation of being betwixt and between social states.

15. The formulation of *tristes paysans* is clearly a play on Lévi-Strauss's foundational travelogue-*cum*-ethnography of cultural dissolution and social displacement in South America, *Tristes tropiques* (1955).

16. See Partha Chatterjee's discussion of Indian anticolonial nationalist discourse, which emphasized a distinction between "spiritual" and "material" domains of cultural life, granting British superiority in the former, but maintaining the latter as a space of Indian authenticity (1993).

17. We are grateful to Jeremy Lane for calling our attention to this question. While a fuller treatment is surely called for, it is beyond our capacities in this book.

18. On Algeria's Agrarian Revolution see Benhouria (1980); Dahmani (1979); Martens (1973); and Raffinot and Jacquemot (1977).

19. Sayad (2002: 68) later recalled the outrage elicited by Bourdieu's 1960 Algiers public lecture on "Algerian Culture": "Even well before the event, the few small flyers announcing the lecture were perceived as a provocation, as calls for subversion, as attacks on 'French culture'—such was the only possible

and decent culture—or so one heard in Algiers, within 'French Algeria'. And during and after the lecture there were cries of scandal! . . . How could one speak of culture, even in the anthropological sense, with regards to 'savages', 'ignoramuses', 'fanatics?'"

20. See Lane (2000: 117–19) for a parallel discussion of the tension between "rehabilitation" and "romanticism" in Bourdieu's Kabyle studies.

21. For similar colonial formulations of Berbers' Mediterranean character, see Busset (1929); Demontès (1930); Guernier (1950); and Maunier (1922). For a further discussion of the place of Berbers in colonial constructions of the Mediterranean, see Silverstein (2002).

22. Berber racial identity and origins were a much debated subject in late-nineteenth-century scholarship. See Mercier (1871); Rinn (1889); and Tauxier (1862–63). For a general overview of racial stereotyping in colonial Algeria see Gross and McMurray (1993) and Lorcin (1995).

23. The works of military ethnologists Hanoteau and Letourneux on oral lore and *qanoun* (Hanoteau 1867; Hanoteau and Letourneux 1872–73) are exemplary in this regard and are repeatedly cited by subsequent authors including Bourdieu (1977: 16). For a discussion of their work in the context of French imperialism and Bourdieu's oeuvre, see Goodman (2002 and this volume).

24. Bourdieu's posthumously published autobiographical reflection, *Esquisse pour une auto-analyse* (2004, *Sketch for a Self-Analysis*), is instructive of how clearly self-conscious he was of his own medial class position and its effects on his professional life and scholarly perspective.

25. Biographical information on Sayad can be found on the website of the Association des Amis de Abdelmalek Sayad (AAAS): http://www.abdelmaleksayad .org/f_biographie.html. See also Sayad (2002).

26. "Abdelmalek Sayad gives us an exemplary figure of the sociologist as 'public scribe', who records and broadcasts, with anthropological acuity and poetic grace, the voice of those most cruelly dispossessed of it by the crushing weight of imperial subordination and class domination, without ever instituting himself as a spokesperson, without ever using these given words to give lessons except lessons in ethnographic integrity, scientific rigor, and civic courage" (Bourdieu and Wacquant 2000: 179).

27. "Caught between two worlds, he did not truly recognize himself in one or the other, but did not wish to renounce either, and intensely experienced a 'sociological doubling' or perhaps rather a permanent tension between systems of contradictory obligations and influences which constrain emigration but also the position of the critical sociologist. Defying all illusions, Sayad, who became a sociologist at the moment of the war of liberation, was always in the position

of the outsider, the marginal, the trickster (*porte-à-faux*) even when he became research director at the CNRS and was recognized by the international scientific community" (Saint-Martin 1999: 36).

28. For an incisive analysis of the marginal character of emigration that picks up exactly where *Le Déracinement* leaves off, see Sayad's "Les trois 'âges' de l'émigration algérienne en France" (1977, translated and republished as "The Three Ages of Emigration" in Sayad 2004).

29. The Service des Centres Sociaux was the brainchild of Jacques Soustelle, governor general of Algeria beginning in 1955; however, it was Germaine Tillion who created a specific plan for educational reform and recruited Feraoun. For a history of the Service des Centres Sociaux, see LeSueur (2005: chap. 5).

30. Mammeri was active in the anticolonial resistance as early as the 1930s when he was a member of the maverick "Group of 7" whose mission was to "get France to leave" no matter the cost. Although World War II clearly interrupted their plans, Mammeri saw it as an opportunity to train himself in the art of war. See Yacine (1990b).

31. Some of these texts appear in Yacine (1990b: 112–35). See also Djeghloul (1990).

32. We are grateful to Jeremy Lane for helping us to clarify this point.

33. Bourdieu's support for Kabyle scholars continued into his later years with the founding of the Committee for the Support of Algerian Intellectuals (CISIA) after the 1993 assassination of Kabyle journalist/novelist Tahar Djaout.

34. On the place of the "Berber" in Algerian nationalist ideology, see McDougall (2003).

35. For a history of Kabyle cultural politics in France, see Slimani-Direche (1997) and Silverstein (2003, 2004).

36. Bourdieu published an insightful analysis of the events as they were occurring, with Didier Eribon in the French socialist daily *Libération* (1980; see Lane 2000: 114–15).

Works Cited

Addi, Lahouari. 2002. *Sociologie et anthropologie chez Pierre Bourdieu*. Paris: La Découverte.

Adnani, Hafid and Tassadit Yacine. 2003. L'autre Bourdieu. *Awal* 27/28: 229–49.

Ageron, Charles-Robert. 1960. La France a-t-elle un politique kabyle? *Revue Historique* 223: 311–52.

Arkoun, Mohamed. 1990. Mouloud Mammeri à Taourirt Mimoun. *Awal* spécial: 9–13.

Asad, Talal. 1973. *Anthropology and the Colonial Encounter*. London: Ithaca Press.

Balandier, Georges. 1951. La situation coloniale. *Cahiers Internationaux de Sociologie* 11: 44–79.

Barthes, Roland. 1957. *Mythologies*. Paris: Seuil.

Benhouria, Tahar. 1980. *L'Economie de l'Algérie*. Paris: Maspero.

Bianco, Lucien and Tassadit Yacine. 2003. On n'avait jamais vu le 'monde': Nous étions une petite frange de gauche entre les communistes et les socialistes. *Awal* 27/28: 267–77.

Bourdieu, Pierre. 1958. *Sociologie de l'Algérie*. Paris: Presses Universitaires de France.

———. 1959. Le choc des civilisations. In *Le Sous-développement en Algérie*. pp. 52–64. Algiers: Secrétariat Social.

———. 1961. Révolution dans la révolution. *Esprit* 1 (1): 27–40.

———. 1962a. Les relations entre les sexes dans la société paysanne. *Les Temps Modernes* 195: 307–31.

———. 1962b. Célibat et condition paysanne. *Etudes Rurales* 5/6: 32–136.

———. 1962c. De la guerre révolutionnaire à la revolution. In *L'Algérie de demain*, ed. François Perroux. pp. 5–13. Paris: Presses Universitaires de France.

———. 1962d. *The Algerians*. Boston: Beacon Press.

———. 1966. The Sentiment of Honor in Kabyle Society. *In Honour and Shame: The Values of Mediterranean Society*, ed. J. G. Peristiany, trans. Philip Sherrard. pp. 191–241. Chicago: University of Chicago Press.

———. 1970. La maison kabyle ou le monde renvversé. In *Echanges et communications. Mélanges offerts à Claude Lévi-Strauss à l'occasion de son 60è anniversaire*. Paris: Mouton.

———. 1972. *Esquisse d'une théorie de la pratique*. Geneva: Droz.

———. 1977a. *Outline of a Theory of Practice*. Cambridge: Cambridge University Press.

———. 1977b. *Algérie 60. Structures économiques, structures temporelles*. Paris: Minuit.

———. 1988 [1984]. *Homo Academicus*. Stanford: Stanford University Press.

———. 1989. Mouloud Mammeri ou *la colline retrouvée*. *Awal* 5: 1–3.

———. 1990 [1980]. *The Logic of Practice*. Cambridge: Polity Press.

———. 1991. Préface. In *L'Immigration ou les paradoxes de l'altérité*, Abdelmalek Sayad. Brussels: De Boeck.

———. 1996 [1989]. *The State Nobility: Elite Schools in the Field of Power*. Stanford: Stanford University Press.

————. 2000 [1997]. *Pascalian Meditations*. Cambridge: Polity Press.

————. 2001. *Masculine Domination*. Stanford: Stanford University Press.

————. 2002. *Le Bal des célibataires: Crise de la société paysanne en Béarn*. Paris: Points Seuil.

————. 2003a. *Images d'Algérie: Une affinité élective*, ed. Franz Schultheis. Arles: Actes Sud.

————. 2003b [2000]. Entre amis. *Awal* 27–28: 83–88.

————. 2003c. Participant Objectivation. *Journal of the Royal Anthropological Institute* 9: 281–94.

————. 2004a. *Esquisse pour une auto-analyse*. Paris: Raisons d'Agir.

————. 2004b. Algerian Landing. *Ethnography* 5 (4): 415–44.

————. 2008 *Esquisses algériennes*, ed. Tassadit Yacine. Paris: Seuil.

Bourdieu, Pierre, et al. 1993. *La Misère du monde*. Paris: Seuil.

Bourdieu, Pierre, Alain Darbel, Jean-Pierre Rivet, and Claude Seibel. 1963. *Travail et travailleurs en Algérie*. Paris: Mouton.

Bourdieu, Pierre and Didier Eribon. 1980. Clou de Djeha: Des contradictions linguistiques léguées par le colonisateur. *Libération* 19–20 April: 13.

Bourdieu, Pierre and Mouloud Mammeri. 2003 [1985]. Du bon usage de l'ethnologie. *Actes de la Recherche en Sciences Sociales* 150: 9–18.

Bourdieu, Pierre and Jean-Claude Passeron. 1970. *La Réproduction: Eléments pour une théorie du système d'enseignement*. Paris: Minuit.

Bourdieu, Pierre, Franck Poupeau, and Thierry Discepolo. 2002. *Interventions, 1961–2001: Science sociale et action politique*. Marseille: Agone.

Bourdieu, Pierre and Abdelmalek Sayad. 1964. *Le Déracinement. La Crise de l'agriculture traditionnelle en Algérie*. Paris: Minuit.

————. 1972. Stratégie et rituel dans le marriage kabyle. In *Mediterranean Family Structures*, ed. John G. Peristiany. Cambridge: Cambridge University Press.

————. 2004 [1964]. Colonial Rule and the Cultural Sabir. *Ethnography* 5 (4): 445–86.

Bourdieu, Pierre and Loïc Wacquant. 2000. The Organic Ethnologist of Algerian Migration. *Ethnography* 1 (2): 173–82.

Briggs, Charles. 1988. *Competence in Performance: The Creativity of Tradition in Mexican Verbal Art*. Philadelphia: University of Pennsylvania Press.

Busset, Maurice, et al. 1929. *Maroc et l'Auvergne*. Paris: Imprimerie Nationale.

Calhoun, Craig, Edward LiPuma, and Moishe Postone, eds. 1993. *Bourdieu: Critical Perspectives*. Chicago: University of Chicago Press.

Chaker, Salem. 1998. *Berbères aujourd'hui*. Second Edition. Paris: Harmattan.

Chatterjee, Partha. 1993. *Nationalist Thought and the Colonial World: A Derivative Discourse?* Minneapolis: University of Minnesota Press.

Clifford, James and George Marcus, eds. 1986. *Writing Culture: The Poetics and Politics of Ethnography.* Santa Fe NM: SAR Press.

Colonna, Fanny. 1975. *Instituteurs algériens, 1883–1939.* Paris: Presses de la Fondation Nationale des Sciences Politiques.

———. 1987. *Savants paysans: Eléments d'histoire sociale sur l'Algérie rurale.* Algiers: Office des Publications Universitaires.

———. 1995. *Les Versets de l'invincibilité: Permanence et changements religieux dans l'Algérie contemporaine.* Paris: Presses de la Fondation Nationale des Sciences Politiques.

Comaroff, Jean. 1985. *Body of Power, Spirit of Resistance.* Chicago: University of Chicago Press.

Cooper, Frederick and Ann Laura Stoler, eds. 1997. *Tensions of Empire: Colonial Cultures in a Bourgeois World.* Berkeley: University of California Press.

Corcuff, Philippe. 1995. *Les Nouvelles sociologies: Constructions de la réalité sociale.* Paris: Nathan.

Dahmani, Mohamed. 1979. *L'Algérie: Légitimité historique et continuité politique.* Paris: Editions Le Sycomore.

de Certeau, Michel. 1984. *The Practice of Everyday Life.* Berkeley: University of California Press.

Demontès, Victor. 1930. *L'Algérie économique.* Volume 3. Algiers: Gouvernement Général d'Algérie, Direction de l'Agriculture, du Commerce, et de la Colonisation.

Dermenghem, Émile. 1954. *Le Culte des saints dans l'Islam maghrébin.* Paris: Gallimard.

Dirks, Nicholas, ed. 1992. *Colonialism and Culture.* Ann Arbor: University of Michigan Press.

Djeghloul, Abdelkader. 1990. Le courage lucide d'un intellectuel marginalisé. *Awal* 6/7: 79–98.

Eickelman, Dale. 1977. Time in a Complex Society: A Moroccan Example. *Ethnology* 16 (1): 39–55.

Feraoun, Mouloud. 1954 [1950]. *Le Fils du pauvre.* Paris: Editions du Seuil.

———. 1992 [1954]. *Jours de Kabylie, suivi de Le Fils du pauvre.* Algiers: ENAG.

———. 2000 [1962]. *Journal 1955–1962: Reflections on the French-Algerian War*, ed. James D. Le Sueur, trans. Mary Ellen Wolf and Claude Fouillade. Lincoln: University of Nebraska Press.

Free. Anthony. 1996. The Anthropology of Pierre Bourdieu: A Reconsideration. *Critique of Anthropology* 16 (4): 395–416.

Garcia-Parpet, Marie-France. 2003. Des outsiders dans l'économie de marché. Pierre Bourdieu et les travaux sur l'Algérie. *Awal* 27/28: 139–52.

Goodman, Jane. 2002. Writing Empire, Underwriting Nation: Discursive Histories of Kabyle Berber Oral Texts. *American Ethnologist* 29 (1): 86–122.

———. 2005. *Berber Culture on the World Stage*. Bloomington: Indiana University Press.

Greenhouse, Carol J., Elizabeth Mertz and Kay B. Warren, eds. 2002. *Ethnography in Unstable Places: Everyday Lives in Contexts of Dramatic Political Change*. Durham: Duke University Press.

Gross, Joan and David McMurray. 1993. Berber Origins and the Politics of Ethnicity in Berber North Africa. *PoLAR: Political and Legal Anthropology Review* 16 (2): 39–57.

Guernier, Eugène. 1950. *La Berbérie, L'Islam, et la France*. Paris: Editions de l'Union Française.

Guilhaume, Jean-François. 1992. *Les Mythes fondateurs de l'Algérie française*. Paris: Harmattan.

Hammoudi, Abdellah. 2000. Pierre Bourdieu et l'anthropologie du Maghreb. *Awal* 21: 11–16.

Hanoteau, Adolphe. 1867. *Poésies populaires de la Kabylie du Jurjura*. Paris: Imprimerie Impériale.

Hanoteau, Adolphe and Aristide Letourneux. 1872–73. *La Kabylie et les coutumes kabyles*. 3 volumes. Paris: Imprimerie Nationale.

Héran, François. 1987. La seconde nature de l'*habitus*. Tradition philosophique et sens commun dans le langage philosophique. *Revue Française de Sociologie* 28 (3): 385–416.

Herzfeld, Michael. 1987. *Anthropology through the Looking Glass*. Cambridge: Cambridge University Press.

———. 1997. *Cultural Intimacy*. London: Routledge.

Honneth, Axel, Hermann Kocyba and Bernd Schwibs. 1986. The Struggle for Symbolic Order: An Interview with Pierre Bourdieu. *Theory, Culture and Society* 3 (3): 35–51.

Huntington, Samuel. 1996. *The Clash of Civilizations and the Remaking of the World Order*. New York: Simon and Schuster.

Lacoste-Dujardin, Camille. 1976. A propos de P. Bourdieu et de l'*Esquisse d'une théorie de la pratique*. *Hérodote* 2 (2): 103–16.

Lahire, Bernard, ed. 1999. *Le Travail sociologique de Pierre Bourdieu. Dettes et critiques*. Paris: La Découverte.

Lane, Jeremy F. 2000. *Pierre Bourdieu: A Critical Introduction*. London: Pluto Press.

Le Sueur, James. 2005 [2001]. *Uncivil War: Intellectuals and Identity Politics during the Decolonization of Algeria*. Lincoln: University of Nebraska Press.

———. 2000. Introduction. In *Journal 1955–1962: Reflections on the French-Algerian War*, Mouloud Feraoun. pp. ix–xlviii. Lincoln: University of Nebraska Press.

Lévi-Strauss, Claude. 1955. *Tristes tropiques*. Paris: Plon.

Lewis, Bernard. 1990. The Roots of Muslim Rage. *The Atlantic Monthly* 266 (3): 47–60.

Lorcin, Patricia. 1995. *Imperial Identities: Stereotyping, Prejudice, and Race in Colonial Algeria*. London: I. B. Tauris.

Lucas, Philippe and Jean-Claude Vatin. 1975. *L'Algérie des anthropologues*. Paris: Maspero.

Maddy-Weitzman, Bruce. 2001. Contested Identities: Berbers, "Berberism," and the State in North Africa. *Journal of North African Studies* 6 (3): 23–47.

Mahar, Cheleen. 1990. Pierre Bourdieu: The Intellectual Project. In *An Introduction to the Work of Pierre Bourdieu: In the Practice of Theory*, ed. Richard Harker, Cheleen Mahar and Chris Wilkes. pp. 26–57. London: Macmillan.

Mammeri, Mouloud. 1980. *Poèmes kabyles anciens*. Paris: Maspero.

———. 1989. Une expérience de recherche anthropologique en Algérie. *Awal* 5: 15–23.

———. 1991 [1938]. La société berbère. In *Culture savante, culture vécue: Etudes 1938–1989*. Algiers: TALA.

Mammeri, Mouloud and Pierre Bourdieu. 2004 [1978]. Dialogue on Oral Poetry. *Ethnography* 5 (4): 511–51.

Martens, Jean-Claude. 1973. *Le Modèle algérien de développement: Bilan d'une décennie*. Algiers: Société Nationale d'Edition et de Diffusion.

Maunier, René. 1922. Leçon d'ouverture d'un cours de sociologie algérienne. *Hespéris* 11: 93–107.

McDougall, James. 2003. Myth and Counter-Myth: The "Berber" as National Signifier in Algerian Historiographies. *Radical History Review* 86: 66–88.

Mercier, Ernst. 1871. Ethnographie de l'Afrique septentrionale. Notes sur l'origine du peuple berbère. *Revue Africaine* 40: 420–33.

Nordstrom, Carolyn and Antonius C. G. M. Robben, eds. 1995. *Fieldwork under Fire: Contemporary Studies of Violence and Survival*. Berkeley: University of California Press.

Nouschi, André. 1961. *Enquête sur le niveau de vie des populations rurales constantinoises*. Paris: Presses Universitaires de Frances.

———. 2003. Autour de *Sociologie de l'Algérie*. *Awal* 27/28: 29–36.

Pinto, Louis. 1998. *Pierre Bourdieu et la théorie du monde social*. Paris: Albin Michel.

Raffinot, Marc and Pierre Jacquemot. 1977. *Le Capitalism d'État algérien*. Paris: Maspéro.

Redfield, Robert, Robert Linton and Melville J. Herskovits. 1936. Memorandum for the Study of Acculturation. *American Anthropologist* 38: 149–52.

Reed-Danahay, Deborah. 1995. The Kabyle and the French: Occidentalism in Bourdieu's Theory of Practice. In *Occidentalism: Images of the West*, ed. James Carrier. pp. 61–84. Oxford: Oxford University Press.

———. 2005. *Locating Bourdieu*. Bloomington: Indiana University Press.

Rinn, Louis. 1889. *Les Origines berbères. Etude linguistique et ethnologique*. Algiers: Jourdan.

Roberts, Hugh. 1980. Towards an Understanding of the Kabyle Question in Contemporary Algeria. *Maghreb Review* 5 (5–6): 115–24.

Said, Edward. 1978. *Orientalism*. New York: Vintage.

Saint-Martin, Monique de. 1999. Un sociologue critique. *Migrance* 14: 36–39.

Sanson, Henri. 2003. "C'était un esprit curieux." *Awal* 27/28: 279–86.

Sayad, Abdelmalek. 1977. Les "trois ages" de l'émigration algérienne en France. *Actes de la Recherche en Sciences Sociales* 15: 59–79.

———. 1992. Minorités et rapport à l'état dans le monde méditerranéen: le "mythe kabyle". In *Connaissance de l'Islam*. pp. 135–81. Paris: Syros.

———. 2002. Entretien avec Hassan Afraoui. In *Histoire et recherche identitaire*. pp. 45–105. Algiers: Bouchène.

———. 2004 [1999]. *The Suffering of the Immigrant*, trans. David Macey. Cambridge: Polity Press.

Scheele, Judith. 2007. Recycling *Baraka*: Knowledge, Politics, and Religion in Contemporary Algeria. *Comparative Studies of Society and History* 49 (2): 304–28.

Shepard, Todd. 2006. *The Invention of Decolonization: The Algerian War and the Remaking of France*. Ithaca NY: Cornell University Press.

Shusterman, Richard, ed. 1999. *Bourdieu: A Critical Reader*. Oxford: Blackwell.

Silverstein, Paul A. 2002. France's *Mare Nostrum*: Colonial and Post-Colonial Constructions of the French Mediterranean. *Journal of North African Studies* 7 (4): 1–22.

———. 2003. Martyrs and Patriots: Ethnic, National, and Transnational Dimensions of Kabyle Politics. *Journal of North African Studies* 8 (1): 87–111.

———. 2004. *Algeria in France: Transpolitics, Race, and Nation*. Bloomington: Indiana University Press.

Slimani-Direche, Karima. 1997. *Histoire de l'émigration kabyle en France au XXe siècle: Réalités culturelles et politiques et appropriations identitaires.* Paris: Harmattan.

Sprecher, Jean. 2003. "Il se sentait bien avec nous . . . cela signifiait qu'il était de notre bord." *Awal* 27/28: 295–305.

Tauxier, Henri. 1862–63. Etudes sur les migrations des tribus berbères avant l'islamisme. *Revue Africaine* 18: 35–37.

Temime, Emile. 1999. Un homme-frontière. *Migrance* 14: 28–34.

Tillion, Germaine. 1957. *L'Algérie en 1957.* Paris: Minuit.

———. 1958. *Algeria: The Realities.* New York: Knopf.

Turner, Victor. 1967. Betwixt and Between: The Liminal Period in *Rites de Passage.* In *The Forest of Symbols. Aspects of Ndembu Ritual.* Ithaca NY: Cornell University Press.

Vandenberghe, Frédéric. 1999. "The Real is Relational": An Epistemological Analysis of Pierre Bourdieu's Generative Structuralism. *Sociological Theory* 17 (1): 32–67.

Wacquant, Loïc. 1993. Bourdieu in America: Notes on the Transatlantic Importation of Social Theory. In *Bourdieu: Critical Perspectives,* ed. Craig Calhoun, Edward LiPuma, and Moishe Postone. pp. 235–62. Chicago: University of Chicago Press.

———. 2002. The Sociological Life of Pierre Bourdieu. *International Sociology* 17 (4): 549–56.

———. 2004. Following Pierre Bourdieu into the Field. *Ethnography* 5 (4): 387–414.

Yacine, Tassadit. 1990a. Aux origines de la quête: Mammeri parle . . . *Awal* 6/7: 67–77.

———. 1990b. Mouloud Mammeri dans la guerre. *Awal* 6/7: 105–41.

———. 2004. Pierre Bourdieu in Algeria at War: Notes on the Birth of an Engaged Ethnosociology. *Ethnography* 5 (4): 487–510.

———. 2008. Aux origines d'une ethnographie singulière. In *Esquisses algériennes, Pierre Bourdieu.* pp. 21–53. Paris: Seuil.

ONE

The Phantom of Dispossession

From The Uprooting to The Weight of the World

FANNY COLONNA

Translated by Patricia Fogarty

Should we take Pierre Bourdieu at his word when, in an interview he gave at the end of his life and published posthumously, he refers to his research on Algeria as "at once his oldest and most current work" (Bourdieu 2003: 14)? Or when he adds that *Le Déracinement* (The Uprooting, 1964) "has a strong resemblance to *La Misère du monde* (The Weight of the World, 1993)" (2003: 40)? Can we do more than just note the strong family likeness between these two texts, which were written thirty years apart about such very different societies? Can we draw on Bourdieu's own statements to argue that it was his initial discovery of radical deprivation of the weakest (in *Le Déracinement*) that gradually opened the way to his theory of domination as keystone of all social relations? The theory has gained ever since in its power of generalization, and, perhaps unfortunately, has had even greater success than the work itself.

Or should we instead follow Philippe Corcuff, who, invoking Foucault's critique of the "ready-made syntheses" entailed in the categories of "work" and "author,"[1] prefers to focus on the fighting spirit of Bourdieu's science as a "combat sport"[2] and on the absence of uniformity in his "variegated" thinking "criss-crossed with fault lines" (Corcuff

2003: 11–13, 129)? This is the knotty aporia I propose to look into
in this chapter, an undertaking that entails a careful and, if possible,
"fresh" re-reading of texts that have already been critically discussed
countless times. To circumscribe even more precisely what we might
expect from an exploration of the alternatives that I have perhaps too
simplistically sketched: Is our task to read Bourdieu's corpus as a closed
and deterministic system (to state it perhaps too baldly), or is it to look
into how, when, and through what means Bourdieu, his successors,
and even his adversaries were able to promote one of the most novel
and substantial theoretical projects of the twentieth century, which
extends well beyond the horizon of the social sciences?

After Bourdieu's somewhat esoteric beginnings in philosophy,
the indissociably theoretical, empirical, and epistemological project
that Bourdieu and his research team(s) developed became—in less
than twenty years (from *Les Héritiers* in 1964 to *Le Sens pratique*
in 1980)—the primary point of reference in the "field" of sociology
in France and, gradually, elsewhere. When Bourdieu first turned his
attention to this field (shortly after the end of World War II), he was
acutely aware of the state of decay and dependence—in a word,
impoverishment—in which this science found itself: perceived by
the layman as resembling a kind of journalism by virtue of its object
of study, and denigrated as vulgar in relation to philosophy due to
its scientific, even positivistic, "airs" (Bourdieu 2004: 14). Bourdieu
thus began what he would envision as a long-term project to reha-
bilitate and reinvigorate the discipline. In reconstituting the field, he
not surprisingly adopted a piece of advice that Claude Lévi-Strauss
would often offer in his seminars: bracket off everything that did not
concern the "invention" to be defended. Hence the almost obsessive
concern with evoking the coherence of Bourdieu's oeuvre. Need we
add that from his first texts on Algeria, something like a "tragic

vision" of the social world—quite Spinozan—was already in play, producing and reinforcing the theme of domination.

And yet, Bourdieu was quite wary of the overly "violent" uses of models—his own or others'—and he frequently cautioned against this in his teaching. It may be worth mentioning here that Bourdieu's "oral oeuvre" (constituted in seminars, doctoral defenses, or even in student advising sessions) is every bit as significant as his written one, and much more nuanced or "variegated," as Corcuff would say. The problem is that—by Bourdieu's choice of research subjects and thus of problematics—he has almost always, if not always, privileged relations of domination. But it's unclear whether this was in spite of or against himself! As I see it, it was more a matter of a conscious strategy of a somewhat crude primitive accumulation.

For the last ten years or so, most of the currents of what is called in France the "new sociologies" (Corcuff 1995) have stemmed from the salutary "shock" that Bourdieu's work produced, even if these currents claim that their inspiration lies elsewhere, particularly outside of France (e.g., Elias, Schutz, etc.). At the same time, resistance began appearing to what was taking shape as a hegemonic ambition, at least in terms of its claim to describe social reality. In a word, Bourdieu's was an "exclusive" thought, which is difficult to contest.

With the passing of time, this "exclusive" thought has been rightly perceived as a *limit* out of and/or against which new ideas have developed. A sociologist of Indian societies will underscore how important the notion of domination is for his work; another, Algerian, might feel entirely at home with the concept (and for good reason). But a third, also Algerian, will invoke the *historicity* of that society, which has been so very "revolutionized" (the word is Bourdieu's)[3] to contest the effectiveness of a category like "the sense of honor," for instance. It is in this third category—as will become apparent below—that my reading is located, even if the foundations of my training owe a great deal to my long relationship with Bourdieu, first as his student and later as a researcher. Even during those years, however, there was always one area of contention between us: the time and importance that I accorded to the field in my work. And this latter point explains the former one.

Bourdieu taught his students that "situations of beginnings" (of institutions, of colonization, and of capitalism) are especially important and require particularly attentive analytical work—witness the studies he inspired on early education and pediatrics, or on the origin of intellectuals, at the end of the nineteenth century. So we are doubtless justified in taking a closer look at beginnings where theoretical paradigms are concerned. We do have here a Durkheimian guideline (see *L'Evolution pédagogique en France*), inherited in turn from the historian Fustel de Coulanges.[4] In this essay, I trace a line that begins in Bourdieu's earliest works on Algeria, runs through *Le Sens pratique* (The Logic of Practice), and culminates in his 1993 work *La Misère du monde* (The Weight of the World). These studies, I argue, constitute significant landmarks in Bourdieu's extreme and agonistic vision of the social world. At the same time, I will attend to some of the "lateral by-ways" (as Corcuff calls them) through which Bourdieu—more in his practice than in his theory—attempted to escape from this implacable model. All the while bearing in mind, as I alluded to above, that Bourdieu was not unaware that the world and the human condition were less "dark" than his corpus might suggest.

The Shock of the Algerian Field: Encounter with the Third World, or Merely with a Third World

In 1958, only three years after his arrival in Algiers, where, following his military service, he was teaching sociology at the University of Algiers, Bourdieu published *Sociologie de l'Algérie* (Sociology of Algeria). This work, "torn" (as he says)—by means of what he later termed a "critical culturalist" reading—from the texts of his predecessors, already contains the essence of what interests us here: the theme of the disintegration of "indigenous" society and the theme of *habitus*, which is not yet named as such but referred to as "real psychological dispositions" inculcated through cultural apprenticeship, apparently with the aim of keeping improvisation at bay (see in particular chapters 6, "Désagrégation et désarroi" (Disintegration and dismay), and 5, "Le fond commun" (Common ground). In brief, Bourdieu elaborated a proto-theory of domination. Then came his encounter with rural Algeria through the group investigations conducted by the ARDES (Association pour la Recherche Démographique, Economique et Sociale)[5] on selected resettlement camps—that is, camps housing refugee populations displaced from their homes on the orders of the French army during the Algerian revolution. The two resulting books, *Travail et travailleurs en Algérie* (Work and Workers in Algeria, 1963) and *Le Déracinement* (The Uprooting, 1964) provided Bourdieu with an empirical basis for what had initially been no more than a set of hypotheses, or even intuitions, inspired by a deep reappropriation of philosophic and sociological paradigms.

I will not enter here into the detailed reappraisal of these paradigms that I was led to make over the course of my own research in rural Algeria (in the Aurès area from 1973, and later in the Gourara; see Colonna 1978, 1987, 1995). Suffice it to say that, as I was a student of Bourdieu's in the late 1950s, wrote a thesis under his supervision in the early 1970s, and was living in Algeria at the height of the Agrarian Revolution,[6] when I carried out these investigations, the process of distancing myself from Bourdieu's approach to rural Algeria was doubly painful. In 1989—that is, after Algeria's so-called "democratic opening"[7]—a high-ranking official of the Education Department, who was close to government circles, read my chapter entitled "Le déracinement comme concept et comme politique" (Uprooting as Concept and Policy) (Colonna 1978) and told me, only partly in jest, "You're lucky our bosses don't read or you would have landed in prison!" The model I was questioning was so strongly regarded as legitimate in Algeria that to this day I have not managed to persuade many of my colleagues there to examine it more critically.

The reason that Bourdieu's model of radical deprivation of the peasantry appeared to me to have little heuristic validity for my own field site (the Aurès mountains) was that its way of describing and especially of theorizing the consequences of spatial and social exclusion brought about by colonization left the peasants' own cultural resources entirely out of the picture. To me these resources were readily apparent in their memorized and even written traditions, in their carefully preserved scriptural religion, and above all, in an endogenous reflexivity with regard to past and present historical experience that effectively challenged the model's presumption that the peasants were not in a position to reflect critically on their own lives. Moreover, the political implications of the "deprivation" model were especially dramatic in Algeria because they resonated dangerously with the extremely radical vision of the leaders of the Algerian revolution and, paradoxically, with the theses of its main theorist Frantz Fanon, about which Bourdieu had, quite early on, expressed very lucid reservations (Bourdieu 1960).[8]

For all this, *Le Déracinement* is a book both rich and strange. In retrospect, the reader cannot help but be struck by the gap between the real empirical complexity of some chapters (e.g., chapters 3 and 7), the shrewd and painstaking way of posing questions, the care taken in comparing the different areas studied, and the simplicity of the theses proposed by way of explanation. In the end, however, it was not the empirical detail but the book's synthetic "theoricist" reasoning that was accepted as the "truth" about the situations depicted. This reasoning was then extended, without any real support or justification, to the Algerian peasantry as a whole. The last chapter goes so far as to extrapolate from the wartime situation to make incautious predictions about post-independence Algeria, prophecies that were not supported by any references to specific dated or situated studies.

Retrospective reviews and re-readings have a distinct advantage in that they impel us to look for the reasons and origins of theoretical developments that have since come to be taken for granted. The posthumous work invoked above, *Images d'Algérie, une affinité elective* (Images of Algeria: An Elective Affinity, 2003), invites this kind of reflection. It is a book of photographs taken by Bourdieu in 1958 and 1959, in and around Algiers and in the resettlement camps that were the subjects of *Le Déracinement* and *Travail et travailleurs*. It contains intriguing reflections on the role of the photograph in ethnological work, and on "those photographs" in particular. There are also numerous long quotations, drawn primarily from *Travail et travailleurs* and *Le Déracinement*. Finally, the book includes an article initially written in 1960, in which Bourdieu takes issue with the theses of Frantz Fanon (later published in a much milder form in *Esprit*) (Bourdieu 1961). Clearly the text and photos were meant to be read together. However, for anyone familiar with present-day Algeria, the pictures could have been taken just yesterday. Sadly Algeria's cities and countryside (especially countryside) have changed very little since the 1950s, aside from ending the horror of the resettlement camps (and again, even here, some of the "socialist villages" built during the Boumediene years were not much better[9]). What we see above all through the eyes of the photographer is his discovery of an "other world." For obvious reasons, we see almost nothing that suggests the presence of a foreign army. Instead, we are shown a society of the South, clearly impoverished and underdeveloped but above all *different*. In the accompanying interview, Bourdieu confesses that he found his experience in Algeria "overwhelming"—even "tragic"—and that he lived there in a permanent state of feverish tension. Tension because of the exceptional nature of the experience coupled with a feverish desire to understand. But isn't this kind of state more generally and largely attributable to the unsettling and unsettled nature of any first experience of fieldwork together with, in Bourdieu's case, the surprise of encountering such alterity in a "French department," a land that was juridically part of France?[10] Photographs, according to the professionals, are interpreted primarily through their captions. In the present case, it's only the quotations accompanying the photographs that bring the themes of "disintegration," "uprooting," or "economy of misery" into focus in an exaggeratedly synchronic presentation.

Admittedly, it was wartime, and it was a war that left at least a million dead. But what the pictures show primarily are other ways of dressing, other body postures (carrying a child on one's back), inequality between sexes (a woman walking beside a man riding), small trades, rudimentary crafts, technology of another age—in short, a world living in a culture and a temporality that were different, though not totally different. Yet this culture and temporality are presented in the text only in terms of lack, loss, and discrepancy, as an atemporal non-culture. They are crushed by an interpretative frame that leaves them no place.

Furthermore, no Europeans are ever shown, even in town, and they were practically absent from the 1958 book (*Sociologie de l'Algérie*) as well. The omission is serious for it amounts to ignoring an important dimension of the daily life of the Algerians Bourdieu felt it was his mission to understand. In underlining this absence, my aim is not to take issue with Bourdieu or to advance my own ideas but to draw attention to what a cinematographer might call the "frame." For in Bourdieu's approach as it appears in this book, there is not the least attempt at any "close-up" anthropology. He sometimes refers in passing to "westernized" and town-dwelling Algerians in his 1958 study (124), as people "in-between," tempted "by anxious identification or rebellious negativism," who don't know their country any better than do the French left-wing intellectuals (such as Sartre, in particular, and also Fanon) who were close to Algeria's National Liberation Front (Front de Libération Nationale, FLN[11]). He sometimes invokes the memory of the novelist Mouloud Feraoun, assassinated by the Organisation de l'Armée Secrète (OAS)[12], or his collaboration with Abdelmalek Sayad (with whom he wrote *Le Déracinement*). On the whole, however, it "is as if" (to use one of his own favorite expressions) all that really counted for Bourdieu was to depict a uniquely deprived population, not clearly linked to any temporal context or involved in any meaningful dialogue with different Others.

"I didn't keep a journal," Bourdieu said in the course of the interview, pleading the urgency of the situation. Reading this, an ethnologist, who never lets his/her field notebook out of sight day or night, is at a loss to know what to make of this regret or oversight. It is indeed surprising, especially considering the plethora of sophisticated techniques, ingenious observation grids (even Rorschach tests!), visual records, and sketches that Bourdieu mentions using, and in light of his stated intention of grasping the whole of the unsettling reality by any and all means. It appears, in fact, that he was careful to keep records of everything . . .

except himself and his feelings. Bourdieu claimed he was not there just to see and feel but to understand. Point taken; but for him, to understand was to theorize: "I wasn't going to satisfy myself with the sort of account a good journalist could make, I wanted to discover the logic and transhistorical effects of these great forced displacements of population" (2003: 40). What comes next in the interview is curious and unexpected for anyone who knew Bourdieu—perhaps there is some virtue in free association in interviews even when the subject is a master of the technique! It is a passage on censoring and self-censoring, on the fashion in Paris at the time of suppressing "anything to do with philosophy and literature," and on the prevailing academic etiquette, which meant that there were all sorts of things one didn't even think of describing. All the "little" things that in fact could have been jotted down from day to day and that might have provided some opening into what his central thesis left obscure.

Second-Level Developments

Habitus and Practice, or Doing Things without Knowing Why One Does What One Is Doing

> What one can require in all rigorousness (*en toute rigueur*) of the eth-nologist is that he attempt to restore (*restituer*) to other men the meaning of their behaviours, of which the colonial system, among other things, dispossessed them.—Foreword of *Travail et travailleurs* (1963)

My aim is to outline the "dark slope" of Bourdieu's thinking and to discern it under the more elaborate guise he gives it in his later theoretical constructions, in particular those of *Le Sens pratique* (1980). To do this correctly, we need to place ourselves in the border zone between anthropology and sociology that Bourdieu himself always claimed to occupy: "I didn't make any distinction between sociology and ethnology" he would say. In the case of the subjects of *Le Déracinement*, dispossession was historical and political. Domination existed for them as a "pre-constructed object," to use another of his favorite expressions. There was no need to search for or guess at it. The problem was that he extended the use of this construction in a way that concealed too much, a point I will come back to. In the case of the actors of *Esquisse d'une théorie de la pratique* (Outline of a Theory of Practice) or of *Le Sens pratique* (The Logic of Practice) the question is not really the same, and there is also the matter of situating them in time and space (see Goodman, this volume). Just who are these Kabyles? Where, when, and how did he meet them? Here, as in the case of the child referred to in *Sociologie de l'Algérie* (The Algerians),[13] misrecognition of the motivations of practice is presented as ontological, natural, and structural. In fact *Esquisse* and *Le Sens pratique* propose generalizations that go far beyond those applicable to the paroxystic situation of uprooting.

Rather than argue from the example of the agrarian calendar, as I did elsewhere (Colonna 1995: chapter 7; see also Goodman, this volume), I will take up the fascinating episode of Bourdieu's "famous" dialogue with Mammeri and the invention of "*oralité savante*" (oral wisdom). In 1978 a discussion between Bourdieu and the Algerian novelist Mouloud Mammeri appeared in *Actes de la Recherche en Sciences Sociales* (Bourdieu and Mammeri 1991 [1978]). The piece was titled "Dialogue on Oral Poetry in Kabylia" (Dialogue sur la poésie orale en Kabylie), but the summary on the cover of the issue referred more enigmatically to "Berber poets and the Homeric question." The Homeric problematic was in fact foregrounded in the exchange. Mammeri had studied classics at the University of Algiers and completed a diploma of advanced studies (Diplôme d'Etudes Supérieures) in Greek under the eminent Durkheimian Greek scholar Louis Germet, who was teaching in Algiers at the time; he thus willingly engaged in a discussion of Kabyle poetry along Homeric lines. It was Bourdieu, however, who constantly oriented the discussion so as to emphasize the importance of orality and minimize the long-standing presence of scriptural culture, be it Arabic and Islam or French from the end of the nineteenth century—despite the fact that Mammeri gave one example after another of scriptural practices. Once again "close-up" anthropology is sadly missing, for nothing in the dramaturgy of the dialogue gives any idea of how much Mammeri's docility owed to his personal interest as an "organic intellectual" of the Kabyle cause.

The key point, however, is this: the sophistication of the Kabyle poetic tradition, the genuinely sapiential role of the poets, and, as Mammeri very rightly emphasized, the known horizontality of cultural practice in this culture (all men, whatever their status, assist at the public performances of the epic poets or "aèdes," as Bourdieu calls them) all went counter to any depiction of culture as something merely incorporated in and reproducing itself mechanically through practice. And yet Bourdieu formulated it in this way, for the first time (at least systematically) in *Esquisse d'une théorie de la pratique*, published in 1972:

> The value system of honour is acted rather than thought and the grammar of honour can inform acts without being formulated. Thus when Kabyles spontaneously seize on this or that behaviour as dishonourable or ridiculous they are in a situation like that of a person who seizes on a linguistic mistake though he has no command of the syntactic system that has been transgressed. (41)

Or, further:

> Every agent whether or not he knows or intends it is a producer and reproducer of objective meaning: because his actions and his

works are the product of a *modus operandi* of which he is not the producer and over which he does not have conscious mastery they contain an "objective intention" as the Scholastics would say, which always exceeds his conscious intentions . . . it is because, strictly speaking, subjects do not know that what they are doing means more than they know. *Habitus* is the universalising mediation which ensures that practices without explicit reason and meaning intended by an individual actor are nonetheless "sensible," reasonable, and objectively orchestrated . . . that is to say that the process of objectivation cannot be described in the language of interaction and mutual adjustment, because the interaction itself owes its form to objective structures. (182–83)

This was a targeted critique, by the way, of interactionism and ethnomethodology.

One does not need to be of a particularly suspicious turn of mind to see straight away that the oft-cited reflexivity and historicity of the poetic message of the Kabyle *imusnawen* (professional poets) is not at all consistent with the "logic of practice" model. It is unthinkable that in spite of immigration, military conscription, and a century of French republican schooling (of which Mammeri was by no means the unique product), history had not touched the Algerian peasants over the centuries—indeed, well before the Algerian revolution. The fact is, moreover, that well before 1980, Bourdieu had read a manuscript that I conveyed to him: Mammeri's introduction to *Poèmes kabyles anciens* (Old Kabyle Poems, Mammeri 1980), a magnificent poetry corpus that was published only two years after Bourdieu and Mammeri's discussion—thus at the same time as *Le Sens pratique* (The Logic of Practice). The introduction was written in 1976 during the period of then-President Boumediene's triumph: following extremely contentious and vibrant nationwide discussions over the new National Charter (Charte Nationale), and in particular the role of the Berber language and culture in Algeria, Boumediene's government effectively foreclosed any possibility that Berber would have a place in Algerian public discourse.[14] Mammeri's text constitutes a eulogy in the classical sense of the term, a tribute to "Kabyle-ness" (*kabylité*) as a living, constantly evolving entity. The piece is so overwhelmingly sincere, politically courageous, precisely documented, and poetically powerful that, as a sociologist and perceptive reader, Bourdieu could not have helped but be deeply affected by it.

1980: Le Sens pratique (The Logic of Practice)

We cannot examine in detail the whole of this ambitious work here. It is very difficult and finally, in spite of what one might think at first, very Lévi-Straussian in its desire to tie everything together, without ever letting us know what the actors concerned think and do about it all. We can, however, look at how Bourdieu manages to carry on in the face of two major implicit challenges to the mechanical nature of the *habitus*/practice relationship, ones that are especially interesting in light of who wrote them. The *habitus*/practice relationship is asserted very early on and very firmly:

> In social formations in which the reproduction of relations of domination (and economic or cultural capital) is not performed by objective mechanisms, the endless work required to maintain relations of personal dependence would be condemned to failure if it could not count on the permanence of *habitus*, socially constituted and constantly reinforced by individual or collective sanctions. In this case the social order rests mainly on the order that reigns in people's minds, and the *habitus*, i.e., the organism

as appropriated by the group and attuned to the demands of the group, functions as the materialization of the collective memory, reproducing the acquisitions of the predecessors in the successors. . . . The *habitus*—embodied history, internalized as a second nature and so forgotten as history—is the active presence of the whole past of which it is the product. (91n4, 94)[15]

These lines send a chill down the spine and make us feel we wouldn't want to live in the society of the sort described! If, that is, a society exists that actually fits the description. It can also be noted that we have here in a nutshell, the formulation of the relation between *habitus/practice and domination*. The implication is that, at least in this type of social formation, domination constitutes the very essence of the social. We will take up this point again below.

But let us return to the implicit challenges. Besides Mammeri's work mentioned above, there is a chapter in Jack Goody's *The Domestication of the Savage Mind* titled "Intellectuals in Societies without Writing." Bourdieu had included Goody's work in his series Sens Commun (Common sense) of the Editions de Minuit press, published in French translation with the rather abstract title *La Raison graphique* (Goody 1979). We must note, to Bourdieu's credit, that he did instigate the debate with Mammeri (even though it was not really a debate since they, at least apparently, agreed on every point), that he published it in his own journal, and that he also had Goody's work translated. In so doing he accepted a confrontation with theses he could have chosen merely to glance at or mention in passing in *Le Sens pratique*. For that was the work Bourdieu felt to be his major and definitive theoretical statement, as is clearly evident from the long, self-justifying Preface.

It seems to me highly significant that the first mention of a possible controversy comes in the Preface itself, which includes a note of self-criticism (a rare event for this author) in which Bourdieu regrets that his "Durkheimian" tendency led him to underestimate the part played by Kabyle poets in a cultural practice he had up until then taken to be "collective and impersonal, in short, without producers" (35n23).[16] This implicit challenge "from the field" of a society that was also his own was felt by him to be particularly important, and rightly so. After this first comment, Mammeri is invoked three more times in the work, always as having contributed something utterly new in his "revelation" of the role of the poets (35n24, 35n164, 35n177).[17] Mammeri does not appear, however, in the final bibliography (which, admittedly, does not include literary references). And yet many of Mammeri's novels, like most of the literary production of the "in-between" writers of his day, provide invaluable documentation of and testimony to the "adjustments" between *habitus* and practice on the part of both men and women that resulted from *local* historical change; in this vein, the most heuristic of Mammeri's novels was probably *Le Sommeil du juste* (The Sleep of the Just, Mammeri 1955), which deals with the advent of French republican schooling (operating in Kabylia since 1883). Also worth mentioning, along the same lines, is Feraoun's *Les Chemins qui montent* (The Ascending Paths, Feraoun 1957).

However, even taken together, Bourdieu's acknowledgments of indebtedness may add nuance and complexity to his model but do not alter its overall shape. We cannot see here much in the way of what Philippe Corcuff might call "fault lines" or "variegations." However, one passage deserves more attention: a plea for "ethnology of Algeria by Algerians" and a tribute to the early work done under the auspices of the Center for Archaeological, Prehistoric, and Ethnological Research (CRAPE), which Mammeri directed for a number of years (Bourdieu 1980: 35n24[18]).[19] The testimonial is surprisingly "indigenist" and probably to be understood in connection with the unfailing support Bourdieu gave Mammeri from 1983 on. After the major Berber uprising known as the Berber Spring in Algeria in 1980–81,[20] Mammeri wanted to create a structure in Paris for research and publication on the world of the Berbers; this eventually led to the launching of the journal *Awal*. We can assume, even though Bourdieu himself never clearly acknowledged it, that his relationship with Mammeri, which lasted until the death of the latter in 1989, and his readings of Mammeri's later works, led him to become aware of the "obsolete" character of his earlier assertions, at least as far as the Kabyle region was concerned. By then a lot of water had flowed under the bridge, and a strongly intellectual Berber movement had come into being (see, for example, the profile of the Rassemblement pour la Culture et la Démocratie or RCD, a Berberist political party created by Algerian Francophone intellectuals).[21] From then on he could accept other models, albeit without questioning the basis of his own works. In his practice he could in fact go against his own scientific *habitus*. To this extent, Corcuff may not be entirely wrong.

Then there is the further implicit challenge of Goody's *La Raison graphique* (The Domestication of the Savage Mind), a heterogeneous work structured as a series of articles. *La Raison graphique* is quoted only once in *Le Sens pratique* (Bourdieu 1980:24).[22] But the chapter by Goody that Bourdieu referred to is not the one that really "hurts." Bourdieu's two other references to Goody (1980: 214–15, 223)[23] contain only statements about which everyone can agree: for example, that writing changes societies when it arrives. However, chapter 2, on intellectuals in societies without writing, goes further. It is, if not a veritable bombshell, at least a hand grenade in the field of *Le Sens pratique* (Colonna 1987b). Goody's remarks are not aimed explicitly at Bourdieu; indeed, there is no way of knowing whether Goody had read *Esquisse d'une théorie de la pratique* or what he thought of it. They are aimed at Durkheim and Mauss via Lévi-Strauss (who is in fact the main target) and, more generally, at the propensity of the "French school" (imitated later by some Anglo-Saxons) to consider "only the social aspects of intellectual operations, to the exclusion of individual aspects" (68). With his usual capacity for getting right to the point, Goody indicates what he considers to be the source of this propensity: the founding text of the Durkheimian theoretical genealogy, *Primitive Classification (De Quelques formes primitives de classification)*, written by Durkheim and Mauss and published in 1903 in volume 6 of the *Année Sociologique*. Here, very briefly, the authors underscore the social nature of thought categories and of the perception of the world:

> The first logical categories were social categories, the first classes of things were classes of men into which things were integrated. And if the totality of things is conceived as a single system it is because society itself is conceived in like manner. It is a whole or, rather, it is *the* one and only whole to which everything else is related and the unity of knowledge is nothing other than the unity of the collectivity itself extended to the universe. (1971: 224, 225)

Here, though Bourdieu never makes any specific reference to it, we can see the cornerstone of the whole undertaking of *The Logic of Practice*, which, we may recall, ends with these lines:

> The theoretical model that makes it possible to reproduce the whole universe of recorded practices, in so far as they are

sociologically determined, is separated from what the agents
master in the practical state, and of which its simplicity and
power give a correct *idea*, by the infinitesimal but infinite distance
that defines awareness or (it amounts to the same thing) explicit
statement. (1990: 270)

Obscure, but emphatic nonetheless! To sum up while simplifying
greatly: it was possible, for Bourdieu, to construct a theoretical model
to account for *all* practices in a given society. Practices are socially
determined. Actors have no access to their logic, either through
immediate awareness or reflexive reasoning. This is final. In other
words, as Goody says, the meaning for the actors—the "apparent"
logic—is less important than the underlying themes detected by the
observer, or the "deep logic" that allows the observer to explain an
utterance, a ritual, or an interactive situation. A view of this sort,
Goody concludes, leaves scant room for any but the most superficial
creative activity on the part not only of intellectuals but of any social
actors (see 1979: 70).

Fin de Siècle France "From Below": *La Misère du monde* (The Weight of the World)

> Yet I do not think we felt "deprived." We knew even if we did not
> articulate, and knew from an early age, that we were "out of most
> things" . . . I think our mother would have resented and rejected the
> word "deprived" in its common modern usages; it would have suggested
> that she was being seen from outside as a social problem, by people
> who felt they had a right to make such judgments, a right she would
> have resisted.—Richard Hoggart, A Local Habitation

What a disconcerting title—The Weight of the World! The text itself
is no less disconcerting. To reproduce so many interviews at length if

not in entirety was at the time exceptional in French sociology. This
was probably the primary reason for the book's success. Sales went
into the tens of thousands (eighty thousand, it was said), and it was
taken up by the media—a television appearance with Abbé Pierre,
icon of humanitarianism in France—and brought out in a paper-
back edition very soon after publication. The international audience
was astoundingly broad: in 1996 a leading Egyptian sociologist told
me—in the middle of an interview in which he contended that there
was no point in my interviewing provincial intellectuals in Egypt (a
project I was trying at the time to get under way) because nothing
happened in the provinces—that his own sociological model was
henceforth *The Weight of the World* because it homed in directly on
the "truth" about people's lives, and that was just what the public
wanted. In this paradoxical situation, his enthusiasm was somewhat
comical and rather dubious. Bourdieu's work was also daring in its
claim to give voice to a multiplicity of "sometimes irreconcilable"
viewpoints on the "same realities," after the fashion of the most
canonical literature (Faulkner, Joyce, and Virginia Woolf are cited
right at the beginning, 1993: 13). There is no doubt that students
and ordinary readers alike felt that here was a veritable revolution
in a discipline usually deemed rather tedious: they gained access for
the first time to an author whose work was reputed to be hermetic,
yet who was here writing in "(almost) natural language" and to
material in which ordinary people described their ordinary lives in
their own words.

The work produced a very different effect on me when I first read
it ten years earlier. I was reminded of this when I came across an interview with a young British film director, author of *The Magdalene
Sisters* (*Le Monde*, February 4, 2003). He recounted how, after four
attempts at short films, all very poor and politically very angry, he

one day had the misfortune to hand over one of his scripts—a comedy about adolescence—to another director. He was horrified at the result, which he termed "unbelievable"; and yet, he fumed, "they kept my own dialogues." This young man, of Glasgow working-class background, had previously won an acting award at the Cannes Film Festival for his role in Ken Loach's 1998 film *My Name Is Joe*. To his mind, the gaze directed at the characters—the ways they were labeled and depicted—radically changed the way they were interpreted.

The point is important. If *La Misère du monde* reminds us rightly and so strongly of *Le Déracinement*, it is primarily through its construction. The actors—those subjected to the book's *mise-en-scène*—are construed as occupying the margins of affluent society, or even of citizenship. But in his construction of "the dominated" of the France of the 1990s, Bourdieu did not use the traditional tools of the social sciences. Nor is the domination he discusses presented as a preconstructed object like the historic domination of the Algerian peasants. Instead, Bourdieu reinvokes a distinction he made in a brilliant article (Bourdieu 1966) between "class condition" and "class position" and introduces the notions of "*petite misère de position*" (minor position hardship, people who are having a hard time of it) and "*grande misère de position*" (major position hardship, the really poor). He then includes both types in the very wide spectrum of "hardships" to be found in a particular social order, that of contemporary France, which has, to his mind, entailed an unprecedented proliferation of all forms of inequality. The extensive category of hardship(s) here targeted has a great deal to do with what he calls "self-despair" (1993: 86[24]) but, strictly speaking, the indefinable, unfathomable nature of uprooting.

His use of meta-text leaves no doubt about the label or frame

intended to qualify all of the persons selected, dissimilar though they
may be. They range from the Maghrebi immigrant to the graduate
of the elite Ecole Polytechnique who is not really sorry, but sorry all
the same, that he chose to work for the National Scientific Research
Center (CNRS)[25] rather than for a private firm. By meta-text I mean
the titles of the book itself and of most of the chapters, which vie with
one another in "catastrophism": "*une famille déplacée*" (a displaced
family), "*un mauvais placement*" (a bad investment), and "the last
difference," to mention only those in the first part. Above all we
find several reminders, in Bourdieu's own chapter titles, of the rigid
line of reasoning behind the system expounded in the book: the link
between social structures, mental structures, and spatial structures
("Site Effects"); the grave dereliction of the authoritarian and irresponsible neoliberal state (also the topic of one of his first annual
lectures at the Collège de France, "The Desertion of the State" [*La
démission de l'Etat*]). Here again, the headings are striking—"An
Impossible Mission" (*une mission impossible*), Institutional Bad Faith
(*la mauvaise foi de l'institution*), Double Binds (*porte à faux et double
contrainte*); the question of social reproduction is treated in a very
broad and varied sense ("The Contradictions of Inheritance") (*Les
contradictions de l'héritage*). Here are reminders that for Bourdieu,
habitus has lost none of its potency and, in spite of a few nuances
(1993: 717[26]), it plays a central part, functioning "like a language,"
imposing "a particular mode on desire, which is then converted into
a specific illusion" (1993: 718[27]). As a picture of fin-de-siècle France
from below, the very structure of the book, from its chapter titles to
its layout, incites readers to see the persons interviewed as losers, as
screwed-up, disappointed failures, which is often far from being the
case. What prevails here is the underlying intention—that is, the book
invites readers to look at and categorize these people in a particular

way. We do not need to stress the terrifying effects of this orienting frame on some of Bourdieu's disciples, nor those of the extensive and repetitive use of the phrase "the dominated" in most chapters.

In spite of its general orientation, the corpus itself is fascinating—any social science professional no doubt will feel that the investigation must have been an extraordinary human experience for everyone, including Bourdieu. It entailed a collective effort that investigated all sorts of corners of French society in depth. The team of researchers were experienced and highly qualified, and some are well-known for other outstanding studies. Occasionally, their voices and their ways of looking at people succeeded in eluding the iron framework of the general design, just as what the people who were interviewed had to say sometimes gave a different color to their account of themselves than the one pre-intended. It is, however, by no means easy for readers to become really immersed in the interviewees' accounts. This is because of the layout, which reserves the full page and most visible type for the researcher's presentation, which is often highly redundant with the dialogue, as though the public could not be trusted to read the latter with any degree of proper attention. The interview itself is reproduced in two columns in smaller type.[28] This presentation is by no means innocent. Indeed, it is part of the author's strategy and it clearly echoes the dominant principle of the whole approach: *people don't know why they do what they do*, and thus *both* they *and* the readers need to have it explained to them. For Bourdieu—and this point must be stressed—the task of *translation*, of reframing, was the *raison d'être* for social science. He said so repeatedly for as long as he had been writing, and it constituted a central element in the scheme of his work as a whole. The logic of social life is unconscious for the actors and for the general public. Here we are reminded once again of the critique mentioned above (expressed by Goody and also formulated here and there by many other commentators). The question is, too, whether any degree of social awareness or social struggle is conceivable in a society of the sort described.

And yet is that all there is to be said? Since 1995 there have been countless discussions about the famous strikes and the social unrest that resulted finally in the dissolution of the Assemblée Nationale in France, about Bourdieu's "belated militantism" and his unexpected engagement on the public scene.[29] We should at least point out that no matter what the author said after the fact, the almost nine hundred pages of *La Misère du monde* did not give the slightest inkling of what was to come: the whole country in the streets for three weeks, not only in Paris but also in the provinces (and provincial background was a major autobiographic theme for Bourdieu; in his 1993 work it played an often decisive part in the domination and distress interviewees were alleged to have suffered; see also Reed-Danahay this volume). Admittedly, in his "political" interventions from 1988 to 1995 (Bourdieu 2002), we do find a certain number of fairly general declarations in favor of the engagement of intellectuals across Europe toward what he calls "the reinvention of a collective intellectual." This led to the launching in 1995 of an international supplement, *Liber*, to the journal *Actes de la Recherche en Sciences Sociales*. But something even more decisive would transpire, once again linked to Algeria. From 1993 to 1997, Bourdieu chaired the CISIA (Comité International de Soutien aux Intellectuels Algériens) to provide support for Algerian intellectuals fleeing assassination threats.[30] The committee was set up in Paris by a handful of researchers and university teachers, myself included. There can be no doubt that the international impact and (relative) effectiveness of this small undertaking owed a great deal to the prestige of Bourdieu's name, though Habermas, Gellner, Derrida, and others of like reputation also took part. Bourdieu's four years with the CISIA, the experience of openly engaging in a crisis situation, of exposure to the media—he claimed he loathed television—certainly changed his relationship to public action.

The dynamics of the social movement of 1995 did the rest. This movement brought about an "objective encounter" between Bourdieu's desire to communicate what his "knowledge of the social world," oft proclaimed and very real (witness his long research experience) had taught him and the urgent social demand expressed by the intellectual fringe of the movement. This fringe was made up of trade unionists and militants belonging to far-left associations or political groups who were discouraged and at a loss because of the connivance or neglect of those leaders whose role it should have been to react in both words and deeds. In that kind of situation one doesn't worry about nuances. So it may be that the speech Bourdieu made to the railway workers at the Gare de Lyon in December 1995[31] as well as what followed the speech were a response to the *practical* challenges that led, among other things, to the founding of the group "Raisons d'Agir" (Reasons to Act). But Bourdieu's speeches and writings in this period (1995–2001) offer no self-criticism of the "misérabilisme" of the 1993 publication, which came under attack more than once. On the contrary there were some serious relapses (e.g., *La Domination Masculine*, 1998, and the lively reactions it provoked among French feminists). However, taken together, his actions on the public scene can be considered as *practical* responses to some *conscious* theoretical biases in his work. Once again, "how can one go against one's *habitus*!" Simply do more or less as he did with the Algerian material: when confronted with complex historical evidence, hold on to stubborn theoretical convictions but consent at the same time to practical engagements that relativize the former without denying them.

Conclusion

Of course, this general presentation of the "byways" from theory towards practices that are in contradiction with it is no more than a set of hypotheses. The texts are still the texts. The theses, too. If read too rapidly and without reference to the context in which it was produced, Bourdieu's work is still an edifice fortified from beginning to end by the strong theme of domination, even more so than the works of Durkheim and his direct heirs, to whom he owes so much. And, after all, it is Bourdieu who can take the real credit of having given his discipline—that is, sociology, but not also, as he would have wished, anthropology—an ambition and a consistency it had never had before his day.

That may be where the problem lies. Even as he opens up new avenues of thought and lays down paths that had formerly only been roughly outlined, a genius closes doors, sets up strong themes that tend to overtake all the space, bars the way to promising exploration even for himself. Any hegemonic system is bound to conceal as well as reveal. This has already been said, of course, in connection with Freud or Blanchot, for example. A (social) world of domination would be uninhabitable and, notwithstanding his pessimism, Bourdieu was not unaware of that. Furthermore, social science cannot be reduced to the description and theorization of this type of violence. The general question (the very same one as that posed by *Le Déracinement* on the very modest scale of Algerian peasantry) is not whether inequalities and power relations exist: they do. It is whether in our disciplines we should take them as central or sole objects of study or, on the contrary, extend our scope, adopt a frame that gives visibility to whatever there is in daily life that enables people to counteract these forces or at least to "get by", and to how they go about this. Whether social science should talk about nothing but "that" violence, or of the multitude of other things that make up everyday life: invention, belief, love, friendship, self-mockery, humor, considered from the point of view of the actor and not that of a divinity called "the social."

For the last twenty years, this task of reframing has been tackled from many varied theoretical angles by what, in France, are called "the new sociologies" (Corcuff 2003; Barthe and Lemieux 2002). Here the engaged scholar's task is not primarily to articulate a critique of systems of domination from a privileged sociological vantage point. Rather it is to attend to the multiple and plural forms of "critical competencies" (Barthe and Lemieux 2002: 36) on which all social actors regularly draw. Only by "following the actors" (Barthe and Lemieux 2002: 37) can we hope to understand the varied and, above all, *different* critical resources that people have brought to bear on conditions of domination and injustice.

Notes

1. Corcuff refers here to Foucault's *Archeology of Knowledge* as well as to the essay "What Is an Author?" to argue that metadiscursive concepts such as "work" and "author" tend to foster a unitary and coherent reading of Bourdieu's writings. In contrast Corcuff seeks to attend to the "cracks and fissures" (Corcuff 2003: 13) that traverse Bourdieu's work.

2. In calling Bourdieu's science a "combat sport," Corcuff refers to the title of a film by Pierre Carles, "La sociologie est un sport de combat—Pierre Bourdieu" (Carles 2001).

3. The term *révolutionnée* can also be understood as "revolutionized" or subjected to revolution.

4. The lineage from Durkheim to Fustel de Coulanges is direct. Durkheim: "For in each one of us, there is the man of yesterday, and it's even the man of yesterday who—by the force of things—is predominant in us" (Durkheim 1938: 16); Fustel de Coulanges: "Fortunately, man's past never completely dies. . . . For even as [man] is constituted in each era, he is the product and the summary of all the previous epochs" (Fustel de Coulanges 1864: 4) (our translation).

5. ARDES (Association for Demographic, Economic and Social Research)

was a research unit linked to the Institut des Statistiques d'Alger (Institute of Statistics of Algiers) developed by former students of France's prestigious Ecole Polytechnique and the Ecole Nationale d'Administration (ENA), who had come to Algeria from metropolitan France to work under the Plan de Constantine—a program of planned development conceived at the request of General de Gaulle to help Algeria emerge from underdevelopment, initially under the auspices of France.

6. The Agrarian Revolution entailed a redistribution of cultivable lands confiscated from French land owners under the terms of a March 1962 order, followed by a series of measures designed to put in place a collectivist use of the land—following the Soviet model—in the form of state farms.

7. That year (1989) marked the beginning of the "democratic opening" that followed significant urban riots that occurred in the fall of 1988; this opening was signaled by the adoption of a new constitution that ostensibly put in place a pluralist political system.

8. Fanon (1925–61), a psychiatrist born in the French overseas department of Martinique, came to Algeria in 1953 following his medical studies in France. He argued in *The Wretched of the Earth* (1963) that peasants were the "revolutionary class" in Algeria because, dispossessed of everything including itself, the peasantry occupied the place of the proletariat in the Marxist schema.

9. Subsequent creation of the Agrarian Revolution (see note 6) in which peasants who had been newly allotted lands were grouped together in "modern" villages equipped with running water, electricity, and paved roads, which were all constraints in ordinary peasant life.

10. With the advent of the Third Republic (1871), northern Algeria was divided into three French departments—Algiers, Oran, and Constantine—that were in principle governed by the same laws as metropolitan France. The Algerian Sahara remained under military jurisdiction.

11. The Front de Libération Nationale (National Liberation Front) was created by a group of twenty-two activist militants who called the Algerian people to armed revolutionary struggle against the French occupation on November 1, 1954.

12. The Organisation de l'Armée Secrète, OAS (Secret Army Organization), was created in 1961 after the French military putsch of April 21 failed; the goal of the OAS was to fight against Algerian independence by any means, including armed struggle and torture.

13. "Within his family the child also learns the rules of politeness and, to be more exact, the words he must say in each circumstance. . . . In short, *the cultural apprenticeship tends to produce true psychological sets or prepared attitudes,*

the purpose of which is to guard against, or even to forbid, any improvisation" (Bourdieu 1962: 15, emphasis added).

14. The 1976 National Charter was a series of official doctrinal texts produced by the FLN (or more precisely, produced in its name by party intellectuals). The National Charters outlined the overall ideological, political, and social orientations of each regime—a model inspired by the Nasserian state in Egypt. Each Charter expressed the dominant tendencies of the team in power at the time.

15. The first part of this quotation appears on 291n3, of *The Logic of Practice*. The second part of this quotation (following the ellipsis points) appears on p. 56 of *The Logic of Practice*. In the French edition the note appears on the same page as the text it refers to, whereas in the English edition the note comes at the end. We have used Richard Nice's translation.

16. See p. 286n10 in the English edition.

17. See pp. 286n11, 296n17, and 296n104 in the English edition. Note that the footnoted reference on p. 177 was incorporated into the text of the English edition, and thus does appear in the bibliography to the English edition.

18. See p. 286n11 in the English edition.

19. Center for Archeological, Prehistoric, and Ethnological Research, located in Algiers and directed by Mouloud Mammeri from 1971 to 1981.

20. Significant social movement marked by major street protests in the cities of Tizi-Ouzou and Algiers during March and April of 1980—the first of its kind since Algerian independence. It brought about police and institutional repression and marked a notable hardening of Algerian cultural and linguistic politics with regard to Berbers. It also marked the beginning of a more violent "Arabization" of the Algerian population.

21. Rassemblement pour la Culture et la Démocratie (Assembly for Culture and Democracy), an avowedly secular party in Algeria created in 1989 (see note 7).

22. See p. 11 of the English edition.

23. See pp. 125 and 286n12 in the English edition.

24. See p. 64 of the English edition.

25. The Centre National pour la Recherche Scientifique (National Center for Scientific Research) is a public French institution for research created following French liberation from German occupation in World War II. It is the only institute of its kind in Europe. Scholars at the CNRS are relatively poorly remunerated in relation to their degrees and their scholarly production.

26. See p. 512 of the English edition.

27. See pp. 512–13 of the English edition. We have used the translation of Priscilla Parkhurst Ferguson et al.

28. In the French edition the type of the interview is considerably smaller than it is in the English edition, making the difference between these sections even more prominent.

29. Important social movement in France that lasted throughout November 1995, marked by significant street protests throughout the country and a massive transit strike. It ended with the dissolution of the French National Assembly and new legislative elections, which brought the Left to power.

30. Between February 1993 and March 1994 dozens (probably more than one hundred) reporters, academics, musicians and singers, doctors, and other intellectuals—all "democrats" opposed to an Islamist regime but also disturbing to the military government—were victims of assassinations or targeted disappearances. Most of those who felt targeted emigrated abroad, and many never returned to Algeria.

31. During a mass demonstration organized by railway workers who occupied the Gare de Lyon (one of the largest train and public transit stations in Paris) in December of 1995 (see note 29), Bourdieu—generally ill at ease as an orator—gave a lengthy speech that was very well received by the crowd.

Works Cited

Barthe, Yannick and Cyril Lemieux. 2002. Quelle critique après Bourdieu? *Mouvements* 24 (Nov.–Dec.): 33–38.

Bourdieu, Pierre. 1958. *Sociologie de l'Algérie*. Paris: Presses Universitaires de France.

———. 1960. Guerre et mutation sociale en Algérie. *Etudes Méditerranéennes* 7 (Spring).

———. 1961. Révolution dans la révolution." *Esprit* 1 (January): 27–40.

———. 1962. *The Algerians*. Boston: Beacon Press.

———. 1966. Condition de classe et position de classe. *Archives Européennes de Sociologie* 7(2): 201–23.

. 1972. *Esquisse d'une théorie de la pratique: Précédé de trois études d'ethnologie kabyle*. Geneva, Switzerland: Librairie Droz.

———. 1980. *Le Sens pratique*. Paris: Minuit.

———. 1993. *La Misère du monde*. Paris: Seuil.

———. 1998. *La Domination masculine*. Paris: Seuil.

———. 2002. *Interventions 1961–2001: Sciences sociales et action politique*, ed. Franck Poupeau and Thierry Discepolo. Marseilles: Agone.

———. 2003. *Images d'Algérie. Une affinité élective*, ed. Franz Schultheis. Arles, France: Actes Sud.

Bourdieu, Pierre, Alain Darbel, Jean-Paul Rivet, and Claude Seibel. 1963. *Travail et travailleurs en Algérie*. Paris: Mouton.

Bourdieu, Pierre and Mouloud Mammeri. 1991 (1978). Dialogue sur la poésie orale en Kabylie. In *Culture savante, culture vécue: Etudes 1938–1989*. pp. 93–115. Algiers: Editions Tala.

Bourdieu, Pierre and Abdelmalek Sayad. 1964. *Le Déracinement. La Crise de l'agriculture traditionnelle en Algérie*. Paris: Minuit.

Carles, Pierre. 2001. La Sociologie est un sport de combat—Pierre Bourdieu. Montpellier: C–P Productions. 2h26min.

Colonna Fanny. 1978. *Le Déracinement comme concept et comme politique. Questions de sciences sociales*. Algiers: ONRS.

———. 1987a. *Savants paysans. Elements d'histoire sociale sur l'Algérie rurale*. Algiers: Office des Publications Universitaires.

———. 1987b. En finir avec le débat sur "literacy." Notes de relecture sur J. Goody, *La Raison graphique. L'Espace culturel*. Oran: LAHASC.

———. 1995. *Les Versets de l'invincibilité. Permanence et changements religieux dans l'Algérie contemporaine*. Paris: Presses de l'Institut National de Sciences Politiques.

Corcuff, Philippe. 1995. *Les Nouvelles sociologies: Constructions de la réalité sociale*. Paris: Nathan.

———. 2003. *Bourdieu autrement: Fragilités d'une sociologie de combat*. Paris: Textuel.

Durkheim, Emile and Marcel Mauss. 1971 (1903). De quelques formes primitives de classification. In *Marcel Mauss. Essais de sociologie*. Paris: Minuit.

Fanon, Frantz. 1963. *The Wretched of the Earth*, trans. Constance Farrington. New York: Grove Press.

Feraoun, Mouloud. 1957. *Les Chemins qui montent*. Paris: Seuil.

Fustel de Coulanges. 1864. *La Cité antique*. Paris: Hachette.

Goody, Jack. 1979. *La Raison graphique: La Domestication de la pensée sauvage*. Paris: Minuit.

Hoggart, Richard. 1988. *A Local Habitation. Life and Times, Vol. 1, 1918–1940*. Oxford: Chatto & Windus.

Mammeri, Mouloud. 1955. *Le Sommeil du juste*. Paris: Plon.

———. 1980. *Poèmes kabyles anciens*. Paris: Maspero.

Rivière, Marie-Christine and Yvette Delsault. 2002. *Bibliographie des travaux de Pierre Bourdieu*. Pantin: Le Temps des Cerises.

TWO

The Proverbial Bourdieu

Habitus and the Politics of Representation
in the Ethnography of Kabylia

JANE E. GOODMAN

> The separation of sociology and history is a disastrous division, and one totally devoid of epistemological justification: All sociology should be historical and all history sociological.—Bourdieu and Wacquant, *An Invitation to Reflexive Sociology*

What is the relationship between fieldwork, ethnography, and theory—the unequal trinity at the heart of Bourdieu's adopted discipline of anthropology? How germane was Bourdieu's fieldwork to the development of his anthropological theory? Since at least the publication of Edward Said's *Orientalism* in 1978, an ongoing dialogue about the politics of ethnographic representation has been central to the discipline (see, among others, Breckenridge and Van der Veer 1993; Clifford and Marcus 1986). During the same period, the work of Pierre Bourdieu became increasingly significant as anthropologists turned to his notions of "*doxa*," "practice," and "*habitus*" to challenge prevailing conceptualizations of structure and to rethink social inequality. As the epigraph above suggests, Bourdieu was himself centrally concerned with the relationship of historical context to empirical analysis. Indeed, he was among the first to view ethnography in political terms.

Given Bourdieu's contributions and commitments, it is somewhat surprising that his work has remained largely outside the purview of the literature attentive to the political and ethical responsibilities of ethnographic representation.[1] This seems particularly significant given the historical and political context of his ethnographic work: Bourdieu was introduced to Algeria via his military service in the French army; much of his fieldwork was conducted during the Algerian revolution in resettlement camps to which thousands of Algerians were forcibly moved by the French army. Despite this, Bourdieu's "theory of practice" is now essentially free-floating, traveling widely across disciplines and geographies, unmoored from the society in which it was developed.

In this chapter I explore whether key premises of Bourdieu's theory can be supported by historical and ethnographic evidence from the Kabyle Berber region where he carried out most of his Algeria-based field research. I seek to reconnect elements of the theoretical apparatus that Bourdieu developed in Kabylia—in particular, his notions of "*habitus*," "misrecognition," and "practice" itself—with the conditions of his own fieldwork as well as with Kabyle social history. If, as I suggest, Bourdieu's fieldwork did not fully support the conclusions he drew in *Outline of a Theory of Practice* (1977), what questions does this raise about the fieldwork–theory relationship? What does it suggest about his central concepts?

To explore the relationship between Bourdieu's own theory and practice, I focus on a central discrepancy in his representation of the Kabyle population of Algeria. Bourdieu presents two very different "Kabylias": One is the idealized version found in the *Outline*, the work that many consider his most important ethnography of Kabylia; the other pertains to the disenchanted Kabyles of his earlier works, such as those discussed in *Travail et travailleurs en Algérie* (Bourdieu et al. 1963) and *Le Déracinement* (Bourdieu and Sayad 1964). I argue that these representations are largely constituted through the form of language Bourdieu privileges in each. Whereas proverbs and sayings are the primary genres through which the Kabyles of the *Outline* are made to speak,[2] the Kabyles of Bourdieu's earlier works are represented through prose. These latter Kabyles speak at length about the difficulties of finding work, the high cost of living, the racism they faced on a daily basis, and their experiences in the resettlement camps built by the French army during the last years of the Algerian revolution.

As I will demonstrate, Bourdieu's split portrayal of Kabyle discourse corresponded to separate political projects, both intended to contribute, albeit problematically, to Algeria's political future. To make this case I first examine the role of proverbs in the *Outline* to assess how they support Bourdieu's claims about misrecognition, learned ignorance, *habitus*, and practice itself. I then read across Bourdieu's early studies of Kabylia to reconstitute aspects of his methodology.[3] How did he find the proverbs and sayings that punctuate the *Outline*? Whom did he speak with? Where? When? In reconnecting Bourdieu's representations of Kabyle discourse with his own fieldwork practices, I draw primarily on four studies: (1) *The Algerians* (1962 [1958]); (2) "The Sentiment of Honour in Kabyle Society" (1966) and its later incarnation as "The Sense of Honour," published in *Algeria 1960* (1979 [1972]); (3) *Travail et travailleurs en Algérie* (Work and workers in Algeria), a study of wage labor and unemployment among Algerian peasants (Bourdieu et al. 1963); and (4) *Le Déracinement* (The Uprooting), an account of the French army resettlement camps, which Bourdieu wrote with his Kabyle colleague Abdelmayek Sayad in 1964. I also consider how Bourdieu's position as a young social scientist attempting to grapple with his own role in a colonial wartime situation may have led him to privilege his interlocutors' graphic accounts of contemporary Kabylia in some studies while expunging them from others. Finally I examine the presumption of orality that underwrites Bourdieu's analysis of the Kabyle *habitus* against historical evidence of literacy in the Kabyle region. In so doing, I consider the political implications of Bourdieu's portrayal of orality for the Kabyle Berber population,[4] a linguistic minority in predominantly Arabic-speaking Algeria that was progressively marginalized in part on the grounds that the Berber language lacked writing traditions.

Practice and Metapragmatics

As is well known, one of Bourdieu's major concerns in the *Outline* was with the relationship between practice and its metapragmatic representation. For Bourdieu, knowledge of practice and discourse about practice represent two almost incommensurable phenomena. In his view, when Kabyles provide an account of their practices, they typically draw on normative representations (rules) that uphold and reproduce the group's official view of itself while denying strategy and self-interest.[5] Bourdieu would have us believe that official knowledge— characterized by a vocabulary of honor, equality, and generosity and by a logic of morality, law, and rule—is the only kind of knowledge that is available to Kabyles as metapragmatic discourse, or as discourse about how they understand their own practices. He contrasted official knowledge with practical knowledge—the tacit understandings and strategies, or the felt sense of how the social world works—that all Kabyles engage but that by definition can never be metadiscursively articulated. This kind of knowledge *"goes without saying because it comes without saying"* (1977: 167); it reveals itself not in words but in the organization of space and time, the movements of the body, the strategic moves of challenge and riposte, of gift and counter-gift. Practical knowledge, of course, characterizes the *habitus*, the structured and structuring "system of lasting, transposable dispositions which . . . functions at every moment as a *matrix of perceptions, appreciations and actions*" (1977: 82–83).[6]

On the one hand, *habitus* is powerfully constraining: It constitutes a universe beyond which it is almost impossible to think (*doxa*). Yet it is also fragile, for as soon as the practical logics and generative schemes through which it operates are objectively formulated in discourse, the whole system collapses: The language of theory "destroys the truth it makes available to apprehension" (1977: 117). Describing the objective logic of practice "disenchants" it; metadiscourse, in short, causes its referent to disintegrate or, at best, to "be subject . . . to an essential alteration" (1977: 203n49). To avoid such a disaster, the savvy Kabyles never allow themselves to state explicitly what they nonetheless know in a tacit or embodied sense to be true. Bourdieu referred to the gap between practice and metapragmatic discourse (discourse about practice) as *learned ignorance*: While "agents must not be entirely unaware of the truth of their exchanges . . . they must refuse to know and above all to recognize it" (1977: 6).[7]

Bourdieu thus faced a methodological quandary: His informants could not speak to him about practice, the very subject of his inquiry; they could provide only "the misleading discourse of a speaker himself misled" (1977: 19). One kind of discourse, however, was apparently exempt from such misrecognition: oral lore such as proverbs, sayings, riddles, and gnomic poems. This "spontaneous semiology" (1977: 10)—a "semi-learned grammar of practice" (1977: 20)—became part of Bourdieu's evidence for the claims he made about Kabyle *habitus*. According to Bourdieu, proverbs and sayings are "the product of the same generative schemes as the practices they claim to account for"

(1977: 20); they "reinforce the structures by providing them with a particular form of 'rationalization'" (1977: 20; see also Bourdieu 1990a: 66–79). Through proverbs, then, Kabyles unknowingly could give voice to the "truth" of practice. Thus, while in official language they might describe an "equality in honor" among all Kabyle men, for example, in a proverb they would acknowledge inequalities and social hierarchies that they otherwise deny: "The moustache of the hare is not that of the lion" (1977: 13).

Because Bourdieu located proverbs and sayings as unmediated signs of *habitus*, he had no need to attend to the pragmatics of their use. Most proverbs in his text are unattributed or attributed to a generic speaker: For example, Bourdieu commonly used phrases such as "say the Kabyles" (1977: 11) and "says the proverb" (1977: 12). The only proverbs connected to individuals are drawn from texts and are attributed to the author of the text rather than the speaker. One of these was Yamina Aït Amar ou Saïd, a Kabyle woman who had converted to Christianity, attended mission schools, and wrote an account of a Kabyle wedding for a missionary journal (Yamina 1960, 1961). Bourdieu called Yamina an informant, a statement that is methodologically misleading at best (1977: 212n101). Another source was Adolphe Hanoteau, a French colonel who headed up the Bureau Arabe (Office for Indigenous Affairs) in Fort Napoléon (now Larbaa n At Iraten) in the early 1860s and subsequently published works on Kabyle poetry, grammar, and customary law (see Bourdieu 1977: 49, 211n96, 212n100).[8] Although Bourdieu's primary material was sourced in Kabylia (itself a region that is far from homogeneous), apparently other Berbers would do just as well. For example, a proverb from "Moroccan Berbers" that Bourdieu found in a 1941 text by G. Marcy made an appearance (Bourdieu 1977: 12, 199n13). Via such entextualization strategies (Briggs and Bauman 1990; Silverstein and Urban 1996), Bourdieu created the Kabyles—indeed, "the Berbers"—as a collective, undifferentiated subject (cf. Raheja 1996, 2000). Despite Bourdieu's elegant theorizing about the strategic importance of time and space, when it came to proverbs and sayings he collapsed temporal and spatial considerations, conflating oral texts gathered across a hundred-year period by different individuals and in diverse locations.

In sum, because Bourdieu believed that proverbs were located in a collective *habitus*, he also thought that they required no contextualization. They were not considered in terms of the pragmatics of the situations in which they were used but instead were seen as momentary verbal instantiations of the logic of practice. To borrow a term from Michael Silverstein (1993), Bourdieu saw proverbs as being "nomically calibrated" to practice: That is, proverbs and sayings made available an invisible realm—the *habitus*—that supposedly stood behind them and of which they were verbal signs. The way Bourdieu used proverbs can also be likened to what Susan Stewart, citing Carl Zigrosser (1965), has called "*multum in parvo*," or the "miniaturization of language." In this "miniaturization of language," "compressed" genres like the epigram, the quotation, or the proverb are used in a free-floating capacity to represent entire domains of life "in such a way as to seem to transcend lived experience and to speak to all times and places" (Stewart 1993: 53). In so doing they work in a univocal manner "to close down discourse" (1993: 53). Clearly the Herderian tenet that oral lore represented an unmediated native spirit was among the structuring principles that informed Bourdieu's own approach to Kabyle discourse. In that sense, he was interpreting Kabyle discourse practices through the lens of the Eurocentric language ideology of which he was already a product (see Hanks 2005).

Reconstituting Bourdieu's Fieldwork Practices

When, from where, and how did Bourdieu get these proverbs and sayings? To whom was he speaking? In the *Outline*, Bourdieu made reference to his fieldwork locations in a single footnote, telling us that the research initially took place "in various villages in Kabylia, then in the Collo region, and finally in the Chélif valley and Ouarsenis" (1977: 204n54). This trajectory mirrors Bourdieu's work in the French army's resettlement camps, about which I will have more to say below. Initially seeking to collect genealogies, Bourdieu later turned to the ritual of matrimonial exchange, attempting "to reconstitute a family's social history" (1977: 204 n.54). In *The Logic of Practice* (1990a), Bourdieu made reference to fifteen hundred punchcards that he began to construct in 1962. On these cards, he aggregated data about the agricultural calendar, weddings, weaving, time, space, games, rituals, labor, colors, and so on (1990a: 8). He first wrote down published data; "as a last stage" he "questioned informants . . . about symbolic practices" (1990a: 8). One can readily imagine that he might have asked informants, during that last stage, for proverbs about particular objects or domains of life, given his conviction that proverbs provided a direct conduit to *habitus*.[9] A brief note in the *Outline* supports this conjecture: There Bourdieu referred to a "rough count" he made of "codified sayings, proverbs, and rites" (1977: 219n3). Clearly, then, he had recorded these texts in a way that made them readily countable. He may also have learned proverbs from Abdelmalek Sayad, coauthor of *Le Déracinement*. Sayad was initially Bourdieu's student at the University of Algiers; the two would soon become close collaborators.[10] It was to Sayad that Bourdieu dedicated the initial *Esquisse* (a dedication formulated, I might add, as a proverb).

Table 1. Locating the *Outline* Villages

Village	Outline of a Theory of Practice (1977)	The Sentiment of Honor in Kabyle Society (1966)	Le Déracinement (1964, with Abdelmalek Sayad)	The Algerians (1962); Sociologie de l'Algérie (1958)
Ait Hichem (Greater Kabylia)	X	X		X
Tizi Hibel (Greater Kabylia)	X	X		
Aghbala (Lesser Kabylia)	X	X	X Resettlement Center	
Ain Aghbel (Collo region)	X	X	X Resettlement Center	
Djemaa Saharidj (Greater Kabylia)	Referenced but not named; see note 17	X	X Resettlement Center	
Agouni n Tesellent (Greater Kabylia)	From Hanoteau and Letourneux (1872–73)			
Ighil Imoula (Greater Kabylia)	From Hanoteau and Letourneux (1872–73)			

Sayad's collaboration raises a further question: To what degree was Bourdieu's approach to proverbs solely a reflection of European metadiscourses concerning oral lore,[11] and to what degree might it have been motivated by the Kabyles themselves? Kabyle intellectuals had been collecting their own oral texts since at least the turn of the century (Goodman 2002c). By the 1940s they had a sophisticated understanding of the importance of their own language and folk traditions within the anticolonial nationalist project (Amrane n.d.;

Amrouche 1994; Ouerdane 1990). One of these intellectuals, the novelist and poetry afficionado Mouloud Feraoun, read and annotated many of Bourdieu's early works on Kabylia (Bourdieu 2002b: 7); such annotations may well have included proverbs. The novelist Mouloud Mammeri, with whom Bourdieu was also in dialogue, served as the director of the Center for Archeological, Prehistoric, and Ethnological Research in Algiers and is well known for his series of works on Berber oral literature (Mammeri 1969, 1980, 1985). By virtue of their formal properties, proverbs travel well; they lend themselves to ready insertion into a variety of contexts and conversations (Briggs and Bauman 1992; cf. Keane 1995). During my own stay in Algeria in the early 1990s, one of my interlocutors, a forty-something man from a maraboutic (religious) lineage who had been working in France since the 1960s, would repeatedly invoke proverbs as a way of creating links between new situations and a wider cultural memory. Even if Kabyles privileged proverbs, however, the fact remains that Bourdieu chose to interpret them as unreflexive, momentary manifestations of *habitus* in speech, with Kabyles serving as the mere media of their presentation.[12]

Where in Kabylia—a region of some fifteen hundred villages—might Bourdieu have gathered these bits of lore? As Table 1 shows, much of the work on which the *Outline* was based took place among two primary groups of informants: those living in resettlement centers and those who had relocated to the city of Algiers.[13] One village, Tizi Hibel, was the natal village of the novelist Mouloud Feraoun,[14] who had annotated Bourdieu's early studies; Feraoun was among the informants Bourdieu consulted in Algiers. Three of the villages received a good deal more attention in *Le Déracinement*. Here, we discover that Ain Aghbel, Aghbala, and Djemaa Saharidj were all resettlement centers, or villages to which hundreds (and in the case of Djemaa Saharidj, thousands) of Algerians were forcibly relocated during the war; Aghbala was Sayad's natal village.[15] *Le Déracinement* was Bourdieu and Sayad's ethnography of a dozen of these centers, six of which were in or near Kabylia. Carried out by a team of interviewers who were supervised by Bourdieu and Sayad, the project was related to Bourdieu's study of labor conditions that was funded by and conducted under the auspices of Association pour la Recherche Démographique, Economique et Sociale (ARDES), a government research center similar to the French service INSEE (see Bourdieu et al. 1963: 13; Bourdieu and Sayad 1964: 61n1). It was, in other words, sponsored research produced for the very state that had created the centers in the first place.

Kabyle Ethnography: Between Politics and Theory

If proverbs and sayings punctuate Bourdieu's *Outline*, they are virtually absent from *Le Déracinement* and *Travail et travailleurs*. Here, Kabyles speak in prose, and they speak at length. *Travail et travailleurs* contains an extraordinary set of appendices that comprise some seventy pages of direct quotations focused largely on labor conditions.[16] To cite just one man, a charcoal seller: "There aren't many jobs, the population has doubled and people from the rural areas are in the cities. . . . If there were more factories people would have jobs. How many are dying of hunger with their children?" (Bourdieu et al. 1963: 483). Speakers quoted in *Le Déracinement* emphasize the loss of agricultural lifeways: "I want to continue cultivating my land with all my being," said M. A. Yersan in the resettlement center Ain Aghbel. "But it's too far away, and it's in the 'forbidden zone' (*zone interdite*). You have to be there to supervise" (Bourdieu and Sayad 1964: 115n1). According to another: "We don't have the courage to continue to plant even our gardens. For whom? For the animals, the wild pigs? For the guerillas [i.e., those fighting in the *Armée de Libération Nationale* (ALN)], the shepherds, the *harkis* [Algerians fighting on the side of the French]?" (Bourdieu and Sayad 1964: 115). Indeed, according to Bourdieu, such "de-peasanted peasants" were incapable of proverbial speech: "The young men, thrown into an urban way of life, no longer learn from their elders the precepts, the customs, the legends or the proverbs which formed the soul of the community" (Bourdieu 1962 [1958]: 185).

Why didn't the Kabyles' graphic depictions of life in the resettlement centers make it into the *Outline*?[17] Clearly, it was not because Bourdieu did not have access to Kabyle discourse. On one level, the duality that characterizes Bourdieu's representation of speech may stem from the fact that he was moving between the methodological conventions of two disciplines (see Addi 2002).[18] Bourdieu's home field of sociology privileged statistical analyses and interviews, an orientation that clearly informed his early studies. Bourdieu was also drawn to ethnology, in which he considered himself an "autodidact" (Honneth et al. 1986: 38). Following his return to France from Algeria in May of 1961, Bourdieu attended lectures at the Musée de l'Homme and sat in on Lévi-Strauss's seminars at the Collège de France (Honneth et al. 1986: 39), where he was clearly marked by structuralism's emphasis on underlying principles discernible to the trained observer through rituals, myths or legends but unavailable in the direct discourse of informants.

Bourdieu's dual representations of Kabyle discourse relate more fundamentally, however, to the intertwined political and philosophical positions he was beginning to formulate and, in particular, to his differences with Frantz Fanon and Jean-Paul Sartre. Bourdieu strongly opposed what he viewed as the "utopianism" embraced by Fanon, Sartre, and much of the French left in regards to the Algerian war.

"I was appalled," Bourdieu said, "by the gap between the views of French intellectuals about this war . . . and my own experiences" (Honneth et al. 1986: 38; see also Bourdieu 1990b: 3–7). He was particularly troubled by their Marxist conviction that the Algerian peasantry represented a revolutionary class (Le Sueur 2001: 253; Bourdieu 2002a) that would be freed through the violence of the war from all traces of colonialism, leaving a *tabula rasa* on which a postcolonial socialist state could be built (Le Sueur 2001: 249–55; see Fanon 1963). Bourdieu maintained that the revolt of the Algerian masses was motivated not by a "rational revolutionary consciousness" (Bourdieu 2002a: 34) or by a celebratory affiliation with an international proletarian revolution (Le Sueur 2001: 250) but by a passionate rejection of the insufferable conditions of their lives: "The 'Algerian peasantry' was 'overwhelmed by the war, by the concentration camps, and by the mass deportations. To claim that it was a revolutionary peasantry was completely idiotic'" (Bourdieu, cited in Le Sueur 2001: 254). To counter Fanon's "utopian delirium," Bourdieu sought to "highlight . . . the plight of the Algerian people" (Honneth et al. 1986: 38) both for the benefit of the French left and to provide future Algerian leaders with tools that would help them "make the best choices" (Le Sueur 2001: 254).

If Bourdieu attempted to depict the brutal conditions of life in wartime Algeria in his initial studies, why did he choose not to represent colonial social reality in the *Outline*?[19] The preface to *Travail et travailleurs* provides one hint. Across from a photograph of a worker at a steel plant in Oran, whose back is to the camera as sparks fly around him, Bourdieu engaged with an article by French intellectual Michel Leiris (1950) about the responsibilities of an ethnographer from the metropolis working among colonized populations. In Bourdieu's words, "What one can require in all rigourousness [*en toute rigueur*] of the ethnologist is that he attempt to restore [*restituer*] to other men the meaning of their behaviors, of which the colonial system, among other things, dispossessed them" (Bourdieu et al. 1963: 259; see also Bourdieu 1979: ixn1, where he claimed that he sought to understand the "original social and economic structures"). In a 1985 interview with Kabyle novelist and oral literature specialist Mouloud Mammeri entitled "Du bon usage de l'ethnologie" ("On the Proper Use of Ethnology"), Bourdieu further elaborated: "I think that ethnology, when it's done well, is a very important instrument for self-knowledge, a sort of social psychoanalysis permitting [one] to grasp the cultural unconscious, which all who are born into the particular society have in their heads: mental structures, representations" (Mammeri and Bourdieu 1985: 20).[20] In light of these discussions, the *Outline* and related works can be understood as Bourdieu's attempt to conceptualize what Kabyle society may have been like before French colonization. To access the past from the data of the present, however, he was forced to rely on methodological premises that from today's vantage point would be considered problematic. Among these was the notion that proverbs and sayings index a past social order, of which they were among the few remaining signs. That he persisted in so situating them is clear in a discussion with Mammeri, where he acknowledged that "this original state,[21] no doubt a bit mythical, is [now] totally abolished, and to want to bring it back to life is a bit of a mystification" (Mammeri and Bourdieu 1985: 22). Nevertheless, he went on,

> I think that a certain number of things must continue to function according to the old traditions. . . . [Although] the mythico—ritual structure, the oppositions between the dry and the wet, the masculine and the feminine, no longer operate the way they did

when the great collective rituals were still practiced . . . they still exist in people's heads, in the language, *through sayings* [Mammeri and Bourdieu 1985: 22, emphasis added].[22]

In other words, Bourdieu saw a temporal lag: Practice changes before oral lore. As survivals of a past social order, proverbs and sayings could point to and help to unveil its logic.

While Bourdieu's *habitus*-based theory of practice had a long and productive career in social philosophy, did it have any political usefulness to the Kabyles themselves? As Sayad has noted, to talk about "Algeria" and "culture" in the same breath during the war was already a provocative proposition. When Bourdieu gave a talk on "Algerian culture" during his years at the University of Algiers, the announcements alone were seen as subversive and even scandalous; to acknowledge a unique Algerian culture was implicitly to advocate for Algerian independence and against supporters of a "French Algeria"[23] (see Introduction, this volume). When Bourdieu's *Esquisse* first came out in 1972, the situation of Berbers in post-independence Algeria was precarious at best: not only did the Berber (Tamazight) language have no institutional support but it was not even tolerated in public spaces. To advocate for Berber culture at that time was to risk imprisonment and even torture (see Goodman 2004). Under such conditions Bourdieu's portrayal of an authentic, precolonial Berber culture may have been intended to lend support to the Berbers' claims to a unique cultural heritage. Certainly some of the major figures in the Berber Cultural Movement, including Mouloud Mammeri, shared that vision, for authenticity was one of the few ways that an indigenous culture could gain political recognition.[24]

Yet to portray an imagined precolonial Kabylia in support of a particular political vision is a somewhat different project than to "restore to other men the meaning of their behavior" (Bourdieu et al. 1963: 259). The latter project locates contemporary Kabyles solely in terms of loss and dislocation, unable to develop a critical and conceptual understanding of their own culture and history (see Colonna, this volume). Moreover, if the *Outline* was intended to support a Berber political project in Algeria, it is hard to imagine that many Algerians were reading it. Bourdieu's primary interlocutors were in the French academy where the notion of *habitus* was the theoretical arm Bourdieu used to transcend what he perceived to be a "false dichotomy" (Lane 2000: 88) between a Sartrian subjectivist epistemology rooted in free will and phenomenological experience, and a Lévi-Straussian objectivist epistemology that looked to formal linguistic and semiotic structures as the overarching mechanisms that governed human behavior (see Lane 2000, chapter 4). The *Outline* was Bourdieu's attempt to demonstrate that human beings were neither animated by a kind of existentialist free will nor regulated by "a mysterious cerebral and/or social mechanism" (Bourdieu 1977: 29). The Kabyles became conduits for Bourdieu's contention that practical knowledge—tacitly learned via generative schemes, analogical logics, and embodied dispositions—constituted a doxic lifeworld within which individuals could improvise but from which they could never escape.

In the end it was the *Outline* and related pieces, not the sociological studies, that became the primary works through which representations of Kabyles have circulated in Bourdieu's corpus. Yet the *Outline* located Kabyles in a time out of time, stripping them of even the most basic ability to reflect on their condition. For Bourdieu the possibility of cultural critique required a particular kind of education, and it is to a discussion of Kabyle literacy that I now turn.

Literacy: The Great Divide?

Deborah Reed-Danahay has already noted that Bourdieu drew a sharp dichotomy between so-called modern and traditional societies: Kabylia represented a "pre-industrial, 'traditional' peasant society" (Reed-Danahay 1995: 71) that operated through personalized networks requiring continuous re-creation, in contradistinction to the rationalized, institutional forms of power operative in France and other industrialized nations. A related dichotomy,[25] I suggest, characterizes Bourdieu's works on Kabylia, with the proverb-citing Kabyles of the *Outline*, *The Logic of Practice*, the "Sentiment of Honor," the "Kabyle House" (1970), and related pieces standing as the traditionalized Others to their prose-spewing counterparts, the fragmented Kabyles of *Le Déracinement* and *Travail et travailleurs*. Literacy, for Bourdieu, constituted one of the central pivots on which this dualism rested (see also Reed-Danahay 1995). Bourdieu drew on the hypothesis advanced by Jack Goody and Ian Watt (1968), which posits that literacy (in particular, that associated with phonetic, alphabetic writing) ushers in certain changes in consciousness, including the development of a new mode of abstract reasoning, an increase in individualization, and a "more conscious, comparative, and critical attitude" (Goody and Watt 1968: 48). With the advent of writing, the individual is no longer bound by a "single, ready-made orientation to life" (Goody and Watt 1968: 63) but develops the capability to stand outside the cultural system, which then becomes subject to critique. As Bourdieu put it: "Until language is objectified in the written text, speech is inseparable from the speaker's whole person, and in his absence it can be manipulated only in the mode of *mimesis*, which is not open to analysis or criticism" (1977: 236n41). This statement makes explicit a claim that underwrites the argument of the *Outline*: that the Kabyles (along with other supposedly oral peoples) are incapable of critical metadiscourse; that informed reflection on their own language practices is impossible before the advent of written text.

If Bourdieu endorsed Goody and Watt's thesis, he did not go even as far as they did in acknowledging situations of so-called restricted literacy (Goody 1968).[26] From Goody's perspective, even "ancient Kabylia" would have qualified under this category. When Muslim religious notables (*marabouts*) settled among Berber populations,[27] they dispensed a religious education that often included at least rudimentary literacy skills. Colonial ethnographies contain a substantial written record of legal codes (Bernard and Milliot 1933; Hanoteau and Letourneux 1872–73; Milliot 1932; Ould-Braham 1986).[28] Archives house numerous examples of letter exchanges (in Arabic) between Kabyle leaders and French officers that date from the earliest moments of the French colonization of the region (1840s–1860s).[29] During those decades, the French also hired Kabyles who were literate in Arabic to work in the Bureaux Arabes (Offices of Indigenous Affairs). Called *khodja* (scribes), these individuals handled correspondence, recorded passports, and were responsible for transcribing in the Bureau's registers "the *decisions written* by the Djemaas (local village assemblies)" (Bureaux Arabes n.d.a, emphasis added).[30] The interpreter, another Bureau Arabe employee, checked the khodja's work against the original text, provided a translation, and "submitted to the Bureau Chief any observations that *the way in which they [i.e., the legal decisions] were composed (redigés) suggested to him*" (Bureaux Arabes n.d.b, emphasis added).[31] Although much of this writing was in Arabic, at least one khodja, Si Moula n At Ameur, transcribed poems in Kabyle Berber (using Arabic characters, as was standard at the time) at the request of a French officer (Hanoteau

1867; also discussed in Goodman 2002a). Sources further suggest that manuscripts of Berber poetry have long been held in private hands (Mammeri 1980; Yacine 1987). The French certainly helped to accelerate the practice of writing down Kabyle texts (Ould-Braham 1986: 69); they were responsible for developing a Roman-alphabet writing system for Kabyle Berber that gradually came to constitute the standard (Hanoteau 1858; Ben Sedira 1887; Boulifa 1913; de Paradis 1844; see also the missionary journal *Fichier de Documentation Berbère*). Yet at least one surviving Kabyle manuscript[32] predates by two decades the French conquest of Kabylia: a Kabyle translation of Genesis and the Gospels, which the U.S. Vice-Consul in Algiers, W. B. Hodgson, had made with the assistance of a Kabyle named Sidi Hamet. Hodgson sold it to the British and Foreign Bible Society in 1831; the Society published a limited edition of the first twelve chapters of the Gospel of St. Luke (Société Biblique Britannique et Etrangère 1833). If one considers Berber regions beyond Kabylia, an even more substantial written record can be documented. Buried in colonial ethnographies lies evidence of written land transactions. Several chronicles from Algeria's Mzab region have been found (Lewicki 1934a, 1943b; Moytlinski 1885, 1907). Morocco's Anti-Atlas region has an especially rich scriptural heritage that dates from at least the seventeenth century and includes manuscripts of poetry, stories, religious texts, grammar texts, and medical texts (Boogert 1992, 1995; Boogert and Stroomer 1993; Chaker 1986; Mountassir 1994).

Despite evidence of a small but undeniable written tradition, Bourdieu's portrayal of Kabylia reinforces an orality–literacy divide. The way that Bourdieu transcribed the Kabyle language itself contributed to this portrayal. Bourdieu used a transcription system based in French phonology[33] instead of employing conventional Roman-alphabet symbols and morphological rules for writing Kabyle Berber that had been under development for over a century and were in standard use among most academics by the 1960s. At times he employed improper morphological segmentation, running words into each other in a way that makes them difficult to decipher.[34] He admitted that he recorded the texts phonetically while in the field; he did not study Berber until after he returned to France (Honneth et al. 1986: 39). His Algerian collaborators may also have used French-oriented transcription practices, as it would have been difficult to formally study Berber in Algeria at the time.[35] Even after he began to learn the language, however, Bourdieu maintained his field transcriptions. His rationale? This would make for easier reading.[36]

Perhaps the most disconcerting aspect of Bourdieu's reluctance to take literacy into account concerns his work on the Kabyle calendar. His analysis began from the claim that informants' discourse is unsystematic: They "may offer two different names (e.g., one Berber, one drawn from the Islamic tradition) for the same moment of the year or give the same name to periods that vary in length or occur at different moments in the year" (Bourdieu 1977: 98). Resisting the "temptation" to combine these different accounts into a composite master calendar, Bourdieu argued that such an artifact would at best be a "synoptic illusion" that existed only on paper (1977: 98). Not only would it have little to do with practical experience, but it was imaginable only from the totalizing vantage point of the analyst. "True rigor," according to Bourdieu, "does not lie in an analysis which tries to push the system beyond its limits, by abusing the powers of the discourse which gives voice to the silence of practice and by *exploiting the magic of writing* which tears practice and discourse out of the flow of time" (1977: 155, emphasis added). Instead, Bourdieu sought to uncover the "generative schemes" that connected various temporal and ritual dimensions of Kabyle life, from the agricultural cycles to women's activities, from ploughing rituals to marriage rites, from the structure of the day to the cycle of reproduction.

While Bourdieu's approach has merit, it neglects a key piece of empirical data: The literature suggests that Kabyles did indeed have written calendars, which they used alongside other forms of calendrical knowledge (Genevois 1975; Servier 1985[1962]; cf. Colonna 1995 for the Aurès region). One might argue that for the kind of analysis Bourdieu was engaged in, the existence of written calendars was not of crucial import: He was interested in establishing parallels between how Kabyles experienced the rhythms of time across multiple domains, not in calendars available to only a few specialists that had little relevance for "practical" time. Yet if Bourdieu was seeking to reconstruct what Kabyle society may have been like before colonialism, Kabyle writing traditions could have figured importantly. This was especially true during the years of the presidency of Houari Boumediene (1965–79), when Berbers were marginalized within Algeria in part on the grounds that they lacked a written language. Berbers were told that they had to be "Arabized"—learn to read, write, and speak Arabic—and that their own language and traditions fell outside the modernizing project of the nation-state, except under the guise of folklore (Goodman 2005). Bourdieu's portrayal thus reinforced the state's presumption of Kabyle orality.

Kabyles appear to have employed several types of calendrical knowledge (cf. Eickelman 1977). One, agrarian, was based on agricultural cycles native to the region. Kabylia's climate is not uniform but varies significantly from valleys to mountain peaks and from northern, Mediterranean-facing terrains to more southerly, desert-facing areas. Given this variability, periods with the same name may indeed have started and ended at different times; for example, plants in the south may have been ready for harvest a few days earlier than those in the north (Genevois 1975: 12–18). Shifts in weather patterns from year to year must also be taken into consideration. Despite this variation, Genevois, a missionary who published the only systematic study of the Kabyle calendar, found a fair amount of consistency (see his comparative chart, 1975: 20bis). The agrarian calendar was cyclical, not cumulative; there are no surviving records of a linear mechanism for counting the years, although internal periods were conceived in measurable units. The Muslims who settled in the region brought with them two additional calendars. A twelve-month Julian (solar) calendar, which did count years (the forerunner of the Gregorian calendar employed today), was used alongside and eventually was combined with the agrarian one. A third, the lunar calendar,[37] was derived from the Coptic calendar and was used, among other things, to calculate religious holy days (this calendar was called *al-aɛjami*) (Genevois 1975: 22; Servier 1985 [1962]: 370). Sources concur that the lunar calendar was written; in Kabylia, it could be found in treatises on astronomy and astrology, which were housed in *zawiya*s (lodges) and *medersa*s (Quranic schools) throughout the region and could be consulted by local specialists (for an example of a related calendar, see Dozy 1961; cf. Chachoua 2001). With the French, of course, came the contemporary Gregorian calendar, which organized civil administration and wage labor beginning in the mid-nineteenth century.

In practice, these calendars were no doubt flexibly mapped onto each other. The "same" period of time could be located either in a solar month (with a Roman-derived name), in a lunar month, or in relation to the agrarian cycle (or all three); the choice of which name to use no doubt depended, as Bourdieu suggested, on practical considerations. This does not mean, however, that there were no specialists who knew and could articulate the differences among these traditions. Genevois notes that an *aḥessab*—an expert in calendrical matters—could once be found in almost every village (Genevois 1975: 17)[38] and was clearly literate: "the aḥessab of Djemaa Saharidj did not hesitate to contradict a local saint, using *a copy of a calendar that had come from Tunisia*, to demonstrate to him that [the period of] 'Boudjember' was colder than 'Yennayer'" (Genevois 1975: 21, also cited in Colonna 1995: 179, emphasis added). It is plausible that by the time Bourdieu was in Algeria, the calendrical knowledge that he found was unsystematic: Agricultural practices had long been subordinated to wage labor in the Kabyle region (Khellil 1979), and during the war, agriculture came to a virtual standstill, particularly in the resettlement centers where he was working. By that time the civil calendar of the Western world governed wage labor and had increasingly interpenetrated with local conceptions of time. Kabyle calendrical knowledges may, however, have been more systematically articulated in the past. Yet instead of looking to historical sources, Bourdieu turned again to proverbs and sayings. It was in part through these oral texts that he established homologies between temporal and ritual domains of Kabyle life.[39] For example, a saying enabled him to link life-cycle and ploughing rites: "From life they draw death, from death they draw life" (Bourdieu 1977: 138). He used a riddle to establish a related homology between planting and death:

> Riddle: "I put a bean in the ground and it didn't come up."
> Answer: "A dead man." [1977: 138]

By removing the calendar from time, Bourdieu set the Kabyles of the *Outline* into an endless, repeating cycle that denied their own historicity.[40] Viewed through Bourdieu's bipolar lens, the Kabyles did not enter history until they were forcibly removed from their "enchanted" universe, literally uprooted from their villages. By that point, it was too late; they came into modernity fragmented and dispossessed. As Colonna has pointed out, this thesis articulates all too unfortunately with Algeria's postindependence agrarian development politics, which have been based on a related split between a precolonial idyll and a postcolonial peasantry imagined only in terms of loss—broken, backward, and marginal to the Algerian nation, with nothing to offer of its own (Colonna 1987: chapter 3; 1995: chapter 1; Colonna, this volume). Social science and development politics thus go hand in hand, both caught up in the same mythical view that perpetuates a figure of the peasant as excluded from the nation-state (cf. Mitchell 1990).

Conclusion

"Interpretations," notes David Bordwell, "often function as allegories or figurations of the theory from which they issue" (Bordwell 1996: 26). Bourdieu's Manichean portrayal of Kabylia appears to be a function more of his own theoretical orientation than of Kabyle practice. His claims about the Kabyle *habitus* and its associated realm of practice relate less to the conditions of Kabyle social life than to his efforts to "develop a theoretical framework that would pave the way toward another kind of anthropology" (Addi 2002: 38)—one that would transcend objectivist and subjectivist epistemologies in the French academy while working to bridge the disciplines of anthropology and sociology. Despite Bourdieu's hope that his works would provide Algerians with tools to build a new future, his accounts were haunted by the orientalist specter of a precolonial order supposedly shattered by its entry into capitalist modernity (see Sahlins 1999; cf. Ivy 1995). Diametrically opposed representations of speech mark this split and serve as a key ethnographic vehicle through which

Bourdieu constructed two "attitudes toward the other" (Tylor 1986: 127): The Kabyles of the *Outline* used proverbs and sayings to play what Stephen Tylor has called an "ennobling role as a therapeutic image" while those of the sociological studies were quoted only to demonstrate the degree to which they were "neutered by the dark forces of the world systems" (Tylor 1986: 127). To produce this sharp dichotomy, Bourdieu had to disregard crucial dimensions of Kabyle social reality and bracket the region's multidimensional 130-year relationship with France. The Kabyles were in a sense locked in their *habitus*, unable to speak about critical aspects of their own society. In his portrayal of "ancient Kabylia," Bourdieu appears to have enchanted a world that in historical reality was never enchanted. It is easy to understand why such an imagined precolonial universe may have fueled anthropological fantasy. It is harder to fathom today why Bourdieu thought that such a portrayal could also serve the interests of the Kabyles.

Bourdieu's studies of Kabylia raise anew the relationship between theory and ethnographic practice on which the discipline of anthropology has rested. For even as the concept of *habitus* has traveled far and wide, its problematic relationship to the ethnographic setting in which it was developed has remained largely unexamined.[41] As I have demonstrated, Bourdieu's ethnographic materials appear to have been selected and perhaps even constructed because they were consonant with the theoretical approach he was seeking to develop (see also Knauft 1996: 122–28; Lane 2000: chapters 4–5). Kabyles were made to speak in proverbs because more sustained attention to their language and literacy practices could have unsettled the very notion of *habitus*, which relies on the linked assumptions that speakers lack critical purchase on central aspects of their own society and that only the trained observer is capable of cultural critique. Beyond simply challenging the historical and ethnographic material on which Bourdieu's analysis is based, then, this chapter calls for renewed attention to the ways in which ethnography is made to mediate between fieldwork and theory in such a way that the latter is generally privileged. Perhaps it is time to reevaluate the relationship between these three foundations of the anthropological discipline.

Notes

Archival research for this study was conducted in 2001 with a grant from Indiana University. I thank the Centre des Archives d'Outre-Mer, located in Aix-en-Provence, France, for allowing me to consult the materials in their collection. Field research in Kabylia and Paris was carried out from 1992 to 1994 with generous funding from the American Institute for Maghrebi Studies, the Fulbright Institute of International Education, the Social Science Research Council, the Wenner-Gren Foundation, and Brandeis University. An earlier version of this chapter was published in *American Anthropologist*, Volume 105, Number 4; this chapter is reprinted with the permission of the American Anthropological Association. Previous versions were presented at the University of Michigan Language Laboratory on March 13, 2003 and at the 100th Annual Meeting of the American Anthropological Association, held in New Orleans from November 20–24, 2002. Participants at both venues offered stimulating questions and comments. This chapter has also benefited from critical readings by Fanny Colonna, Dale Eickelman, Michael Herzfeld, Jeremy Lane, Fran Mascia-Lees, Stefania Pandolfo, Deborah Reed-Danahay, Paul Silverstein, and four anonymous reviewers. Remaining errors or limitations are entirely my responsibility. © 2003 American Anthropological Association.

1. In an important exception, Poupeau and Discepolo have brought together Bourdieu's political and theoretical writings that span the course of his career (Bourdieu 2002c).

2. By my rough count, approximately ninety proverbs, sayings, and riddles can be found in the *Outline*. If anything, this is underestimated.

3. Wacquant (1993) notes that some of Bourdieu's works are rarely read against each other because of both disciplinary-based circulation practices and translation issues.

4. Kabylia is a mountainous region in northern Algeria where much of Algeria's Kabyle Berber population—a linguistic and cultural minority—is concentrated.

A 1986 census estimated 3 million Kabyles of a total Algerian Berber-speaking population of at least 4.5 million (the population of Algeria was then 22 million) (Chaker 1989). On January 1, 2007, the Algerian population was 33.8 million (Office National des Statistiques 2007). Maintaining the same percentages, the Kabyle population would now total 4.6 million.

5. In one of the first reviews of the *Outline*, Eickelman found unconvincing Bourdieu's claim that Kabyles denied material and economic interest (Eickelman 1979).

6. The full quote reads:

> *Habitus*, understood as a system of lasting, transposable dispositions which, integrating past experiences, functions at every moment as a *matrix of perceptions, appreciations, and actions* and makes possible the achievement of infinitely diversified tasks, thanks to analogical transfers of schemes permitting the solutions of similarly shaped problems, and thanks to the unceasing corrections of the results obtained, dialectically produced by those results (Bourdieu 1977: 82–83).

7. The premise that individuals are unable to see the "truth of their exchanges" is one that Bourdieu shared with psychoanalysis. Bourdieu 2000 makes this explicit: "The sociologist has the peculiarity . . . of being the person whose task is to tell about the things of the social world . . . the way they are." In so doing, the sociologist "breaks the enchanted circle of collective denial" and works toward the "return of the repressed" (Bourdieu 2000: 5; see also Dreyfus and Rabinow 1993: 41).

8. One poem Bourdieu cites can be found on p. 305 of Hanoteau's *Poésies populaires de la Kabylie du Jurjura* (Popular Poems of Kabylia of the Djurdjura) (Hanoteau 1867) (Bourdieu located the poem on p. 475; he may have been working with a different edition (Bourdieu 1977: 209n83). Hanoteau attributed the poem to Si Mohammed Said des Ait Mellikeuch; Bourdieu left it unattributed. For more on this nineteenth-century poet, see Goodman (2002a) and Mammeri (2001).

9. In his discussion of the ladle, Bourdieu may provide a clue as to what these punchcards looked like. The text reads:

> Here is a series of scattered, contradictory observations, which were collected in the hope of removing the ambiguity of the ladle but only serve to confirm it. (1) On her wedding day the bride plunges the ladle into the pot: she will bear as many sons as she brings up pieces of meat. (2) A Proverb: 'Whatever there is in the cooking-pot, the ladle will bring it up.' (3) The

ladle is hung on a piece of string so that it balances evenly, in front of a piece of wheatcake; if it dips towards the wheatcake, the hoped-for event will occur. (4) Of a man who cannot do anything with his hands: 'He's like the ladle.' (5) You must never hit anyone with a ladle: either the implement would break (there is only one in the house) or the person struck would break. (6) A man must never eat out of the ladle (to taste the soup, as the women do): the consequence would be storms and rain when he marries. (7) If a man scrapes the bottom of the pot with the ladle, it is bound to rain on his wedding day. (8) To someone using a tool clumsily: 'Would you have eaten with the ladle?'—if one eats with the ladle one is liable to be cheated (Bourdieu 1977: 141).

10. Sayad described this period in an interview published on http://www.abdelmaleksayad.org/f_itineraire.html, accessed January 11, 2007.

11. For a social history of approaches to proverbs in Europe, see Obelkevich (1987). As Reed-Danahay pointed out to me, Bourdieu's use of proverbs may also relate to the communicative environment in which he was raised—the historical French province of Béarn. According to Reed-Danahay, Bourdieu used proverbs in informal conversations she had with him about rural France, and he included proverbs and sayings in his works on Béarn. (See, for example, Bourdieu 1990: 155, 305n3.) Personal communications by email, May 30 and June 4, 2003; see also Reed-Danahay, this volume.

12. I owe this phrase to an anonymous reviewer.

13. Goodman (2002b) provides a more detailed discussion of Bourdieu's fieldwork locations. Yacine offers rich biographical material about Bourdieu's research in Algeria (Yacine 2004, 2008).

14. Feraoun is best known for his series of ethnographic novels beginning with *Le Fils du pauvre* (The Son of the Poor Man, Feraoun 1954). He also wrote a chronicle of his experiences during the war (Feraoun 1962). He was familiar with Kabyle oral literature and published a book of the poems of one of Kabylia's most renowned nineteenth-century poets (Feraoun 1960).

15. As Bourdieu explained it, resettlement began in 1954 but took a "methodical and systematic form" beginning in 1957. The goal was to "empty out non-controlled areas and to extract the population from the rebel influence" (Bourdieu and Sayad 1964: 110, citing an "official directive"). In all, some two million Algerians were resettled (Bourdieu and Sayad 1964: 13). An existing village could become a resettlement center by being forced to receive populations from areas that were being emptied out; Djemaa Saharidj and Aghbala were centers of this type. Alternatively, new centers could be created by the French.

Bourdieu and Sayad were interested in the differences between newly created centers and those that were attached to existing villages.

16. The interview data in *Travail et travailleurs* was recorded by teams of interviewers who handwrote interviewees' responses to a preestablished questionnaire. See pp. 261–67.

17. One exception is on p. 166, where Bourdieu quotes "an old Kabyle woman" whose words also appear in an appendix to *Le Déracinement* (Appendix IV, pp. 215–20); in the *Outline*, the woman's location was not identified; in *Le Déracinement*, we learn that this woman, in her seventies, was from Djemaa Saharidj.

18. Jeremy Lane locates one reason for this split portrayal of Kabylia in Bourdieu's attempt to "work through the opposition between sociology and anthropology" (Lane 2000: 138). Countering arguments that Bourdieu imagined traditional Kabylia as a kind of primitive Other in relation to European modernity, Lane contends that Kabylia constituted for Bourdieu a comparative case study that could usefully illuminate the workings of symbolic domination in western societies. In this sense, Bourdieu's ethnography of Kabylia accomplished the important critical work of "mak[ing] the familiar strange, the exotic quotidian" (Clifford and Marcus 1986: 2). That is, Bourdieu's simultaneous study of familiar and foreign worlds, usually divided on disciplinary grounds, was a way to reduce the space of Othering to which nonwestern subjects were typically assigned in anthropological works at the time, while denaturalizing western practices that may have appeared natural to Euro-American readers. Yet the fact remains, as Lane notes, that in order for Bourdieu's theory to work, he had to constitute traditional Kabylia as a kind of pristine or originary "archetypal instance of the contribution of 'the doxic experience' to the workings of symbolic domination" (Lane 2000: 129). This archetype could be imagined only if key historical and ethnographic empirical data were suspended, such as Kabylia's "relationship with wider networks of religious, political and economic power" (Lane 2000: 138).

19. The *Outline* contains five references to the war, the colonial situation, or immigration, by my count, on pp. 68, 173, 175, 206n70, and 232n6.

20. Here, he went on to say, "It is necessary to include in this cultural unconscious all traces of colonisation, the effect of the humiliations" (Mammeri and Bourdieu 1985: 20).

21. By "original state," Bourdieu was referring to both ancient Kabylia and ancient Béarn, his natal region in France. For an analysis of Bourdieu's work on Béarn, see Reed-Danahay (1985, 2005, and this volume).

22. Bourdieu reiterated this position in a later interview:

This mountain society of North Africa is particularly interesting because it is a genuine cultural repository that has kept alive, through its ritual practices, its poetry, and its oral traditions, a system of representations . . . which survives to this day in our [i.e., Mediterranean] mental structures and, for a part, in our social structures (Bourdieu and Wacquant 1992: 171).

23. See http://www.abdelmaleksayad.org/f_itineraire.html, accessed January 11, 2007.

24. I am grateful to an anonymous reviewer for helping me to clarify this point.

25. On the dichotomy in Bourdieu's work between precolonial idyll and subsequent "uprooting" or fragmentation, see Colonna (1995: 30–31; 1987: 67–68; and this volume). See also Herzfeld (1987: 7–8, 82–87). Lane 2000 chap. 5 offers a contrasting interpretation.

26. For a critique of Goody's work, see Messick (1993); Street (1995, 2001). For more complex accounts of the relation between orality and literacy in North Africa, see Eickelman (1985); and Wagner (1993).

27. This occurred in the seventh and eleventh centuries.

28. That French colonial works contain substantial documentation of indigenous legal institutions (including written codes) should not be understood as disinterested proto-ethnographic research. During the middle decades of the nineteenth century, French officials sought to locate in Kabylia the rudiments of Western democracy (in fact, some went so far as to see the Kabyle legal system as inspired by Roman law). Hanoteau and Letourneux's work on Kabyle law was an explicit attempt to construct parallels between indigenous legal systems and the French Napoleonic Code (the fascinating subtext of this endeavor can be read in Hanoteau and Letourneux's footnotes, which try to establish a 1:1 correspondence between a Kabyle law and its Napoleonic counterpart). This effort supported a wider "divide-and-rule" policy wherein the French viewed Kabyles (and Berbers more generally) as secular subjects and thus as potentially assimilable into the French republican project. In contrast, Algerian Arabs were seen as mired in a retrograde Islamic law that would impede their ability to assume French citizenship. The premise that Kabyles were closer to Europeans than were Arabs became known as the Kabyle Myth. Although the Kabyle Myth's impact on French colonial policy was limited, its hold on the French imagination was more considerable. For more on the Kabyle Myth, see Ageron (1960, 1976); Lorcin (1999); and Silverstein (2002).

29. For example, there is extensive correspondence between the Ou Kassy family and French officials, including several letters addressed to French General

Randon, head of operations in Algeria, during the 1840s and 1850s; this family apparently collaborated closely with the French (Gouvernement Général de l'Algérie n.d.a). The French took Algiers in 1830, but did not make inroads into Kabylia until the 1840s. The Kabyle region was not under nominal French control until 1857; a final insurrection was quashed in 1871.

30. The job description for the *khodja* is recorded as follows in the 1862 annual report of the Arab Bureau in Fort Napoléon:

> The titular khodja handles correspondence and recopies the letters sent out by the Bureau in a special register; he files all those that are sent by the Djemaas. He also transcribes all the acts that are drawn up by the Djemaas, and serves as an interpreter to the officers in charge of government. The second khodja is specially charged with the recording of passports (Gouvernement Général de l'Algérie n.d.b). The position of khodja appears to have been reserved for indigenous hires.

31. The interpreter's job description in 1862 was as follows:

> The interpreter translates tax letters. He ensures that the khodjas transcribe on the ad-hoc registers all the acts that are written by the Djemaas. He translates them and submits to the head of the Bureau Arabe any observations that the way in which they are written suggests to him. He helps the officers in their functions as officers of the judicial police [i.e., legal affairs] and translates the words that the natives selected for their Kabyle interpreter (Gouvernement Général de l'Algérie n.d.b). In 1861, the interpreter appears to have been French, one Monsieur Despinasse.

32. The British and Foreign Bible Society published 250 copies of this document. Copies were sent to North Africa "without satisfactory result," so the effort was halted (Darlow and Moule 1963: 855). A copy of the manuscript is housed in the rare books collection of the University of Michigan.

33. Bourdieu claimed to be using the "most common transcription" (Bourdieu and Sayad 1964: 181). While it may have been common for those without training in Kabyle Berber, it had never been used by academics and other researchers, who had begun to develop a systematic transcription system beginning in the 1850s (see, for example, Hanoteau 1858; and Boulifa 1913). The White Fathers (Pères Blancs) put in place a Roman-alphabet transcription system based on the one-phoneme-equals-one-character principle beginning in the 1940s (see Vincennes and Dallet 1960). Instead of following this system, Bourdieu represented, for example, the "x" phoneme with "kh"; the "j" phoneme with "dj"; the "t" phoneme with "th": "*adrum*" became "adhrum," "*axxam*" became "akham,"

and *"tajaddit"* became "thadjadith" (in the latter case, he also missed the emphatic consonant). He also added silent "e" to final syllables with long vowels, as French would require: *Tiftirin* became "thiftirine." (Bourdieu 1977: 102, 64, 108). In *The Algerians,* a 1962 English translation of the 1958 *Sociologie de l'Algérie,* he added a "Glossary of Arab and Berber Terms" that includes both the French orthography and the standard (Berber) orthography; this appears to be the only place in his corpus that he includes the Berber orthography with relatively accurate diacritics.

34. To cite just a few examples from the *Outline*: p. 68: ta'a n thamgarth, da susmi; corrected: ṭṭaɛs n temɣart d asusmi. Bourdieu combined the first letter of the final noun (asusmi, silence) with the particle "d," meaning "it is." On p. 55, iḥachem udhmis; corrected: iḥacem udem-is; "-is" is the possessive pronoun "his," which Bourdieu joined to the noun "udem" or "face." Furthermore, Bourdieu's system is not internally consistent: He spelled the same word in different ways in different places. Many of Bourdieu's transcription idiosyncracies are found in the Kabyle proverb with which he dedicated the *Esquisse* to Sayad: Addu dusa'dhi, ataghedh disa'dh-s (corrected: ddu d useɛdi at-taɣed di sseɛd-is; see Dallet 1982: 802) (Go with a man of good and you will resemble him).

35. Bourdieu's transcription closely resembles that of Mouloud Feraoun, who annotated Bourdieu's work. See Feraoun (1960).

36. Bourdieu's rationale for the transcription system he uses is spelled out in *Le Déracinement,* Appendix I, pp. 181–85. He claimed that he was using the most common transcription system (Bourdieu and Sayad 1964: 181).

37. Bourdieu made a single reference to this calendar (1977: 106) but did not reference written sources.

38. Genevois's (1975) work on the Kabyle agrarian calendar is curiously absent from Bourdieu's sources. While this is understandable for the *Outline* (1977), which may have been in press when Genevois' publication came out in 1975, it is less understandable for *The Logic of Practice* (published in French in 1980). Nor did Bourdieu take into account Jean Servier's work on the Kabyle calendar (1985 [1962]), which is largely consistent with the work of Genevois, although Bourdieu did refer to other aspects of Servier's study. On calendars, see also Colonna 1995; and Dozy 1961.

39. Servier prefigured Bourdieu's analysis, noting that the agrarian calendar was connected, via similar symbolism, to various domains of Kabyle life, including the labors of the house and the life-cycle rites (Servier 1985 [1962]).

40. On Bourdieu's approach to time, see also Eickelman (1977); Goodman (1999); Herzfeld (1987); Silverstein (this volume).

41. Even those scholars who have questioned the relationship between theory

and fieldwork in Bourdieu's work tend to take his work on Kabylia as more empirically sound than some of his later works. Aaron Cicourel, for instance, in an otherwise well-founded critique of Bourdieu's method, found convincing the "detailed ethnographic evidence" from his study of Kabylia (Cicourel 1993: 95).

Works Cited

Addi, Lahouari. 2002. *Sociologie et anthropologie chez Pierre Bourdieu: Le Paradigme anthropologique kabyle et ses conséquences théoriques.* Paris: La Découverte.

Ageron, Charles-Robert. 1960. La France a-t-elle eu une politique kabyle? *Revue Historique* 1960 (April):311–52.

———. 1976. Du mythe kabyle aux politiques berbères. In *Le Mal de voir: Ethnologie et orientalisme: Politique et épistémologie, critique et autocritique . . . Contributions aux colloques: Orientalisme, africanisme, américanisme (9–11 mai 1974); Ethnologie et politique au Maghreb (5 juin 1975).* pp. 331–48. Paris: Cahiers Jussieu, Union Générale d'Editions.

Amrane, M. I. Aït. n.d. *Ekkr a mmis oumazigh: Mémoire, au lycée de Ben-Aknoun 1945.* Privately published.

Amrouche, Jean El-Mouhoub. 1994. *Un Algérien s'adresse aux Français, ou l'histoire d'Algérie par les textes (1943–61),* ed. T. Yacine. Paris: Awal/Harmattan.

Ben Sedira, Belkassem. 1887. *Cours de langue kabyle.* Algiers: Jourdan.

Bernard, Augustin, and Louis Milliot. 1933. Les qanouns kabyles dans l'ouvrage de Hanoteau et Letourneux. *Revue des Etudes Islamiques* II.

Boogert, Nico van den. 1992. A Sous Berber Poem on Sidi Ahmad Ibn Nasir. *Etudes et Documents Berbères* 9: 121–37.

———. 1995. *Catalogue des manuscrits arabes et berbères du Fonds Roux.* Aix-en-Provence, France: Institut de Recherches et d'Etudes sur le Monde Arabe et Musulman (IREMAM).

Boogert, Nico van den, and Harry Stroomer. 1993. A Sous Berber Poem on the Merits of Celebrating the Mawlid. *Etudes et Documents Berbères* 10: 47–82.

Bordwell, David. 1996. Contemporary Film Studies and the Vicissitudes of Grand Theory. In *Post-Theory: Reconstructing Film Studies,* ed. David Bordwell and Noël Carroll, pp.3–36. Madison: University of Wisconsin Press.

Boulifa, Si Ammar Ben Saïd. 1913. *Méthode de langue kabyle: Cours de deuxième année (Etude linguistique et sociologique sur la Kabylie du Djurdjura).* Algiers: Jourdan.

————. 1990 (1904). *Recueil de Poésies Kabyles*. Paris: Awal.

Bourdieu, Pierre. 1962 (1958). *The Algerians*, trans. A. C. M. Ross. Boston: Beacon Press.

————. 1966. The Sentiment of Honour in Kabyle Society. In *Honour and Shame: The Values of Mediterranean Society*, ed. J. G. Peristiany, trans. Philip Sherrard. pp. 191–241. Chicago: University of Chicago Press.

————. 1970. The Kabyle House or the World Reversed. *Social Science Information* 9(2): 151–70.

————. 1972. *Esquisse d'une théorie de la pratique. Précédé de trois études d'ethnologie kabyle*. Geneva: Droz.

————. 1977. *Outline of a Theory of Practice*, trans. Richard Nice. Cambridge: Cambridge University Press.

————. 1979 (1977). *Algeria 1960*, trans. Richard Nice. Cambridge: Cambridge University Press.

————. 1990a (1980). *The Logic of Practice*, trans. Richard Nice. Stanford: Stanford University Press.

————. 1990b (1987). *In Other Words: Essays Towards a Reflexive Sociology*, trans. Matthew Adamson. Cambridge: Polity Press.

————. 2000 (1997). *Pascalian Meditations*, trans. Richard Nice. Stanford: Stanford University Press.

————. 2002a. De la guerre révolutionnaire à la révolution. In *Interventions, 1961–2001: Science sociale et action politique*, ed. Franck Poupeau and Thierry Discepolo. pp. 29–36. Marseilles: Agone.

————. 2002b. Entre amis. *Awal* 21: 5–10.

————. 2002c. *Interventions, 1961–2001: Science sociale et action politique*, ed. Frank Poupeau and Thierry Discepolo. Marseilles: Agone.

Bourdieu, Pierre, Alain Darbel, Jean-Paul Rivet, and Claude Seibel. 1963. *Travail et travailleurs en Algérie*. Paris and The Hague: Mouton.

Bourdieu, Pierre, and Abdelmalek Sayad. 1964. *Le Déracinement: La Crise de l'agriculture traditionnelle en Algérie*. Paris: Editions de Minuit.

Bourdieu, Pierre, and Loïc Wacquant. 1992. *An Invitation to Reflexive Sociology*. Chicago: University of Chicago Press.

Breckenridge, Carol A., and Peter Van der Veer. 1993. *Orientalism and the Postcolonial Predicament: Perspectives on South Asia*. Philadelphia: University of Pennsylvania Press.

Briggs, Charles, and Richard Bauman. 1992. Genre, Intertextuality, and Social Power. *Journal of Linguistic Anthropology* 2(2): 131–72.

Chachoua, Kamel. 2001. *L'Islam kabyle: Religion, état et société en Algérie*. Paris: Maisonneuve and Larose.

Chaker, Salem. 1986. Ecriture (graphie arabe). *Encyclopédie Berbère* XVII: 2580–83.

———. 1989. *Berbères aujourd'hui.* Paris: Harmattan.

Cicourel, Aaron V. 1993. Aspects of Structural and Processual Theories of Knowledge. In *Bourdieu: Critical Perspectives,* ed. Craig Calhoun, Edward LiPuma, and Moishe Postone. pp. 89–115. Chicago: University of Chicago Press.

Clifford, James, and George E. Marcus, eds. 1986. *Writing Culture: The Poetics and Politics of Ethnography.* Berkeley: University of California Press.

Colonna, Fanny. 1987. *Savants paysans: Elements d'histoire sociale sur l'Algerie rurale.* Algiers: Office des Publications Universitaires.

———. 1995. *Les Versets de l'invincibilité: Permanence et changements religieux dans l'Algérie contemporaine.* Paris: Presses de la Fondation Nationale des Sciences Politiques.

Dallet, Jean-Marie. 1982. *Dictionnaire kabyle-français.* Paris: SELAF.

Darlow, T. H., and H. F. Moule. 1963. *Historical Catalogue of the Printed Editions of Holy Scripture in the Library of the British and Foreign Bible Society.* New York: Kraus Reprint Corporation (for the British and Foreign Bible Society).

de Paradis, Venture. 1844. *Grammaire et dictionnaire abrégés de la langue berbère.* Paris: Imprimerie Royale.

Dozy, R. 1961. *Le Calendrier de Cordoue.* Leiden: E. J. Brill.

Dreyfus, Hubert, and Paul Rabinow. 1993. Can There Be a Science of Existential Structure and Social Meaning? In *Bourdieu: Critical Perspectives,* ed. Craig Calhoun, Edward LiPuma and Moishe Postone. pp. 35–44. Chicago: University of Chicago Press.

Eickelman, Dale. 1977. Time in a Complex Society: A Moroccan Example. *Ethnology* 16(1): 39–55.

———. 1979. The Political Economy of Meaning (review article). *American Ethnologist* 6(2): 386–93.

———. 1985. *Knowledge and Power in Morocco. The Education of a Twentieth-Century Notable.* Princeton: Princeton University Press.

Fanon, Frantz. 1963 (1959). *The Wretched of the Earth.* New York: Grove Press.

Feraoun, Mouloud. 1954. *Le Fils du pauvre.* Paris: Editions du Seuil.

———. 1960. *Les Poèmes de Si Mohand.* Paris: Editions de Minuit.

———. 1962. *Journal, 1955–1962.* Paris: Editions du Seuil.

Genevois, Henri. 1975. Le calendrier agraire et sa composition. *Le Fichier Periodique* 125: 1–89.

Goodman, Jane E. 2002a. The Half-Lives of Texts: Poetry, Politics, and Ethnography in Kabylia (Algeria). *Journal of Linguistic Anthropology* 12(2): 157–88.

———. 2002b. What Talk Conceals, Proverbs Reveal: Bourdieu, Folklore, and the Kabyle *Habitus*. Paper presented at the Annual Meeting of the American Anthropological Association, New Orleans, November 21.

———. 2002c. Writing Empire, Underwriting Nation: Discursive Histories of Kabyle Berber Oral Texts. *American Ethnologist* 29(1): 86–122.

———. 2004. Reinterpreting the Berber Spring: From Rite of Reversal to Site of Convergence. *Journal of North African Studies* 9(3): 60–82.

———. 2005. *Berber Culture on the World Stage: From Village to Video*. Bloomington: Indiana University Press.

Goody, Jack. 1968. Restricted Literacy in Northern Ghana. In *Literacy in Traditional Societies*, ed. Jack Goody. pp. 198–264. Cambridge: Cambridge University Press.

Goody, Jack, and Ian Watt. 1968. The Consequences of Literacy. In *Literacy in Traditional Societies*, ed. Jack Goody. pp. 27–68. Cambridge: Cambridge University Press.

Gouvernement Général de l'Algérie. n.d.(a). Série I, Bureaux Arabes, Division d'Alger, Cercle de Tizi-Ouzou, Sous-Serie 44 I. Alg/gga/71 MIOM 302. Centre des Archives d'Outre Mer, Aix-en-Provence, France.

———. n.d.(b). Série I, Bureaux Arabes, Division d'Alger, Cercle de Fort Napoléon, Sous-Série 43 I, 1 Inspection Général: Rapports d'ensemble, 1861–62. Alg/gga/71 MIOM 288.Centre des Archives d'Outre Mer, Aix-en-Provence, France.

Hanks, William F. 2005. Pierre Bourdieu and the Practices of Language. *Annual Review of Anthropology* 34: 67–83.

Hanoteau, Adolphe. 1858. *Essai de grammaire kabyle: Renfermant les principes du langage parlé par les populations du versant nord du Jurjura et spécialement par les Igaouaouen ou Zouazoua*. Algiers: Bastide.

———. 1867. *Poésies populaires de la Kabylie du Jurjura*. Paris: L'Imprimerie Impériale.

Hanoteau, Adolphe, and Aristide Letourneux. 1872–73. *La Kabylie et les coutumes kabyles*. Paris: L'Imprimerie Nationale.

Herzfeld, Michael. 1987. *Anthropology through the Looking-Glass: Critical Ethnography in the Margins of Europe*. Cambridge: Cambridge University Press.

Honneth, Axel, Hermann Kocyba, and Bernd Schwibs, eds. 1986. The Struggle for Symbolic Order: An Interview with Pierre Bourdieu. *Theory, Culture and Society* 3(3): 35–51.

Ivy, Marilyn. 1995. *Discourses of the Vanishing: Modernity, Phantasm, Japan.* Chicago: University of Chicago Press.

Keane, Webb. 1995. The Spoken House: Text, Act, and Object in Eastern Indonesia. *American Ethnologist* 22(1): 102–24.

Khellil, Mohand. 1979. *L'Exil kabyle: Essai d'analyse du vécu des migrants.* Paris: Harmattan.

Knauft, Bruce M. 1996. *Genealogies for the Present in Cultural Anthropology.* New York: Routledge.

Lane, Jeremy F. 2000. *Pierre Bourdieu: A Critical Introduction.* London: Pluto Press.

Le Sueur, James D. 2001. *Uncivil War: Intellectuals and Identity Politics during the Decolonization of Algeria.* Philadelphia: University of Pennsylvania Press.

Leiris, Michel. 1950. L'ethnographe devant le colonialisme. *Les Temps Modernes* 58: 357–74.

Lewicki, T. 1934a. Quelques textes en vieux berbère provenant d'une chronique ibadite anonyme. *Revue des Etudes Islamiques* 3: 275–96.

———. 1934b. Une chronique ibadite: Kitâb as-Sijar, d'Abû-l (Abbas Ahmad as-Sammahi). *Revue des Etudes Islamiques* 3: 59–78.

Lorcin, Patricia M. E. 1999. *Imperial Identities: Stereotyping, Prejudice and Race in Colonial Algeria.* London: I. B. Tauris.

Mammeri, Mouloud. 1969. *Les Isefra de Si Mohand-ou-Mhand.* Paris: La Découverte.

———. 1980. *Poèmes kabyles anciens.* Paris: Maspero.

———. 1985. *L'ahellil du Gourara.* Paris: Maison des Sciences de l'Homme.

Mammeri, Mouloud, and Pierre Bourdieu. 1985. Du bon usage de l'ethnologie. *Awal* 1: 7–29.

Marcy, G. 1941. Les vestiges de la parenté maternelle en droit coutumier berbère et le régime des successions touarègues. *Revue Africaine* 85: 187–211.

Messick, Brinkley. 1993. *The Calligraphic State: Textual Domination and History in a Muslim Society.* Berkeley: University of California Press.

Milliot, Louis. 1932. Les institutions kabyles. *Revue des Etudes Islamiques* 2: 127–74.

Mitchell, Timothy. 1990. The Invention and Reinvention of the Egyptian Peasant. *International Journal of Middle East Studies* 22: 129–50.

Mountassir, Abdallah El. 1994. De l'oral à l'ecrit, de l'ecrit à la lecture: Exemple des manuscrits chleuhs en graphie arabe. *Etudes et Documents Berbères* 11: 153–60.

Moytlinski, A. de. 1885. Bibliographie du Mzab. *Bulletin de Correspondance Africaine* 3: 15–72.

THE PROVERBIAL BOURDIEU

————. 1907 (1905). Le manuscrit arabo-berbère de Zouagha. In *Actes du XIVème Congrès des Orientalistes,*Volume II, Section 4. pp. 68–78. Paris.

Obelkevich, James. 1987. Proverbs and Social History. In *The Social History of Language,* ed. Peter Burke and Roy Porter. pp. 43–72. Cambridge: Cambridge University Press.

Office National des Statistiques. 2007. Quelques indicateurs économiques: Statistiques sociales—Population et démographie, Electronic document, www.ons.dz/them_sta.htm, accessed May 25, 2007.

Ouerdane, Amar. 1990. *La Question berbère dans le mouvement national algérien, 1926–1980.* Quebec: Septentrion.

Ould-Braham, Ouahmi. 1986. Un qanoun kabyle recueilli au XIXème siècle. *Etudes et Documents Berbères* 1: 68–77.

Raheja, Gloria Goodwin. 1996. Caste, Colonialism, and the Speech of the Colonized: Entextualization and Disciplinary Control in India. *American Ethnologist* 23(3): 494–513.

————. 2000. The Illusion of Consent: Language, Caste, and Colonial Rule in India. In *Colonial Subjects: Essays on the Practical History of Anthropology,* ed. Peter Pels and Oscar Salemink. pp. 117–52. Ann Arbor: University of Michigan Press.

Reed-Danahay, Deborah. 1995. The Kabyle and the French: Occidentalism in Bourdieu's Theory of Practice. In *Occidentalism: Images of the West,* ed. James G. Carrier. pp. 61–84. Oxford: Clarendon Press.

Sahlins, Marshall. 1999. What Is Anthropological Enlightenment? Some Lessons of the Twentieth Century. *Annual Review of Anthropology* 28: i–xxiii.

Said, Edward. 1978. *Orientalism.* New York: Vintage Books.

Servier, Jean. 1985 (1962). *Tradition et civilisation berbères: Les Portes de l'année.* Monaco: Editions du Rocher.

Silverstein, Michael. 1993. Metapragmatic Discourse and Metapragmatic Function. In *Reflexive Language: Reported Speech and Metapragmatics,* ed. John A. Lucy. pp. 33–58. Cambridge: Cambridge University Press.

Silverstein, Michael, and Greg Urban, eds. 1996. *Natural Histories of Discourse.* Chicago: University of Chicago Press.

Silverstein, Paul A. 2002. The Kabyle Myth: Colonization and the Production of Ethnicity. In *From the Margins: Historical Anthropology and Its Futures,* ed. Brian Keith Axel. pp. 122–55. Durham: Duke University Press.

Société Biblique Britannique et Etrangère. 1833. *Extrait d'une traduction ms. en langue berbère de quelques parties de l'écriture sainte contenant 12 chapitres de Luc.* London: R. Watts, Crown Court, Temple Bar.

Stewart, Susan. 1993. *On Longing: Narratives of the Miniature, the Gigantic, the Souvenir, the Collection.* Durham: Duke University Press.

Street, Brian. 1995. *Social Literacies: Critical Approaches to Literacy in Development, Ethnography and Education.* London: Longman.

———. 2001. *Literacy and Development: Ethnographic Perspectives.* London: Routledge.

Tylor, Stephen A. 1986. Post-Modern Ethnography: From Document of the Occult to Occult Document. In *Writing Culture: The Poetics and Politics of Ethnography,* ed. James Clifford and George E. Marcus. pp. 122–40. Berkeley: University of California Press.

Vincennes, Louis de, Sr. and J. M. Dallet. 1960. *Initiation à la langue berbère (Kabylie).* Fort-National, Algeria: Fichier de Documentation Berbère.

Wacquant, Loïc J. D. 1993. Bourdieu in America: Notes on the Transatlantic Importation of Social Theory. In *Bourdieu: Critical Perspectives,* ed. Craig Calhoun, Edward LiPuma, and Moishe Postone. pp. 235–62. Chicago: University of Chicago Press.

Wagner, Daniel A. 1993. *Literacy, Culture, and Development: Becoming Literate in Morocco.* Cambridge: Cambridge University Press.

Yacine, Tassadit. 1987. *Poésie berbère et identité: Qasi Udifella, héraut des At Sidi Braham.* Paris: Maison des Sciences de l'Homme.

———. 2004. Pierre Bourdieu in Algeria at War: Notes on the Birth of an Engaged Ethnosociology. *Ethnography* 5(4): 487–510.

———. 2008. Aux origines d'une ethnographie singulière. In *Esquisses algériennes,* Pierre Bourdieu. pp. 21–53. Paris: Seuil.

Yamina Ait Amar ou Saud. 1960 (1953). *Le Mariage en Kabylie, Part 1.* Fort National: Fichier de Documentation Berbère.

———. 1961 (1953). *Le Mariage en Kabylie, Part 2.* Fort National: Fichier de Documentation Berbère.

Zigrosser, Carl. 1965. *Multum in Parvo: An Essay in Poetic Imagination.* New York: George Braziller.

THREE

Bourdieu's Ethnography in Béarn and Kabylia

The Peasant *Habitus*

DEBORAH REED-DANAHAY

> I can say that I spent nearly twenty years trying to understand why
> I chose that village ball. . . . I even believe—this is something that I
> would never have dared say even ten years ago—that the feeling of
> sympathy (in the strongest sense of the term) that I felt then and the
> sense of pathos that exuded from the scene I witnessed were surely at
> the root of my interest in this object.—Bourdieu and Wacquant, *An Invitation
> to Reflexive Sociology*

Introduction

The statement above marks the reflexive turn in his writing that Pierre
Bourdieu eventually came to label "auto-analysis." At that moment
in the early 1990s, he signaled his increasing self-awareness about
the motives and positions of his research. Why would he "never
have dared" before to speak of his feelings about the situation of the
peasant bachelors at a dance in the village where he grew up? And
why did Bourdieu begin to talk more about his emotions and feelings
toward his research? Up until the time of his death in 2002, Bourdieu
remained ambivalent about self-revelation among social scientists,
and was scornful of "the diary disease." And yet the autobiographical

writings that he produced in the final decade of his life help shed light on the ways in which his own feelings of being in the world were reflected in his theories and choices of research subject.

There are significant parallels between the ways in which Bourdieu explained human behavior through *habitus* and the ways in which he expressed in his writings his own experiences of action, thought, and feeling. This essay will focus on the origins of Bourdieu's use of the concept of *habitus* in his early ethnographic work on socio-cultural rupture and change in Algeria and in rural France. At that time, in the early 1960s, he was a young man who had experienced dislocation first-hand both through geographical movement (from his native rural France to Paris, and then to Algeria) and through social class movement (in large part by virtue of leaving his modest social background and acquiring a formal education). After some preliminary discussion that sets the stage, I will focus on two articles published in *Etudes Rurales* within two years of each other in the early 1960s (Bourdieu 1962b and Bourdieu and Sayad 1964a) that present striking parallels in Bourdieu's thinking about peasants and his use of the concept of *habitus* in the dual contexts of Kabylia and Béarn. The theme of rupture (as a break with tradition) is prevalent in both articles, despite important differences in the ethnographic contexts.[1] As Bourdieu himself led us to see through his subsequent autobiographical writings about this period in his life, the young sociologist/ethnographer who conducted this research occulted his emotions about the social suffering he observed at the time. He later would make social suffering a major topic of research in *La Misère du monde* (*The Weight of the World*) (Bourdieu and Accardo et al. 1993), and write about a form of "intellectual love" that informs such research. He would write about needing to hide behind the camera in Algeria to hide his emotions (2003b), and he would write, as is reflected in the epigraph at the beginning of this chapter, about the emotions he felt during his research in rural France (see also Bourdieu 2002). But when he was developing his theory of *habitus* in the early 1960s, his project for a reflexive sociology or an auto-analysis had not yet fully surfaced. In this early work, he was exploring (and coming to terms with) some of his own experiences through the lens (or mask) of the experiences of Algerian men and other rural French men.

Bourdieu was born in the interwar year of 1930 and grew up in a rural village in the southwestern region of Béarn. His father was a postman, but his grandfather and uncle were tenant farmers. Despite his somewhat humble, petit-bourgeois background, Bourdieu was a "scholarship boy" (*le miraculé*) who did well in school and was able to attend an elite high school in Pau and then pursue prestigious studies in philosophy at the Ecole Normale in Paris. Although Bourdieu wrote extensively toward the end of his life (esp. Bourdieu 2004a) about some of the emotional strains he felt growing up and moving away from rural life, he had begun to address this in the early 1990s: "I spent most of my youth in a tiny and remote village of Southwestern France, a very 'backward' place as city people like to say. And I could meet the demands of schooling only by renouncing many of my primary experiences and acquisitions, not only a certain accent. . . . The research I did, around 1960, in this village, helped me to discover a lot of things about myself and about my object of study" (Bourdieu and Wacquant 1992: 205).

Bourdieu first made use of the concept of *habitus* as a way to explore the social position and sentiments of the *paysan empaysanné* (em-peasanted peasant)—a tragic figure who could not adapt to urbanizing influences in his rural milieu at mid-century. Bourdieu found a version of this em-peasanted peasant in both rural France and in the resettlement camps of wartime Algeria. He contrasted this type of peasant with the *bon paysan* (Bourdieu 1962b:57) or the "de-peasanted" peasant (Bourdieu and Sayad 1964a), a person who could more easily adapt to urban influences, was less traditional in worldview, and had an identity based more on individualism than on kinship group. Bourdieu was himself a "de-peasanted" peasant, who had left rural life through education and a career in academia.[2] This position left him with what he later called a "split *habitus*" (2004a: 130), which, I argue, made him uncomfortable about adopting a worldview that depended wholly on individual social agency or one that identified social milieu as the main determinant of human action and thought. Having left the confines of rural life himself, through education, Bourdieu was ambivalent about claiming his own social agency in this act. He could understand the criticisms leveled by the older peasants toward the de-peasanted, urban-oriented youth (who had become more individualistic), yet, as an urban man himself, he viewed as inevitable the social changes that would leave the more traditional peasants and their worldview behind. Bourdieu's mixture of nostalgia and guilt about rural France and his own actions in departing for an urban life fueled his sympathies for the *paysan empaysanné*, the figure at the center of his interest. At the same time, Bourdieu's proximity to the experience of peasants shaped the role that emotion and the body played in his theoretical formulation of the *habitus*. In his more developed explications of this concept beginning in the 1970s, Bourdieu wrote of the *habitus* as a set of dispositions, of "structured structures predisposed to function as structuring structures" (1977: 72), but also in terms of feelings, thoughts, tastes, and bodily postures.

Bourdieu made a strong statement regarding his stance toward reflexivity in his Huxley Memorial Lecture delivered at the Royal

Anthropological Institute in 2000 (Bourdieu 2003a). Promoting what he referred to as "participant objectivation," he wrote that "one does not have to choose between participant observation, a necessarily fictitious immersion in a foreign milieu, and the objectivism of the 'gaze from afar' of an observer who remains as remote from himself as from his object" (2003a: 282). In the introduction to a volume published posthumously that collects key writings on Béarn (Bourdieu 2002), Bourdieu explained that he chose to work in France so as to invert the Lévi-Straussian move in *Tristes Tropiques* (1992) to seek "the other." He wrote of "throwing himself" into this very familiar world of his own region that he "knew without knowing" (2002: 10) and which he could now "objectify" because he had distanced himself by immersion in another way of life (and here one can imagine he may have been referring to his previous fieldwork in Algeria, but perhaps also to his life as an academic in Paris). It was this very experience of doing autoethnology, of taking as his object something that he "knew without knowing" and trying to study it as a sociologist, that led Bourdieu to develop a theory of practice (and of feeling/sentiment/emotion) for which the problem of reconciling subjective and objective knowledge is key.

Parallel Worlds: Peasant Society in France and Algeria

As I have discussed in greater detail elsewhere (Reed-Danahay 2005), Bourdieu's earliest ethnographic studies in rural France and in Algeria were carried out in the context of the growing field of Mediterranean studies in social anthropology. The work was published at around the same time in France and operated within, to use one of Bourdieu's own terms, the same intellectual "field." It is significant to point out, however, that the Algerian work reached English-speaking audiences

over a decade earlier than the rural French research, and most of
the latter had not been translated into English until quite recently.[3]
Although his concept of *habitus* developed within this intellectual
field of Mediterranean studies as much as it did within the context
of the European philosophical traditions coming down from Mauss,
Merleau-Ponty, and Elias, Bourdieu himself made little reference to
his position in the field of either Mediterranean or peasant studies in
his later autobiographical writings. He more often distanced himself
from fellow ethnographers of Europe or North Africa (by virtue of
rarely making reference to their work), and positioned himself and
his work within the French academic milieu of philosophy, sociology,
and an ethnology dominated by Lévi-Strauss.

Bourdieu's place within the history of peasant studies in Europe
or, more broadly, in the Mediterranean region has frequently been
overlooked. This can be explained not as solely due to his relative
lack of engagement with other ethnographers, but also because the
sociological work he did beginning in the mid-1960s on French education and university life brought him into a new realm of visibility
during the events of 1968, when the book coauthored with Jean-
Claude Passeron, *Les Héritiers* (1964), came to articulate the crisis
in higher education in France for many in the student movement
(despite Bourdieu's own distancing from this movement). In the post-
1968 phase of his life, Bourdieu's reputation was built upon books
such as *Reproduction* (Bourdieu and Passeron 1970), *Distinction*
(Bourdieu 1979), and *Homo Academicus* (Bourdieu 1984), which
turned his gaze to issues within French society in particular, and the
nation-state more generally.[4]

The field of Mediterranean studies during the early 1960s was
informed by a dichotomy between urban and rural societies, and
influenced by wider historical ideas central to European social thought

(Caro Baroja 1963; Williams 1973). This had been reinforced by scholarship such as Redfield's (1956) rural–urban continuum and suggestion that peasant societies were "part-societies," and by Tönnies's *Gemeinschaft-Gesellschaft* dichotomy (1957), in which the "community" of the village was privileged over the anonymity and anomie of the city. This theme was also, of course, present in the work of Emile Durkheim (cf. 1951 [1897]) and in the work of Frédéric Le Play (whose work on kinship in rural France influenced Bourdieu's analysis of marriage strategies). The concept of honor in Mediterranean studies was tied to a system of ideas claiming that peasants in rural societies had a different worldview from that of people living in urban societies. Bourdieu published essays in two English-language edited collections that resulted from pivotal conferences on the Mediterranean: *Mediterranean Countrymen* (Pitt-Rivers, ed. 1963) and *Honor and Shame: The Values of Mediterranean Society* (Peristiany, ed. 1966). In his introduction to the second volume, John Peristiany articulated the dominant position in this field that "Honor and shame are the constant preoccupation of individuals in small scale, exclusive societies where face-to-face personal, as opposed to anonymous, relations are of paramount importance and where the social personality of the actor is as significant as his office" (Peristiany 1966: 11). Bourdieu's essays in these two volumes drew upon his ethnographic research among the Kabyles (one on concepts of time, the other on concepts of honor) and appeared alongside articles written by ethnographers of rural France, such as Laurence Wylie (working in southern France) and Isac Chiva (who worked in Corsica). Bourdieu's early ethnographic work in both France and Algeria reflects a preoccupation with honor as a staple in the peasant worldview and also reflects the urban/rural dichotomy that organized much thinking about peasant societies and modernity at mid-century.

It was within this intellectual context that Bourdieu started to use the term *habitus*, a context based on a structural–functional view of peasant society as "normally" existing in a state of equilibrium through its value systems, customs, agricultural cycles, and relations of kinship/family. The Mediterranean peasant was also positioned as more traditional in contrast to his northern European neighbors. Bourdieu reinforced this idea in his early writing on the Kabyles, contrasting "the traditionalist attitude" of the Algerian peasant and the "predictive attitude" of the more urbanized person (Bourdieu 1963). As Herzfeld has pointed out, societies in this region of the world are "neither exotic nor wholly familiar" (1987: 7), giving them a unique position in the history of anthropological inquiry. That the notion of "honor" in these societies is seized upon in Mediterranean studies is read by Herzfeld as a Eurocentric move to exoticize the region and differentiate it from a more bureaucratic and rational "modern" Europe. While Bourdieu would go on in later writings to unpack "modern" Europe, particularly in *La Noblesse d'état* (1989), in which he turned the tables and exoticized the *grandes écoles* of Paris, in the early writings under consideration here Bourdieu reproduced the dichotomy of traditional/rural vs. modern/urban in his analysis of peasant societies (see also Reed-Danahay 1995).

That Bourdieu was moving back and forth between two fieldwork sites, not only in terms of travel but also in terms of his own thinking about peasant society and developing theories of *habitus*, is evident in several parallel passages in Bourdieu's writings about rural France and Kabylia. In one example of such twinning, Bourdieu expressed his understandings of peasant life and its emotional implications for the individual in Algeria in ways that might also have been based upon his own life experiences growing up in a French village. In his 1966 article on honor among the Kabyles, Bourdieu referred to Kabylia as a "primary society" in which the group is central to the individual. He described the individual emotions engendered by this: "Penned inside this enclosed microcosm in which everybody knows everybody, condemned without the possibility of escape or relief to live with others, beneath the gaze of others every individual experiences deep anxiety about 'people's words'" (1966: 212).[5] In an article on photography in Béarn coauthored with his wife and published a year earlier, Bourdieu made an almost identical statement to that on Kabyle villages. There he described life in his village in Béarn as an "enclosed world where one senses at each moment without escape that one is under the gaze of others" (Bourdieu and Bourdieu 1965: 172). In both passages we see, perhaps, Bourdieu's own split *habitus*—as someone who has lived in such an environment, he hesitates to romanticize the communal aspects of village life, and understands the ambivalence of a person struggling for some autonomy within it.

There are similar parallels in Bourdieu's writings about the concept of honor among the people of Kabylia and Béarn. In the same article on photography, Bourdieu described the rigid, full-frontal posture and solemn expression among those posing in rural French photographs, especially on the occasion of marriage. He described the village of Lesquire as a society "that holds up the sentiment of honor, of dignity and responsibility" and in which it is important to provide the "most honorable" image of oneself to others (Bourdieu and Bourdieu 1965: 172). In a rare explicit comparison between his two field sites, he added in a footnote that "among the Kabyles, a man of honor is he who faces you, who holds his head high, who looks others straight in the face, unmasking his own face" (1965: 7). There is a similar description in *Outline of a Theory of Practice*, where Bourdieu compared the two societies as those in which frontality and honor are connected (Bourdieu 1977: 94). This focus on honor in the two societies reflects the preoccupation in Mediterranean studies at the time with this notion, but also shows that Bourdieu was seeing French peasants in the faces and bodies of the Kabyles, and perhaps vice versa.

Bourdieu's early ethnographic work focused on the disruption of traditional societies, and he embraced an equilibrium model of social organization as the "natural" state of affairs. He continued to view both his rural French and Algerian fieldsites as places to observe an "experiment" having to do with the before and after of social change in a way that seems to characterize society as not always changing but, rather, being disrupted at certain moments. There are further parallels, therefore, between his characterization of the "experimental situation" (Bourdieu and Bourdieu 1965: 164) of the village of Lesquire in the early 1960s and his statement in a much later publication on Algerian workers that the war offered a "quasi-laboratory situation" (Bourdieu 2000: 17). In the first case he was referring to the diffusion of a "modern technique" (photography) into the "peasant milieu"; in the second, he was referring to the "mismatch" between "precapitalist" and "rationalized" economic systems. His model of peasant societies was marked by nostalgia and by a view of a sort of pristine traditional society (the "before") that most likely never existed.

In his preface to *The Logic of Practice* (1990), Bourdieu made reference to his social origins and the advantage this gave him as a rural ethnographer in Algeria, not so much as an "insider" but as someone who understood that it was not possible to adopt the "native point of view." He wrote: "Perhaps because I had a less abstract idea than some people of what it is to be a mountain peasant, I was also, and precisely to that extent, more aware that the distance is insurmountable, irremovable, except through self-deception" (14). Here Bourdieu legitimized his claims to understand the Kabyles, through reference to both his rural origins and his theoretical stance. He continued in this passage to make a point about the need to be conscious of distancing oneself in the ethnographic situation and to avoid naïve perceptions of understanding "the other" through participant–observation research. He wrote that "the distance lies perhaps not so much where it is usually looked for, in the gap between cultural traditions, as in the gulf between two relations to the world, one theoretical, the other practical" (1990: 14). Having left peasant life to become educated, Bourdieu acquired this theoretical point of view, this "scholastic reason" (Bourdieu 2000) that was, paradoxically, essential to ethnographic understanding or "participant objectivation" (Bourdieu 2003).

It was Isac Chiva, then editor of the French journal *Etudes Rurales*, who published Bourdieu's first ethnographic article on bachelors in rural France in 1962 and who also published his 1964 article on uprooted Algerians (Bourdieu and Sayad 1964a), which was coauthored with Abdelmalek Sayad and extracted from a longer book (Bourdieu and Sayad 1964b). These two articles, to which I will now turn, provide good examples of the ethnographic contexts in which Bourdieu was formulating his theory of *habitus* in the context of two peasant societies, and as an ethnographer who claimed he "had a less than abstract idea . . . of what it is to be a mountain peasant" due to his own rural origins. Bourdieu's theory of *habitus* was formed not only in the field of Mediterranean studies and its dichotomy of traditional vs. modern societies but also in the intellectual milieus of structuralist anthropology and previous writings about notions of embodiment.

The *Habitus* of the *Paysan Empaysanné*

> This is not the place to analyse the motor habits proper to the peas-
> ant of Béarn, that *habitus* which betrays the *paysanás*, the lumbering
> peasant. Spontaneous observation perfectly grasps this *hexis* that serves
> as the foundation for stereotypes. . . . The critical observation of the
> urbanites, swift to spot the *habitus* of the peasant as a synthetic unity,
> puts the emphasis on the slowness and heaviness of his gait.—Bourdieu,
> "Célibat et condition paysanne"

> Because the familiar world is for him his natal world, because all of his
> bodily *habitus* is "made" in this space of his customary movements,
> the uprooted peasant suffers to the core of his being, so profoundly
> that he cannot express his helplessness and less still name the reason
> for it.—Bourdieu and Sayad, "Paysans déracinés"

In the first quote above, we read Bourdieu's first published use of the
term *habitus* in his 1962 article on peasant bachelors. In the second,
he uses the term in the context of displaced and uprooted Algerian
peasants in resettlement camps. In both cases Bourdieu makes use
of the notion of bodily *habitus* to express the condition of being
outside one's familiar setting, the space that one can "know without
knowing." Both cases involve the consequences of urbanization for
peasants, and the *habitus* of the "em-peasanted" peasant—the peasant
who is enclosed within the traditional past. While the French peasant
bachelors have not moved from their natal world, the world around
them has changed. For the Algerians it was geographical displacement and "uprooting" that caused this feeling. *Habitus* thus becomes
more visible when it is not part of the doxa (the taken for granted),
when it appears odd or strange to both onlookers (the urbanites)
and to those who inhabit it and feel out of place. As Bourdieu and

Sayad (1964a: 79) write for the Algerian case: "This urban situation favors 'de-peasanted' peasants, the only ones capable of adapting as well as can be expected, in opposition to the 'em-peasanted' peasants who, committed to perpetuating their peasant values, appear lost and ridiculous." Bourdieu's focus in these two articles was not on the *habitus* of those who were adapting better to the new conditions, or that of the more powerful urbanites (although he would later turn to the bourgeois *habitus* in *Distinction* and the academic *habitus* in *Homo Academicus* and *The State Nobility*). We can presume that the *habitus* of those he labeled explicitly as "de-peasanted peasants" in the Algerian case were better adapted to the new social and economic conditions and were perhaps also helping to foster changing worldviews and social practices. While he did not describe in detail the social position of the de-peasanted peasant in terms of *habitus*, Bourdieu mentioned this figure in his work on Algeria more than he did in the case of rural France.

Toward the end of the chapter called "Disintegration and Distress" in Bourdieu's early book *The Algerians* (1962a), there is a moving passage about the "man between two worlds" that can be read as part-autobiography for Bourdieu (see also Bourdieu and Sayad 1964b). Although the explicit referent in the passage below is the young Algerian intellectual in a rapidly changing Algeria, I think Bourdieu himself was also this "man between two worlds." For Bourdieu the two worlds were the traditional world of rural France in which he grew up and the world of the urban intellectual, the social scientist, he was becoming. In the Algerian context he was able to better understand his own experiences of dislocation brought about through education as he witnessed the dislocation caused by war and urbanization in the lives on young Algerians. Bourdieu wrote:

Constantly being faced with alternative ways of behavior by reason of the intrusion of new values, and therefore compelled to make a conscious examination of the implicit premises or the unconscious patterns of his own tradition, this man, cast between two worlds and rejected by both, lives a sort of double inner life, is a prey to frustration and inner conflict, with the result that he is constantly being tempted to adopt either an attitude of uneasy overidentification or one of rebellious negativism. (1962a: 144)

This figure is compelled, Bourdieu suggested, to make "a conscious examination of the implicit premises or the unconscious patterns of his own tradition"; this was later to be part of the methods involving reflexivity in Bourdieu's work. Although he is expressing this in the context of Algeria, it was through his studies of the peasants of Lesquire, his natal village, that Bourdieu sought the patterns of his own tradition (that of his roots or primary *habitus*). He later did the same thing for his secondary, acquired *habitus* when he studied French elite education/academia in such books as *Homo Academicus* and *The State Nobility* (the traditions he acquired through the pursuit of higher education and a life in academia).

In his peasant studies, Bourdieu focused on the *habitus* of those suffering from social and economic changes and not capable of adapting to them. Their *habitus* was a form of pathology, a stigma. As he wrote about the Algerians, "It is no doubt the language of the body, the way of standing, of holding the head and walking, that expresses better than words, the aberration and disorientation" (Bourdieu and Sayad 1964: 90). Fanny Colonna (this volume) offers a cogent critique of what she refers to as the "deprivation model" of the peasant in Bourdieu's work in Algeria, and also in his later work in *La Misère du monde*. She sees this as a hegemonic discourse in Bourdieu's system of thought that forces out other possible ways of understanding.

Bourdieu's notion of *habitus* is a synthesis of the more psychological theory of *habitus* used by Norbert Elias and that of the theory of bodily habits and *habitus* in the work of Marcel Mauss. Elias's work was first published in the late 1930s, and Mauss first published his key essay on bodily *habitus* in 1935.[6] For Elias, *habitus* was associated with drives and impulses that determine tastes and habits. As Dunning and Mennell point out, for Elias, *habitus* represented "second nature," or "embodied social learning" (1996: ix). Elias described what he called the social *habitus* as a form of "we-feeling" for groups, and he wrote that "in relation to their own group identity, and, more widely, their own social *habitus*, people have no free choice. These things cannot simply be changed like clothes" (Elias 1987: 225). It was also connected to what Elias called the civilizing process, through which he referred to a certain way of understanding the relation of the individual to the social, and the manners and tastes that reflected the perceived "civilized" person. When a lower-status group came into contact with a "higher-order" group, according to Elias, there occurred a sort of "collective destruction and certainly a loss of meaning to the highest degree" (1987: 125). The "we-feelings" for the subordinate group break down. In Bourdieu's description of the *habitus* of the "em-peasanted" French and Algerian peasants (*paysans empaysannés*), he is addressing similar issues regarding a lagging social *habitus* in the face of changing circumstances to those Elias addressed in his work on "we-feelings."

The emphasis on bodily *habitus* in Bourdieu's work in these peasant settings also drew upon the work of Marcel Mauss. In his essay on "Body Techniques," Mauss used the concept of *habitus* to refer to customary habits of moving the body which, as he wrote, "do not vary just with individuals and their imitations; they vary especially between societies, educations, proprieties, fashions, and prestiges. In them we should see the techniques and work of collective and individual practical reason" (1979[1950]: 101). Although Mauss was primarily describing the physical manifestation of this in bodily movement, rather than mental or psychological qualities, he did mention that these body techniques were connected to modes of life and manners. These techniques were the product of training and so could be connected with what he noted was the psychological as well as sociological concept of "dexterity" or cleverness. Here we see some origins of Bourdieu's later use of the term *habitus* as a "feel for the game" in which the individual can exercise various strategies within the generative capacities of his or her *habitus* (see especially Bourdieu 1990). But even in his early 1962 article, Bourdieu speaks of the marriage system in Lesquire as having enough "play" in it to permit "affection or personal interest" to intervene, so that it cannot be viewed as a mechanism (1962b: 47). In his descriptions of the bodily *habitus* of the "em-peasanted" peasants of France and Algeria, Bourdieu emphasizes the connection between the body and social position.

As Bourdieu wrote in the quote cited above, the body can express things better than words. He also stressed that in Lesquire, feelings were expressed primarily in bodily movements rather than in words. One informant tells Bourdieu, for example, that whereas parents did not express much direct verbal affection to children, his father would sometimes take over work for him and thereby express his affection. Bourdieu wrote about this among the Kabyles as well, with a story about a Kabyle who told him that as a boy "he used to go up to [his father] and silently press himself against him, and in this way his father understood he was expected at home" (Bourdieu 1966:

225). As Bourdieu also wrote in his earlier essay about the Kabyles and honor, "Perhaps the essential point is that the norms, felt and experienced so deeply that they do not need to be formulated, have their roots in the system of the most fundamental cultural categories, those which define the mythical vision of the world" (1966: 232). This "practical reason" (a term earlier used by Mauss), or "logic of practice," was a main concern in Bourdieu's work, and he contrasted it to academic forms of reason and expression that were acquired through formal education.

Bachelors in Lesquire: The Ball

"Célibat et Condition Paysanne" ("Bachelorhood and the Peasant Condition") is the title of Bourdieu's 1962 article published in *Etudes Rurales,* a title that links a facet of individual experience (being unmarried) to circumstances in peasant society more generally in southwestern France. The problem of bachelors was not just something the sociologist noticed; it was a preoccupation for many of his informants, who mention this over and over again in interviews. The bachelor had become the lived symbol of all that had gone wrong in this village at mid-century: "the bachelor appears as the most visible sign of the crisis that affects the social order" (Bourdieu 1962b: 59). This long essay (over one hundred pages) alternates between statistical facts and the narratives of those living in these conditions in the village of Lesquire. While the marriage system in Lesquire always produced bachelors and the rate of bachelorhood had not varied considerably since the late nineteenth century, in the past the unmarried were usually younger sons and/or men from remote villages in the mountains. Families always had to slough off some members in order to keep viable farms. To be a younger son and a

149

bachelor was considered a necessary sacrifice for the good of the family patrimony.

Bourdieu charts changes in the marriage system since the late nineteenth century that intensified after the First World War and again after the Second World War. These changes opened up the villages and hamlets to a new opposition between rural and urban life, in which urbanism was more highly valued. The external factors of economic changes that occurred after 1914, along with increasing urbanization and the prolongation of education for girls in particular, led to three major changes in the peasant society of Lesquire and its marriage system: the devaluing of the dowry, the breakdown of parental authority (especially the threat of disinheritance), and the growth of individual choice in selection of a spouse. But the main dilemma articulated by males in Lesquire when Bourdieu studied the village in 1960 was that the ideal male (from the perspective of women) had changed from that of the good peasant to that of the urbanite. Urbanization had spread from the city to the village, making the hamlet now the sole province of the peasant (who previously was also associated with, and comfortable in, the village). According to both Bourdieu and his male informants, females were more receptive than males to adopting a changing worldview resulting from urbanization, which in turn influenced their choice of mate (for a critique of this view, see Reed-Danahay 2002).

In the past, a period that Bourdieu locates as before 1914, most marriages were arranged between families, with the assistance of a go-between (often a peddler), and the ideals of a match were accepted by most inhabitants of the region. The marriage system was based on the opposition between first-born and younger sons and between wealthier and less well-off families. Bourdieu notes that the restriction of choice had a positive side—you didn't have to work hard to find a spouse. You could be "oafish, rustic, coarse, without losing any chance of becoming married" (1962b: 57). The ideal male peasant (*le bon paysan*) represented a middle ground between the peasant who tried to act more like a big shot from the city (*un monsieur*) and the peasant who was considered too rustic and backward (*hocou*). The peasant who played the mister ("*faire le monsieur*") was viewed in the collective system of values as not sufficiently serious or hard working and as lacking authority. Girls, Bourdieu claims, were socialized in this worldview from early childhood and shared its values. With a system favoring primogeniture and also gerontocracy, the eldest male, heir to a family farm, did not usually have trouble finding a wife. And this wife would come under the authority of his parents (especially her mother-in-law) after moving to the farm to become his partner. In Bourdieu's ethnographic present of 1960, girls now wanted freedom to marry the man of their choice, and they wanted urban men; they wanted the *monsieurs* and not the peasants. In the new order there is a breakdown of the old system. There is now competition for spouses among the men, and in the competition "the peasant from the hamlet is particularly disarmed" (65). The bachelor is no longer just the younger male from a poor and large family. He can be an eldest male from what was once considered a good house.

This article on bachelors has four major sections: in the first part Bourdieu describes the system and its logic "in the past"; in the second and third parts he describes the changes and consequences of the new logic and influences of urbanization; in the fourth part he focuses on the peasant body and on the village ball at Christmastime in order to underscore the plight of the "em-peasanted peasant" in the new marriage system. It is in this final section called "The Peasant and his Body" that Bourdieu introduces the concept of *habitus* and focuses on the ways that bodily comportment expresses social hierarchy and social position. Bourdieu takes this relatively heterogeneous social space of the dance, in which young rural women, em-peasanted and de-peasanted men, and a smattering of urbanites come together in a social drama (not a term used by Bourdieu; I intend it in Victor Turner's sense) that plays out the contradictions Bourdieu wants to highlight in Lesquire. The ball used to be a space in which the traditional marriage system operated to introduce boys and girls (who normally had little contact with each other), but now it is a space of exclusion and exile for the em-peasanted peasant bachelors.

Bourdieu evoked the concept of *habitus* in the context of the village dance to describe the bodily techniques (after Mauss) of the bachelors. Due to gender segregation in the community, chances for young males and females to socialize together in the past were limited, and the dances permitted a rare occasion for social mixing. Bourdieu explained that the position of the bachelors in the current marriage system (devalued due to their peasantness) made it difficult for them to marry, but that also, the bachelors themselves embodied ways of moving and dressing and acting that made it difficult for them to attract a wife. They were clumsy in their movements, Bourdieu wrote, and their clothing reflected outdated styles. The bachelors had a way of dressing, a way of moving, a way of drinking, a way of singing, etc. that was part of their bodily hexis, or *habitus*. They internalized this devaluation of themselves and became conscious of their position and status as unmarriageable. They were the subjects of a negative judgment of taste on the part of females, who now were able to exercise more autonomy than before in their choice of a mate. Bourdieu, foreshadowing *Distinction*, mentions that girls now held "the monopoly on the judgment of taste" (104). Although he did not use a vocabulary of symbolic or cultural capital, we can also see this emerging here, and could describe the bachelors as lacking in valued forms of symbolic capital even if their farms were prosperous.

Uprooted Algerian Peasants: The Camp

Two years after the appearance of his article on bachelors in Lesquire, Bourdieu coauthored an article published in the same journal, *Etudes Rurales*, titled "Paysans déracinés" (uprooted peasants). In this article based on ethnographic research in Algerian resettlement camps (*le regroupement*), which predated the ethnographic research in rural France, Bourdieu and Sayad describe what they viewed as the "cultural contagion" that had occurred as a result of peasant groups from the mountains being resettled with other groups with whom they would not normally have had contact. Bourdieu and Sayad write that "with the resettlement, those peasants attached to the system of traditional values find themselves placed in continuous contact with those peasants who have already taken certain liberties with tradition" (60). Here the authors refer in particular to an increase in individualism. The resettlement camps brought together whole villages of peasants removed from their land and placed together with people from other mountain communities. The authors draw an analogy between these resettlement camps and cities—both of which were contrasted with patrilineally based social organization. Algerian peasants mixed with those having had more contact with the city in these camps, and Bourdieu and Sayad note the "devaluation of peasant virtues, the breakdown of 'collective controls'" (1964a: 79) on behavior, generational conflicts, and changes in women's roles. Changes in greetings, café behavior, food, and eating habits were all noted as settings in which the peasant felt ill at ease. In the abstract to the article, Bourdieu and Sayad even refer to "the death of the peasant" (56).

The article begins with a chronicle of how the transition of peasant kin systems had already gone from the clan to the household (a more "occidental" model, according to Bourdieu and Sayad), and that the current transition is from the rural peasant household to the urban-like setting of the camp. Some members of families, moreover, took this opportunity to flee to cities. These changes are associated with a breakdown of "community" and a more individualistic orientation that leads to increased interpersonal conflict. While the authors do note that new forms of solidarity (based "on the sentiment of sharing the same conditions of existence, on the consciousness of a communal misery and on a common revolt against misery" [1964a: 74]) were replacing the older forms based on genealogy and kinship, they focus more in this article on the breakdown of the older systems than on emergent ones. The "loosening of collective controls" (80) led to an economic individualism that ignores obligations to the family.

It is the traditional peasant (*paysan empaysanné*) who is left most emotionally displaced in this setting, according to the analysis, no longer feeling comfortable in his bodily *habitus* (1964a: 87). The language of the peasant body is out of place in the resettlement camp. Bourdieu and Sayad describe the em-peasanted peasants as appearing "lost and ridiculous" in contrast to the de-peasanted peasants favored by the "urban situation" (79). Like the figure of the bachelor at the ball, the de-peasanted Algerian in the resettlement camp is a tragic figure for Bourdieu, lost in the streets of the camp, lost in the new cafés there, lost in the new forms of greeting that leave behind the codes of honor used before. The same language of being "disarmed" that was used to describe French bachelors is used here by Bourdieu and Sayad for the elderly Algerian peasants (79) who are similarly not able to adapt to the new conditions. In a slightly different register from that used in the article on French peasants, Bourdieu and Sayad focus on the more urbanized spaces of the resettlement camp, bringing these more to the forefront in the analysis of the de-peasanted Kabyle peasant *habitus*.[7] Drawing upon Bachelard (whom he cites in a footnote), Bourdieu talks about changes in space in the resettlement camp that lead to melancholy and anxiety. As the de-peasanted peasant moves through the new streets and new spaces, he feels ill at ease. It is not just the changes of interpersonal relations that cause him to be more aware of his *habitus* and the ways in which it is out of sync with the system, but also the new spaces in the camp. For the peasant bachelors of Lesquire, it is the space of the ball, not a new physical space for them but one whose meaning has changed, in which they feel out of place.

Bourdieu presents a parallel set of victims of changing economic forces in his work in Algeria and in France. In Algeria the traditional male peasant dislocated in resettlement camps (Bourdieu and Sayad 1964b) was the subject of a developing theory of *habitus*. In rural France (Bourdieu 1962b) Bourdieu studied the figure of the perpetual rural bachelor who could not attract a wife due to the lures of urban life for women and internalized self-loathing of the peasants (in which dominant values were adopted by the peasants who, as Bourdieu later wrote, participated in their own domination) and changing economic relations in the village itself. Bourdieu has more to say about the inner life of the French peasant bachelor than the Algerian peasant, placing the accent on this idea of internalized symbolic domination (a term that he had not yet used but a concept he was obviously developing with this work), most likely due to his shared social background. In both cases, Bourdieu argued, there was a breakdown of patriarchal society and traditional family socioeconomic relations. An ethos based more on free choice and individualism was replacing one based on family obligations and traditional values. Bourdieu also wrote about this in terms of a loosening of group obligations related to changing orientations to time (1963) and to honor (1966). *Habitus* comes to symbolize in these settings the position of an anomaly, of a "structured structure" that is no longer also a "structuring structure."

At the same time that Bourdieu was writing about the displaced older peasants among the Kabyles, he also addressed the plight of the unemployed youth created by changing economic conditions and urbanization in Algeria in the collaborative work *Travail et travailleurs en Algérie* (Bourdieu et al. 1963). These themes concerning youth would also preoccupy Bourdieu in research on French education (i.e., Bourdieu and Passeron 1964 and 1970) that he conducted right after the ethnographic work in Algeria and rural France, when he began to turn his attention to the plight of working class students in the French educational system. This theme was also addressed in a later collaborative work on social suffering (Bourdieu and Accardo et al. 1999).

Conclusions

Bourdieu worked on both shores of the Mediterranean and as both insider and outsider ethnographer. He was a pioneer of "multi-sited" ethnography (see Reed-Danahay 2005: 157) and he was also a "native anthropologist," an autoethnologist. Algeria and Béarn served as parallel worlds in which he worked on similar themes while developing his theoretical perspectives, but they also served as his own personal worlds, and Bourdieu moved back and forth between them, with Paris forming the mediating point in-between. His roots in rural France informed both the Algerian and French work.

Bourdieu's concept of *habitus* likewise is informed by his own experiences in the world, as one who made a transition from rural to urban himself (parallel to the processes of urbanization he was describing in the Algerian and French cases mentioned in the articles under discussion here). Over and over again in his subsequent work, Bourdieu made the point that he rejected methodological individualism, and in his later criticisms of neoliberalism, the individualistic ethos of this economic system made him uncomfortable. He developed a theoretical concept to understand human action that mediated between subjective experience and objective conditions, one that privileged neither the agency of the individual nor the determinism of the society. His own peasant worldview (his primary *habitus*) depended on the link of the person to the collectivity, and the breakdown of this ethos is what he described in his early ethnographic writings. It is personified in the two figures of the Algerian peasant in the resettlement camp and the French peasant bachelor. Bourdieu's own feelings about this are strong. This is due, I argue here, in part to his own background. He is uncomfortable with individualism, contradicting the "secondary" *habitus* he acquired in schooling that promoted ideas of free choice (an idea that Bourdieu noted is an illusion anyway). Grémion (2005) makes a telling point that North Americans are uncomfortable with *habitus*, and I suggest this is a reverse image of Bourdieu's stance. While Bourdieu was uncomfortable with theories that privilege the individual, many North Americans are uncomfortable with theories that deny individual autonomy and free choice. Bourdieu, nevertheless, came to see that he had a "split" *habitus*. And he was not a good peasant, but instead one of those who left for urban life. His narratives of rurality and urbanization, and of tragic peasant figures, are not that different from those of several other male rural writers in France who adopt a similar mixture of nostalgia and guilt about having distanced themselves from their origins (see Reed-Danahay 2002 and 2006). Bourdieu wrote late in his life that he experienced "social estrangement" (2004a: 121) during his secondary school years, as he would go back and forth between the city where he boarded during the week and the village to which he would return on weekends. Although Bourdieu never puts this in quite such explicit terms, I suggest that in his early ethnography of his own natal village and the resettlement camps in Algeria where he first began to develop the concept of *habitus*, he was drawing upon his own personal experiences of urbanization in order to make sense of the situations he encountered.

To present the genesis of *habitus* or any other feature of Bourdieu's work solely in terms of his own autobiography would, however, betray his own theories that worked against seeing the individual life trajectory outside of its social system or structure. Bourdieu's work was informed by a combination of factors including the intellectual and social fields in which it was produced: Mediterranean studies, structuralism, and previous work on embodiment, to name just a few. Bourdieu synthesized various ideas and produced a unique vision of peasant society in his ethnography, and his own life trajectory can only be viewed as one influence—albeit, I would argue, fairly major—on his approach to the study of peasants and his theory of *habitus* that developed in this context. To return to the question I posed earlier in this essay about why Bourdieu began to write more reflexively about his work in the early 1990s and onward, I suggest that this was a result of subjective and objective conditions, a combination of his own tendency toward self-reflection, based on his "split *habitus*," and wider trends in ethnography at that time, despite his constant disavowels of autobiography, toward confession.[8]

Notes

This chapter had its origins as a presentation at the 2002 American Anthropological Association meetings, in a session organized by Jane Goodman and Paul

Silverstein. That presentation, entitled "Bourdieu's Peasant Studies: Ethnography 'at home and away' in Béarn and Kabylia," was eventually revised and published (Reed-Danahay 2004), and themes from it were also incorporated in my book, *Locating Bourdieu* (Reed-Danahay 2005). This chapter reflects my further thinking about Bourdieu's work since those two publications. I have been interested in the relationship between Bourdieu's French and Algerian ethnography for over a decade (see Reed-Danahay 1995). I would like to thank the reviewers for their helpful comments and suggestions.

1. Bourdieu's focus on the stability of the *habitus* among the Kabyles, detailed in *Outline of Theory of Practice* (his classic work on this concept), contrasts with the earlier work analyzed in this chapter that focused on the problems of the peasant *habitus* in an urbanizing world. See Silverstein, Goodman, and Hammoudi (this volume) and Reed-Danahay (1995) for analyses that unpack and critique the overemphasis on tradition in Bourdieu's work among the Kabyles.

2. One could make the argument that Bourdieu's close colleague and collaborator in the Algerian research, Abdelmalek Sayad, was also a de-peasanted peasant. As Goodman (this volume) points out, he was also a main informant for Bourdieu.

3. As this book goes to press, two key texts upon which I draw here appeared in English translation, *Sketch for a Self-Analysis* (Bourdieu 2008a), originally published in 2004 (Bourdieu 2004a), and *The Bachelors' Ball* (Bourdieu 2008b), originally published in 2002 (Bourdieu 2002). As for the earlier work, the English translation of *The Algerians* appeared in 1962, and other articles on the Algerian work appeared in English translation during the 1960s. The earliest French article dealing with Bourdieu's rural French ethnography also appeared in 1962 (Bourdieu 1962b), but it has not been translated into English (although an excerpt was published recently—see Bourdieu 2004b). It was not until 1976 that the first English-language publication of the Béarn research appeared, in an article on "marriage strategies" included in a compilation of *Annales* articles translated into English. Although *Outline of a Theory of Practice* (1977), a translation of a book first published in 1972, is devoted strictly to the Algerian material, the reworking of some of this material in the *Logic of Practice* was accompanied by a chapter on marriage strategies in Béarn—but this did not appear in English until 1990; moreover, it is from the same *Annales* article already translated in 1976, cited above. With the exception of another recent translation of Bourdieu's article on photography in Béarn (Bourdieu and Bourdieu 2004), little of the French work has been available to the wider Anglophone audience until quite recently. Perhaps due to the lags in translation, for a long time little attention was paid by scholars of Bourdieu to either Bourdieu's rural ethnographic work in France

or to the connections between the French and Algerian work. In addition to my own work (Reed-Danahay 1995, 2004, 2005), recent exceptions in the first case include Jenkins (2006); and in the second, Wacquant (2004).

4. See Grémion (2005) for a recent appraisal of Bourdieu's intellectual trajectory and the various stages of his work.

5. Unless otherwise specified, all translations from Bourdieu's texts published in French are my own.

6. Although originally published in 1935, Mauss's essay was later anthologized in 1950, with a later English edition in 1979 (see Mauss 1935 and 1979).

7. Bourdieu did not ignore issues of space and time in his analysis of rural French society, and his 1962 article on bachelors includes photos of the village, a diagram of a house in the village (*bourg*), and discussion of the changing meaning of the relationship between village and hamlet. It was in the context of his work among the Kabyles, however, that he first integrated his theory of *habitus* with that of space through the idea of "learning through the body" or the body as "memory pad" (Bourdieu 1977). Even though he does not use the term *habitus* in that context, in his "structuralist" analysis of the Kabyle house (Bourdieu 1970), Bourdieu is dealing explicitly with issues of embodiment and space.

8. For example, see *Anthropology and Autobiography* (Okely and Callaway 1992) published the same year as *An Invitation to Reflexive Sociology* (Bourdieu and Wacquant 1992). In the case of French scholarship, two examples are sociologist Florence Weber's (1989) use of a reflexive voice in an ethnography of the French working class, and Jeanne Favret-Saada's (1980) much earlier book bringing a self-reflexive approach to the study of witchcraft in rural western France.

Works Cited

Bourdieu, Pierre. 1958. *Sociologie de l'Algérie*. Paris: Presses Universitaires de France.

———. 1962a. *The Algerians*, trans. Alan C. M. Ross. Boston: Beacon Press.

———. 1962b. Célibat et condition paysanne. *Etudes Rurales* 5–6: 32–135.

———. 1963. The Attitude of the Algerian Peasant Toward Time. In *Mediterranean Countrymen*, ed. Julian Pitt-Rivers. pp. 55–72. Paris: Mouton and Co.

———. 1966. The Sentiment of Honour in Kabyle Society. In *Mediterranean Countrymen*, ed. J. G. Peristiany, trans. Philip Sharrard. pp.192–211. Paris: Mouton and Co.

———. 1970. La maison kabyle ou le monde renversé. In *Echanges et communications. Mélanges offerts à Claude Lévi-Strauss à l'occasion de son 60éme anniversaire*, ed. J. Puillon and P. Maranda. pp. 739–59. Paris: Mouton and Co.

———. 1972. Les Stratégies matrimoniales dans le système de reproduction. *Annales* 4–5: 1105–27.

———. 1977 (1972). *Outline of a Theory of Practice*, trans. Richard Nice. Cambridge: Cambridge University Press.

———. 1979. *La Distinction: Critique social du jugement*. Paris: Editions de Minuit.

———. 1984. *Homo academicus*. Paris: Editions de Minuit.

———. 1989. *La Noblesse d'état: Grandes écoles et esprit de corps*. Paris: Editions de Minuit.

———. 1990 (1980). *The Logic of Practice*, trans. Richard Nice. Stanford: Stanford University Press.

———. 2000 (1997). *Pascalian Meditations*, trans. Richard Nice. Stanford: Stanford University Press.

———. 2002. *Le Bal des célibataires: Crise de la société paysanne en Béarn*. Paris: Editions du Seuil.

———. 2003a. Participant Objectivation. *Journal of the Royal Anthropological Institute* 9: 281–94.

———. 2003b. *Images d'Algérie: Une affinité élective*, ed. Franz Schultheis. Arles: Actes Sud.

———. 2004a. *Esquisse pour une auto-analyse*. Paris: Editions Raisons d'Agir.

———. 2004b. The Peasant and His Body. Translated and adapted by Richard Nice and Loïc Wacquant. *Ethnography* 5 (4): 579–99.

———. 2008a (2004). *Sketch for a Self-Analysis*, trans. Richard Nice. Chicago: University of Chicago Press.

———. 2008b (2002). *The Bachelors' Ball*, trans. Richard Nice. Chicago: University of Chicago Press.

Bourdieu, Pierre and Alain Accardo, Gabrielle Balazs, Stéphane Beaud, et al. 1999 (1993). *The Weight of the World: Social Suffering in Contemporary Society*, trans. Priscilla Parkhurst Ferguson, Susan Emanual, Joe Johnson, and Shoggy T. Waryn. Stanford: Stanford University Press.

Bourdieu, Pierre and Jean-Claude Passeron. 1964. *Les Héritiers: Les Etudiants et la culture*. Paris: Editions de Minuit.

———. 1970. *La Reproduction: Eléments pour une théorie du système d'enseignement*. Paris: Editions de Minuit.

Bourdieu, Pierre and Marie-Claire Bourdieu. 1965. Le paysan et la photographie. *Revue Française de Sociologie* 6 (2): 164–74.

————. 2004. The Peasant and Photography. Translated and adapted by Loïc Wacquant and Richard Nice. *Ethnography* 5(4): 601–16.

Bourdieu, Pierre and Alain Darbel, Jean-Paul Rivet, and Claude Seibel. 1963. *Travail et travailleurs en Algérie*. Paris and The Hague: Mouton and Co.

Bourdieu, Pierre and Abdelmalek Sayad. 1964a. Paysans déracinés: Bouleversements morphologiques et changements culturels en Algérie. *Etudes Rurales* 12: 56–94.

————. 1964b. *Le Déracinement. La Crise de l'agriculture traditionnelle en Algérie*. Paris: Editions de Minuit.

Bourdieu, Pierre, and Loïc J. D. Wacquant. 1992. *An Invitation to Reflexive Sociology*. Chicago: University of Chicago Press.

Caro Baroja, Julio. 1963. The City and the Country: Reflections on Some Ancient Commonplaces. In *Mediterranean Countrymen*, ed. Julian Pitt-Rivers. pp. 27–40. Paris: Mouton and Co.

Dunning, Eric and Stephen Mennell. 1996. Preface. In *The Germans*, by Norbert Elias. Oxford: Blackwell Publishers.

Durkheim, Emile. 1951 (1897). *Suicide: A Study in Sociology*, trans. J. A. Spaulding. New York: Free Press.

Elias, Norbert. 1982. *The Civilizing Process*, trans. Edmund Jephcott. New York: Pantheon Books.

————. 1987. *The Society of Individuals*, trans. Edmund Jephcott. Oxford: Basil Blackwell.

Favret-Saada, Jeanne. 1980 (1977). *Deadly Words: Witchcraft in the Bocage*, trans. Catherine Cullen. Cambridge: Cambridge University Press.

Grémion, Pierre. 2005. De Pierre Bourdieu à Bourdieu. *Etudes* 1/4021: 39–53.

Herzfeld, Michael. 1987. *Anthropology Through the Looking-Glass: Critical Ethnography in the Margins of Europe*. Cambridge: Cambridge University Press.

Jenkins, Tim. 2006. Bourdieu's Béarnais Ethnography. *Theory, Culture and Society* 23 (6): 45–72.

Lévi-Strauss, Claude. 1992 (1955). *Tristes Tropiques*, trans. John and Doreen Weightman. New York: Penguin.

Mauss, Marcel. 1935. Les techniques du corps. *Journal de Psychologie Normale et Pathologique* 3–4: 271–93.

1979[1950] Body Techniques. In *Sociology and Psychology: Essays*, trans. Ben Brewster. pp. 97–123. London: Routledge and Kegan Paul.

Okely, Judith and Helen Callaway, eds. 1992. *Anthropology and Autobiography*. London: Routledge.

Peristiany, J. G., ed. 1966. *Honour and Shame: The Values of Mediterranean Society*. Chicago: University of Chicago Press.

Pitt-Rivers, Julian, ed. 1963. *Mediterranean Countrymen*. Paris: Mouton and Co.

Redfield, Robert. 1956. *Peasant Society and Culture: An Anthropological Approach to Civilization*. Chicago: University of Chicago Press.

Reed-Danahay, Deborah. 1995. The Kabyle and the French: Occidentalism in Bourdieu's Theory of Practice. In *Occidentalism: Images of the West*, ed. James Carrier. pp. 61–84. Oxford: Oxford University Press.

———. 1997. Introduction. In *Auto/Ethnography: Rewriting the Self and the Social*. New York: Berg.

———. 2002. Sites of Memory: Women's Autoethnographies from Rural France. *Biography* 25 (1): 95–109.

———. 2004. Tristes Paysans: Bourdieu's Early Ethnography in Béarn and Kabylia. *Anthropological Quarterly* 77 (1): 87–106.

———. 2005. *Locating Bourdieu*. Bloomington: Indiana University Press.

———. 2006. Becoming Educated, Becoming an Individual? Tropes of Distinction and "Modesty" in French Narratives of Rurality. In *Claiming Individuality: The Cultural Politics of Distinction*, ed. Vered Amit and Noel Dyck. pp. 131–52. London: Pluto Press.

Tönnies, Ferdinand. 1957. *Gemeinschaft und Gesellschaft*. East Lansing: Michigan State University Press.

Wacquant, Loïc. 1993. Bourdieu in America: Notes on the Transatlantic Importation of Social Theory. In *Bourdieu: Critical Perspectives*, ed. Craig Calhoun, Edward LiPuma, and Moishe Postone. pp. 235–62. Chicago: University of Chicago Press.

———. 2004. Following Pierre Bourdieu into the Field. *Ethnography* 5 (4): 387–414.

Weber, Florence. 1989. *Le Travail à-côté: Etude d'ethnographie ouvrière*. Paris: INRA and Editions d'EHESS.

Williams, Raymond. 1973. *The Country and the City*. New York: Oxford University Press.

FOUR

Of Rooting and Uprooting

Kabyle *Habitus*, Domesticity,
and Structural Nostalgia

PAUL A. SILVERSTEIN

Introduction

Pierre Bourdieu's theories of practice revolutionized structuralist methodologies and paved the way for discriminating ethnographic studies of the enactment, rather than merely the form, of culture. In his famous essays on matrimonial strategies and domesticity, Bourdieu (1963a, 1972, 1977, 1979a) underlined how temporality and spatiality, rather than mere structural categories, are manipulated elements of everyday life that organize and are organized by social practice. Bourdieu united Kabyle practices of time and space through the parallel tropes of *enracinement* and *déracinement*, of rooting and uprooting, most notably in his comparative study of village life in late-colonial Algeria, *Le Déracinement*, cowritten with his Kabyle student and collaborator Abdelmalek Sayad. Appropriating these tropes from conservative nationalist discourse into a critical social agenda, Bourdieu and Sayad outlined a culturally-unified, antebellum Kabylia.

The deployment of tropes of rooting and uprooting is moreover evident in Bourdieu's classic study of the "The Kabyle House, or the World Reversed" (1979a [1970]), translated, reprinted, and rewritten on multiple occasions. In this essay a single, concrete social institution stands in as a synecdoche for a rooted cultural unity whose existence the ethnologist cannot (or can no longer) observe directly. Not only had the land expropriations and resulting rural–urban migration entailed by over a century of French colonization brought about sweeping changes to the Kabyle social and physical landscape, but the particular wartime conditions of burned villages, forbidden zones (*zones interdites*), and forced displacement in which Bourdieu conducted his primary field research further guaranteed the receding of any notion of a bounded, "pure" Kabyle culture to an object of "structural nostalgia" (see Herzfeld 1997: 109)—a modern form of social memory to a great extent shared by both Bourdieu and his informants.[1] Moreover, such nostalgia for "a time before time" is likewise maintained to this day by the contemporary Berber cultural movement. Like Bourdieu, Berber activists, operating across North Africa and the diaspora, uphold the Kabyle house (or *axxam aqdim*, or *akham* in Bourdieu's transliteration)[2] as a synecdoche for a precolonial, "rooted" Kabylia whose longed-for cultural integrity is presented as uprooted by the conditions of postcolonial modernity, migration, and "Arabo-Islamic" nationalism.

That nationalist narratives and nostalgic reconstructions of social life should borrow from the language of botany and agriculture is not in and of itself surprising. Tropes of rooting and uprooting have a long genealogy within discourses of culture and nation. Liisa Malkki has argued that the repetitive deployment of arboreal metaphors—from early-modern European national representation (e.g., the English oak tree), to colonial fears of miscegenation and *métissage*,[3] to contemporary theories of nationalism and ecological activism—has served to "naturaliz[e] the links between people and place" (1992: 27; cf. Darian-Smith 1999: 17–19). Anthropological theories of "culture" are likewise embedded in notions of cultivation and rootedness. James

Fernandez, for one, has traced the vagaries of arboreal metaphors through the history of anthropology, from Sir James Frazer through Lévi-Strauss and beyond. Mary Bouquet has further argued that genealogical methods of anthropological representation (e.g., the kinship diagram) draw out older practices of "mapping out ancestry in the form of the tree" and thus present blood relations as part of the natural order of things (1996: 47; cf. Linke 1999: 15).

If root metaphors link people to places in a "national metaphysic," conditions of exile, migration, and "displacement," as Malkki (1992: 32) argues, tend to be pathologized as "uprootedness," as situations of moral breakdown. Uprooting as a gloss for migration and (dis)integration has been normative in French academic literature since at least Georges Mauco's 1932 foundational study of "foreigners" (*étrangers*) in France.[4] In the larger field of migration studies, Oscar Handlin's work on European immigration to the United States, entitled *The Uprooted* (1951), served as the primary metaphoric gloss until at least the mid-1980s when it was superceded by a less violent arboreal image: *The Transplanted* (Bodnar 1985).[5] In spite of this shift, as Malkki argues, metaphors of uprooting continue to predominate in refugee studies, even in those adopting critical social agendas (such as André Jacques's manifesto, *Les Déracinés* [1985, "The Uprooted"]). Bourdieu and Sayad's work on Kabyle displacement and societal disintegration in this way represents but one moment in a longer history of dominance of arboreal metaphors in social theory.

However, perhaps the most important genealogical strain of "rootedness" for Bourdieu's work is located in French rightist, anti-republican discourse that, as Emily Apter (1999: 25–38) has shown, traces itself back to Maurice Barrès's 1897 novel, *Les Déracinés*. In this work, Barrès excoriates the national education system for "uprooting" children from the soil and social group, thus bringing about the moral degeneration of the countryside. This notion of uprooting largely ordered the French *fin-de-siècle* debate over decentralization and administrative reform and quickly became a central pillar of the regional nationalism of Charles Maurras's monarchist, anti-Semitic, and colonialist Action Française movement—a movement that later voiced articulations of an *Algérie française*, a French Algeria (Apter 1999: 35; Ford 1991: 21–23).[6] Supporters of the Action Française included Catholic philosopher Jean Maritain who, like Barrès, opposed radical Republican education as a poor and dangerous substitute for the "rooted," embodied forms of apprenticeship that medieval artists and gothic architects underwent and which he characterized with the Thomist concept of *habitus* (Maritain 1930 [1920]: 34, 61)—a scholastic conceptualization Bourdieu would later borrow for very different political ends via his reading, translation, and commentary on Erwin Panofsky's *Gothic Architecture and Scholasticism* (Bourdieu 1967: 148–59; see Lane 2005: 51–52).[7] In 1942 Simone Weil appropriated this conservative nationalist trope for her humanist critique of the Nazi occupation of France, *L'Enracinement* (Weil 1949), a key text in the postwar development of a global human rights legal discourse and regime.[8] Bourdieu and Sayad's use of the imagery of *enracinement* and *déracinement* follows from Weil's humanism, thus representing a fascinating act of political reappropriation for anticolonialist critique.[9]

In order to explore the uses and consequences of root metaphors in Bourdieu's Kabyle ethnography, this essay begins with a discussion of modes of social reproduction and transformation within Bourdieu's concept of *habitus*. I pay particular attention to Bourdieu's portrayal of Kabyle social doxa as rooted in agricultural practice, and how Bourdieu narrates such practices as disrupted by colonialism, capitalism, and military policy. I then turn to the way in which such processes of rooting and uprooting play out in one cultural form: the "Kabyle house." I discuss Bourdieu's upholding of this form as a synecdoche for a lost or dying Kabyle integrity in terms of his larger focus on social memory as embodied generative schema and in terms of the parallel "structural nostalgia" of contemporary Berber ethnolinguistic nationalists. As such, the essay explores how the language of rooting and uprooting mediates cultural objectifications and discourses of authenticity that are embodied in the *habitus* of group members and later reflexively reified by scholars and activists.

Habitus and Social Reproduction

While Bourdieu devoted much of his later work to the task of describing the complex class dynamics of late-modernity, his early formation as an ethnologist and sociologist of culture occurred in Algeria, first as a young military recruit, and later as a surveyor of Kabyle economic and social life while working for a government agency in the midst of the war. This research experience produced an ethnographic archive from which Bourdieu could draw in his elaboration of increasingly nuanced sociological frameworks: from his early structuralist analyses, through his development of a practice-oriented approach in the *Outline of a Theory of Practice* (1977 [1972]), to his final critiques of theoretical and scholarly reason in *The Logic of Practice* (1990 [1980]) and *Pascalian Meditations* (2000a [1997]). Based on field research (surveys, statistical collections, and interviews) conducted from 1958 to 1961, the early studies and their later revisions can be read as a testament to a society in the process of revolutionary upheaval as the war of decolonization brought violent change to the countryside and laid the groundwork for the construction of a new nation that ideologically sought to transcend regional and ethnic divides. Given this context of radical transformation—what Bourdieu would later refer to as a "quasi-laboratory situation" and a "veritable social experiment" (2000b: 18)—Bourdieu's elaboration of a singular Kabyle symbolic system and *habitus* stands in stark relief. As such, the place of historical change and structural transformation, of temporality *tout court*, in Bourdieu's theoretical schema is critical.

From one perspective structural change may not be possible within the strictures of *habitus* as described by Bourdieu, particularly in the *Outline*.[10] Scholars have chastised Bourdieu for the creation of idealized synchronic analyses that approach culture primarily through the lens of social reproduction (see Comaroff 1985: 5; de Certeau 1984; Eickelman 1977: 40; Free 1996; Herzfeld 1987: 84; Lacoste-Dujardin 1976; Reed-Danahay 1995). Bourdieu's early writings, like all structuralist perspectives, have been especially prone to this line of critique. Although Bourdieu repeatedly underlined the dialectic of incorporation and objectification, of structure and practice, inherent to all social life, he seemed primarily concerned with the way *habitus*, as a system of "structured structures predisposed to function as structuring structures," tended to "reproduce the objective structure of which [it is] the product" (1977: 72). *Habitus*, in this schema, represented "a past which survives in the present and tends to perpetuate itself into the future by making itself present in practices structured according to its principles" (1977: 83).

Kabyle social and economic practices appear to be a case in point of the tendency of *habitus* to foster social stability and reproduction. In contrasting Kabyle economic *habitus* to a capitalist mode of labor, Bourdieu presented Kabyle peasants (*fellahin*) as participating (or having participated) in a "good faith" or gift economy in which individual and collective labor (or *twiza*) remains outside the sphere of rational calculation. Displaying no distinction between work and leisure, Bourdieu characterized the *bou niya*—the man of good faith—as maintaining "an attitude of submission and of nonchalant indifference to the passage of time which no one dreams of wasting, using up, or saving. . . . Haste is seen as a lack of decorum combined with diabolical ambition" (1963a: 57). However, this task-orientation should not imply a lack of work ethic as such. According to Bourdieu and Sayad, "A *fellah* is busy the whole year, every day of every month, and the whole day at that" (1964: 78).

The difference lies, for Bourdieu, in the subsuming of the Kabyle apprehension of time under a more general rubric of "tempo." Work is determined by diurnal cycles of night and day that map in homologous fashion onto the agrarian calendar of planting and harvesting, that itself maps homologously onto the individual lifecycle, that itself maps onto a three-generation cycle of reproduction. These temporal "series" share the same symbolic economy, with the sun's setting and rising, for instance, mapping onto the death and subsequent rebirth of crops and men (1977: 154). In their most synoptic form, the cycles of reproduction link generations of Kabyle men into a single, closed temporal structure, with the grandfather being literally resurrected in the birth of his grandson. Historical change, for the idealized Kabyle peasant, presents itself as thus always already subsumed within the circular logic of time.[11]

Moreover, for Bourdieu, it is this symbolic mapping of social relations onto a stable, potentially infinite temporal structure that creates the condition of possibility for the "misrecognition" of everyday labor and exchange as outside the realm of group interest or exploitation. That is to say, the stability of the Kabyle *doxa* of a good-faith economy depends directly on the *bou niya*'s misrecognition of his own practices (and his own domination) as mere reenactments of social norms as natural cycles. The rooting of social tempos in natural cycles effectively naturalizes cultural forms. Reproduction, in other words, engenders further reproduction.

Déracinement

Can such a closed system nonetheless undergo transformation? Bourdieu has essentially two models of diachrony embedded in his theory of practice. In the first model, social transformation transpires gradually, via the dialectical adjustment of *habitus* to continual shifts in the objective, material conditions of the surrounding social and natural environment. The growth and demise of lineages, the success and failure of crops, the changing political relations with external powers, all alter the landscape upon which dispositions and strategies are generated. The resulting transformed practice contributes to the expansion or contraction of the generative mechanism that is *habitus*. As Bourdieu later noted, "*Habitus* change[s] constantly in response to new experiences. Dispositions are subject to a kind of permanent revision, but one which is never radical, because it works on the basis of the premises established in the previous state. They are characterized by a degree of constancy and variation" (2000a: 161). In other words, Kabyle social life, while inclined towards potentially infinite reproduction, is thus continuously responding to the world in which it is rooted, and subtly changing to meet its demands. While the material conditions of these shifts are essentially exogenous to the mechanisms of *habitus* that tend to root Kabyles in processes of social reproduction, *habitus*, in Bourdieu's revision, "helps to determine what transforms it" (2000a: 149). *Habitus*, as "a product of the durable confrontation with a social world presenting indisputable regularities" (2000a: 214), defines the scope of irregularity and thus effectively anticipates and provides the basis for change.

171

If the first mode of transformation is gradual, largely impercep-
tible, and misrecognized by Kabyle social actors, the second mode
is sudden, dramatic, and ultimately productive of a veritable crisis
in the established order. Processes of culture contact or political
economic upheaval in particular break the "fit between the subjective structures and the objective structures" and thus serve as the
condition of possibility for individuals to break the stranglehold of
misrecognition and question the taken-for-granted everyday order
(1977: 168–70). Once the veil of misrecognition is lifted, the *doxa* can
undergo fundamental transformations. While the lack of fit between
"expectations and experience," as Bourdieu later argued (2000a:
149), is part of the workings of *habitus*, in the Kabyle case the origin
of such change-as-crisis lies quite squarely in the sphere of European
colonialism. Bourdieu and Sayad were particularly concerned with
two interrelated crisis moments: first, colonial land expropriations
that forced thousands of Kabyle peasants to migrate to urban centers
or France; and second, French wartime resettlement policies that
relocated entire Kabyle villages to government camps as part of its
"scorched earth" (*terre brulée*) policy. If the first moment put into
place the necessary structural conditions for the creation of a Kabyle diaspora and, consequentially, the postcolonial Berber cultural
movement that will be discussed below, the second underwrote the
establishment of an Algerian national imaginary itself premised on
the breakdown of ethnoregional differences and the recovery of an
essential Algerian "culture."

It is through the lens of "uprooting" (*déracinement*) that Bourdieu
and Sayad described these crises in "traditional" Kabyle economic
and social life. Through this trope they indicated an interweaving of
Kabyle *habitus* with the physical landscape. "The peasant can only
but live rooted in the land on which he was born and to which his

habits and memories attach themselves. Uprooted, there is a good chance he will die as a peasant, in that the passion which makes him a peasant dies within him" (Bourdieu and Sayad 1964: 115). The destruction of the agrarian cycles and social practices of *twiza* further shattered the misrecognition that "veiled the relationship between labor and labor's product" and underwrote the good faith economy. The resulting social situation was one of "complete disaggregation" and "high instability" (Bourdieu 1963b: 264) in which the Kabyle peasant "painfully experiences the cold and brutal impersonality of work relations (*rapports du travail*)" (Bourdieu 1963b: 280). These processes not only transformed peasants into paupers and eventually into migrant workers who were forced to commodify their labor on colonists' farms or in factories and mines in France, but also led to the "disenchantment of a natural world" (Bourdieu 1977: 176; cf. Bourdieu 1979b) and the introduction of new mental structures based in scarcity, monetary value, and rational calculation (*l'esprit de calcul*). "In the resettlement, the almost total disappearance of agricultural resources and the weakening of traditions of solidarity led one to perceive one's daily meal as the product of one's daily labor" (Bourdieu and Sayad 1964: 82). A general sense that "God will provide," quickly became: "No work, no bread" (Bourdieu and Sayad 1964: 83). Or, as a resettled villager in the Kerkera regroupment center remarked, "I had a cow, which I sold for 400 francs: I replaced it with a moped" (Bourdieu and Sayad 1964: 146).[12]

This is, of course, an old story—a basic modernization narrative with sociological antecedents stretching back at least to Tönnies (1887) and which Bourdieu himself approached through his intervention into the debate between Sombart (1915) and Weber (1924) (cf. Bourdieu 2000b: 25)—though one which Bourdieu and Sayad masterfully tell with a Marxist edge, a structuralist flair, and an eye for historical and ethnographic detail. Although in later work on Algerian emigration to France, Sayad (1977, 1999) recounted a more subtle, dialectical version of this narrative—in which gradual change wrought on Kabyle village *habitus* by successive waves of returned emigrants, whose experiences abroad generate new strategies for future generations' emigration, eventually transforms the *bou niya* into *homo economicus* (one exhibiting *tahrymit*, a "calculating intelligence" (Bourdieu 1977: 173))—the basic tale remains the same: European capitalist modernity uproots Kabyle "traditional" social structure. Focusing on rupture and discontinuity as the generative modality of history is of course central to any critical social theory. Whether this takes the form of a Marxian dialectic, a Kuhnian paradigm shift, or a Foucauldian epistemic break, a philosophy of history-as-crisis has functioned to denaturalize the present and shift attention to the role of political, juridical, and economic formations in producing social reality.[13] Bourdieu and Sayad, in this respect, play a crucial role in recovering the language of rootedness and uprootedness from conservative defenses of nation and culture, and in deploying the evocative power of such language to produce a powerful critique of structures of French capital and colonialism—a critique which also earned Bourdieu scholarly capital and abetted his precipitous rise to the heights of the French academy. However, this deployment also appropriates the objectifying function of arboreal tropes, the reification of the "time before time" as somehow more rooted, integral, and natural than the present uprooted condition.

Akham

One site to examine Bourdieu and Sayad's portrayal of processes of *enracinement* and *déracinement*—the reproduction and rupture of the generative schemas of *habitus*—is the domestic dwelling. Within both

French colonial sociology and contemporary anthropological theory, the Kabyle house (Bourdieu's *"akham"*), has occupied a privileged position as a touchstone of Algerian cultural distance (i.e., *exteriority*) as mediated by particular relations of domestic distinction (i.e., *interiority*).[14] Bourdieu's structural analysis of physical and social relations within the *akham*, variously reprinted and revised by Bourdieu himself, finds itself repeatedly appropriated by authors for the general elaboration of a non-Western model for the organization of social space (see Mitchell 1988: 48–52). In Bourdieu's analysis, the *akham* is a fully structured space whose internal symbolic order reflects and structures—and thus infinitely reproduces—the exterior repertoire underwriting *habitus*. It maps in inverted fashion the fundamental structural oppositions within Kabyle society as a whole: male:female, high:low, dry:wet, day:night, light:dark, human:animal, honor:shame (*nnif:horma*), fertilizing:fertilized (1979a: 140). As such, the Kabyle house, as a site of inverted privacy, simultaneously opposes the public and natural world and embodies its basic values and hierarchies.[15] The symbolic structure of its objects and spaces hence reflects a particular *habitus* and reproduces its constitutive elements for its inhabitants. While for a Kabyle inhabitant the line between public and private— between individual and societal space—is clearly demarcated by a series of thresholds separating the village (*taddart*) from the countryside, the patrilineal agglomeration (*adhrum*) from the *taddart*, and the *akham* from the *adhrum*, Bourdieu's analysis understands these divisions and inversions as participating in a unitary symbolic order and thus exhibiting an overarching continuity. In this sense the practices constituting the *akham* are seen to maintain a relation of synecdoche with Kabyle society as a whole, and be directly rooted in the social and natural landscape on which it is built. As Mohand Khellil has echoed, "The house serves as the centerpiece of all social organization" (1984: 36).

As the natural center of the spatial configurations and differentiations extant within Kabylia, the symbolic order embodied in the Kabyle house functions, within Bourdieu's framework, as a prime generative mechanism for social hierarchy. Internally, binary oppositions of generation and gender (e.g., male:female, parent:child) are seen to be spatially organized in interior living, working, and sleeping arrangements. In his early structuralist analyses (Bourdieu 1979a [1970]), Bourdieu cited proverbs that associate men with the *akham*'s master beam, and women with the central pillar and/or foundation, and sees in the physical intersection of these features a metaphor for sexual reproduction. These domestic spatial divisions moreover structure life-cycle rituals. Marriage enjoins the literal and symbolic making of a house (*adyeg akham*). After the initial wedding celebration, for instance, the bride (*tislit*) participates in a three-day ritual period of liminal separation and feminine visitation that takes place on the mezzanine (*takhana*) floor midway between the animal (*adaynin*) and human (*agouns*) sections of the house. Likewise, birth rites are similarly structured domestically, with the infant's umbilical cord buried in the confines of the *akham*, along the walls associated with each gender.

Bourdieu's initial analysis of the *akham* of course raises a number of questions. In the first place, it glossed over a certain degree of indeterminacy, fluidity, and polysemy within these spatial-sexual designations, over the exact gendering of various features of the house, that Bourdieu acknowledged in his later writings (cf. 1990: 214). While the gendered symbolic opposition of male and female organizes the placement of the house in the world and the features within it, "the products of a second-degree partition, such as the one that divides the (female) house into a female part and a male part, carry within them duality and ambiguity" (1990: 264). Moreover, in discussing its reflection of larger Kabyle social relations, Bourdieu's early analyses may have understated the ways the *akham* functions as a site of counter-hegemony, where younger married men can garner a degree of authority and independence relative to their fathers and elder brothers, where they can constitute themselves as an *argaz n wergazen* ("a man among men") in a parallel space to the village assembly (*tajmaat*).[16] The social imperative to construct one's own house has transcended the advent of massive emigration, as relatively permanent Kabyle residents in Algiers and France continue to build houses (though almost always of modern construction) in their native villages, avowedly for their retirement (cf. Sayad 1999, 2000).

Bourdieu's account of the *akham* as a space of social reproduction must be understood in terms of the work of social memory as concretized in the material objects with which one lives, which can later become the objects of what Herzfeld has called "structural nostalgia" in cases where generative modes of reproduction have been understood to be ruptured. Bourdieu's early presentation of the *akham* as a space of structural stability that mirrors Kabyle culture writ large derived in large part from interviews with Kabyles living in a very different social and architectural setting than the one described in the essay—in the temporary homes of the resettlement camps built by the French military. In other words, his account was largely a post-facto reconstruction of a social institution that, given the wartime violence of his field research, he could only observe in passing, about which many of his informants could only speak of in a language of loss, and for whom the minor architectural features became all the more important as a mnemonic of a series of social relations in rapid transformation. In this respect the nostalgia for the integrity of the Kabyle house and village life was not simply a facet of Bourdieu's political critique of colonialism, of his avowed museological project of cultural rehabilitation, or of his ethnographic bias, but also sprung directly from his informants' own self-essentializing presentation of a "static image of an unspoiled and irrecoverable past" (Herzfeld 1997: 109), of a *doxa* recalled through a threatened architecture.

Resettlement policies, arising from military concerns over the use by National Liberation Front (FLN) guerrillas of mountainous Kabyle village spaces, had as their aim the re-placement of displaced populations and their integration into new structures of European sociality. The government camps built by the army were modular in form, arranged along a rectilinear grid, with no embedded spatial distinctions of moiety (*ssef*) or patriliny (*adhrum*), and no communal space for the *tajmaat*. Walled or surrounded by barbed wire, the resettlement villages were separated from fields and fountains, thus altering the gendered use of these spaces and reinforcing the spatial (if not ideological) division between work and home. Finally, the houses themselves did not follow the same internal, material, and symbolic divides of the *akham* as described by Bourdieu, with no place for livestock or grain storage, no mezzanine *takhana*, and no clear cardinal direction inversion. Stables and storerooms were placed with the guardrooms in the external village walls, enframing the homes instead of uniting intra- and extra-domestic tasks (see Mitchell 1988: 45–48). As described by Bourdieu and Sayad, such transformations in domestic space had an indelible destructive effect on Kabyle *habitus*. "It was as if the colonizers had instinctively discovered the anthropological law which states that the structure of habitat is the symbolic projection of the most fundamental structures of a culture; to reorganize it is to provoke a general transformation of the whole cultural system itself" (Bourdieu and Sayad 1964: 26).

Kabyle scholars, following Bourdieu and Sayad's lead, have described postcolonial Algerian agricultural and urban policies through the same lens of uprooting. In the period immediately after independence, the governments of the victorious FLN actively sought to forge a unified national entity that transcended and overcame local cultural distinctions and divergences. The Algiers Charter, adopted in April 1964 as Algeria's *de facto* constitution, declared Algeria to be an "Arabo-Muslim country" and decried regional identities as "feudal survivals" and "obstacles to national integration." From 1963 to 1965, the Algerian national army fought a ten-month war in Kabylia to disarm Hocine Aït-Ahmed's largely Berberophone Socialist Forces Front (FFS) party and to suture the mountainous region to the nascent nation-state. Berber cultural activists have since narrated this struggle as a key moment in the recolonization of Kabylia by the Algerian state and the implementation of a dominant *Algérie arabe* ("Arab Algeria") ideology over earlier articulations of a pluralist (if not Berberist) *Algérie algérienne* ("Algerian Algeria").

Following its eventual victory, and as part of its agrarian reform program, the FLN established a four-year plan to create 333 collectivized Socialist Agricultural Villages (SVAs) with the goal of disenclaving Kabyle villages and integrating their inhabitants to civic national norms (Benmatti 1982: 157). El-Hadi Iguedelane (1996) has studied one such SVA, simply known as "La Cité," built to relocate inhabitants of the village of Tizouyar in the Bejaïa province (*wilaya*). Like the resettlement camp, the modular houses of La Cité were constructed with imported materials along parallel contours, with no respect for the internal organizing principles of the *akham* or *adhrum* as described by Bourdieu. Following Bourdieu and Sayad, Iguedelane views this spatial transformation as a process of destructuration, as an "overturning (*bouleversement*) of social and familial organization" (1996: 72): "the traditional space [*espace*] or *axxam* is the reflection of an ancient culture, a unique situation where all life functions occur in harmony . . . with the appearance of the 'modern' house, [the Kabyles] witness of the disintegration of their culture" (1996: 100). His study thus shares Bourdieu and Sayad's political ethic of projecting a bounded, timeless Kabyle "culture" in order to highlight the violence of contemporary transformations.

When Iguedelane's ethnography is read against the grain, what proves fascinating about La Cité is the continuity, not the rupture, of Tizouyar modes of social organization even in the new space. In spite of the opportunities for upward mobility engendered by the new possibilities—if not necessities—of labor migration, established patrilines maintained a relative stability of social position, as more wealthy families were better positioned to take advantage of the economic opportunities. Likewise, while no *tajmaat*—the male political space par excellence—was built in La Cité, the new institutions established, particularly the *café arabe* or the residence of the village head (or *ccix*), came to serve as sites for informal village assemblies.[17]

Moreover, while the parallel arrangement of the new houses inscribed a logic of breaking down the insular nature of the patrilineal *adhrum*, lineage still continued to determine the order of residence. In the case of La Cité, two sets of parallel houses were constructed on either side of the national highway that bifurcated the village. The relocated families grouped themselves according to moiety (*ssef*) in inversed spatial order from their original location in Tizouyar, with the road between the two halves replicating the line of division formerly represented by the shared spaces of the mosque, the *tajmaat*, and the cemetery (Iguedelane 1996). In addition, while the houses of La Cité were not built according to the model of the *akham*, their inhabitants imported features from their previous residences. Although there was no distinction between *agouns* and *adaynin*, with the rooms being broken down instead into living room, bedroom, and kitchen, the residents filled the new spaces with storage jars (*ik-oufen*), bridal chests, and sheepskins found normally in an *akham*. Even "European" architectural features, like the kitchen window or the electric range, were denoted with terms borrowed from the idealized *akham*: the *taq takhana* (exhaust vent in the ceiling of the *adaynin*) and the *kanoun* respectively. Finally, the residents of La Cité continued to participate in the everyday social life of Tizouyar, from attending village assemblies, to participating in *twiza* collective labor, to generally being governed by the customary oral laws (*qanoun*) (Iguedelane 1996: 94, 99).

In other words, the building of La Cité—like that of the resettlement camps as described by Bourdieu and Sayad—did not inherently imply the replacement of Kabyle *habitus* by European modes of sociospatial organization, but instead indicated a transformation characterized as much by continuity as by rupture. This perhaps points to the enduring social memory materialized in architectural features which continue to function, in spite of their physical changes, as generative schemes for social *habitus*. Certainly, the wartime context of their writing led Bourdieu and Sayad to critically interpret the changes in the structure of the *akham* as a synecdoche for the uprooting and destruction of an integral Kabyle culture, just as the contemporary state politics of Arabization led Iguedelane to a similar conclusion. Nonetheless, it remains important to emphasize that such transformations operate as yet another moment of historical change for a social form and structure that is surely always already hybridized and subject to a multiplicity of external influences and internal differentiations. It is this internal variation, perpetual accommodation, and larger social historicity irreducible to social class or moments of (colonial) contact that goes underemphasized in Bourdieu's wartime ethnography or, to a certain extent, in his later theoretical rewritings.

Post-Colony

The synecdochal character of the *akham,* by which the domestic dwelling and its transformations come to represent the fate of Kabyle society as a whole, emerges additionally in reflexive, nostalgic narratives of cultural loss, disintegration, and uprooting circulating within the postcolonial Kabyle diaspora. In the mid-1960s, a self-conscious Berber cultural activism arose within the Kabyle immigrant community in France.[18] In these early years, this activism primarily took the form of intellectual endeavors to standardize written Berber (Tamazight) and to record and publish Berber folktales and oral poetry (Direche-Slimani 1992: 138–146). Beginning in the 1970s, politically engaged Kabyle folksingers have put such folklore to music and have written songs set in idealized, antebellum Kabyle villages with imagery drawn from household life. In pursuing these projects of restoration and preservation, the movement has thus echoed Bourdieu in reconstructing a Kabyle culture whose integrality is perceived as disrupted and uprooted by processes of state nationalization, Arabization, and migration. Moreover, like Bourdieu, the movement has privileged the domestic space as the *sine qua non* site for intergenerational cultural transmission.

However, Bourdieu is not merely the intellectual progenitor to this cultural activism. He and his Kabyle students and colleagues have been implicated in the movement throughout its history, as supporters of the foundational 1967 Berber Academy for Cultural Exchange and Research (later Agraw Imazighen) and the 1972 Berber Study Group based at the University of Paris–Vincennes. Moreover, Bourdieu consistently used his academic position in the Collège de France to underwrite Berber intellectual efforts, providing the opportunity for the Kabyle writer/scholar Mouloud Mammeri to establish the Center for Amazigh Study and Research and its journal *Awal* in 1985, and founding the International Committee for the Support of Algerian Intellectuals (CISIA) in 1993 after the assassination of Kabyle playwright/journalist Tahar Djaout. An engaged intellectual throughout, he wrote a stringent critique of the Algerian state repression of Berber culture in the pages of the socialist daily *Libération* during the April 1980 "Berber Spring" demonstrations in Kabylia (Bourdieu and Eribon 1980). Upon Bourdieu's death in January 2002 the president of the World Amazigh Congress, Mabrouk Ferkal, issued a communiqué rendering homage to the scholar as "one of the Kabyles' dearest friends," underlining the importance of Bourdieu's ethnographic work and intellectual support to the cultural movement as a whole.[19]

In exploring how Bourdieu's emphasis on rooted Kabyle cultural forms like the *akham* is replicated and transformed in the structural nostalgia of diasporic Berber culturalism, I draw on my fieldwork with Kabyle residents and activists on the peripheries of Paris, particularly in the neighborhoods of Belleville and Ménilmontant, and the suburbs of Argenteuil, Aubervilliers, Aulnay-sous-Bois, Mantes-la-Jolie, and Nanterre. While my research focused primarily on Kabyles living in state housing projects (*cités*) and active in neighborhood organizations, Kabyles in France are actually represented across the entire social spectrum, with many occupying a staunch middle-class existence. Moreover, in no case are homogenous Kabyle "communities" reconstructed in France; the neighborhoods in question are extremely diverse in terms of ethnicity, nationality, and class.[20] Given this diversity, the association, as I will indicate below, has taken on increased importance as a locus and focus of social organization, as a preeminent space for the production of nostalgic narratives of cultural rooting and uprooting.

That said, the particular residence contexts in which Kabyle emigrants and their families live function as salient sites for the negotiation of cultural difference through the play of domestic synecdoche. In the case of the *cités*, residents map domestic kinship terms onto the multifamilial and multiethnic setting in which they live. In a manner reminiscent of Kabyle villages but also common to larger working class sociability,[21] they look after the children and property of their neighbors, and participate in forms of charity (*sedaqa*) and collective labor (*twiza*) in times of need. For instance, older brothers in the *cités* not only keep an eye on their younger brothers and sisters, but also watch after, lend a hand to, and even punish younger nonrelatives in the housing complex in which they live, much like older family members do for the younger children of a Kabyle *adhrum*. As Pascal Duret has discussed at length, this tendency has produced the generalized phenomenon of *"grands frères,"* authority figures in the *cités* who "take over (*prendre le relais*) from fathers outside of the family home, in the street" (1996: 33). These fictive kin act, in the eyes of the French state, as the primary "cultural mediators" between younger residents and the civic, professional, and educational structures of the housing projects. They are, moreover, the perceived motivators of a putative integration of immigrant populations to eventual national citizenship or, alternately, to ethnic or religious forms of belonging—of an integration, in either case, that begins at home.

During the early 1980s, many such *grands frères* organized themselves into neighborhood associations, building on newly elected socialist President François Mitterrand's experiments with multiculturalism and encouragement of local grassroots development in the *cités* (cf. Parti Socialiste 1981). Groups like the Association Gutenberg in Nanterre, the Association Nouvelle Génération Immigrée in Aubervilliers, and Vivons Ensemble in Mantes-la-Jolie were particularly active throughout the 1980s in providing daycare for children of working parents, after-school tutoring, legal aid, and spaces for communal celebrations. To a great extent, these "Beur"[22] associations served as intermediaries between individual households and state agencies concerned with residence rights and urban renovation. Moreover, they became effectively a home away from home for those Franco-Maghrebis who declared themselves to be forever uprooted from their parents' culture but not fully rooted "French" subjects, to be betwixt and between two identities, to have their symbolic "ass between two chairs" (Aïchoune 1985).[23]

Since the 1990s, the conservative governments that have dominated power in France have for the most part abandoned these experiments in decentralized multiculturalism and grassroots development in favor of more direct intervention and policing in the *cités*. Likewise, the younger generation of *petits frères* have largely rejected the early forms of neighborhood organization as instances of Uncle Tom-ism, accusing former association leaders of being *Beurs de service* in the employ of the state (Bouamama et al. 1994; Boubekeur and Abdallah 1993).[24] As a result, most of the Beur associations described above had gone defunct by the time I began my fieldwork in the mid-1990s. In their place, however, a vibrant milieu of ethnic and religious associations had developed with the explicit aim of re-rooting immigrant populations in their supposed cultures of origin. While these associations do offer some civic and legal services for their members, the majority of the activities they sponsor—from cyclical festivities to language courses to public talks by authors or religious authorities—have a pedagogical imperative of forming the children of immigrants into proper religious or ethnic subjects.

In particular, Berber cultural associations—like the Association de Culture Berbère (ACB) located in the Ménilmontant neighborhood of northeastern Paris, but with branches in a number of suburbs including Argenteuil, Créteil, and Mantes-la-Jolie—have thrived as central nodes in the increasingly transnational Berber cultural movement. In a didactic move designed to teach second-generation Franco-Kabyles about their parents' culture, they offer after-school instruction in the history, language, art, theater, and dance of Berber North Africa (or "Tamazgha"). This instruction draws largely on the imagery of prototypical Kabyle villages and houses as iconic of the referenced culture (see Goodman 2005: 69–72). *National Geographic*–style photos of villages and houses festoon the walls of the associations' headquarters and are featured prominently in the slide shows that almost always accompany the regular ritual celebrations. One of the main textbooks employed in the Tamazight language classes sets its lessons in a mythical village, Tizi-Wwuccen ("Hill of the Jackal"), with each chapter taking place in a different setting: the *akham*, the fountain, the fields, the *tajmaat*, etc.[25] In the process a reified notion of Kabyle culture is presented to the younger generation, one that is rooted in a particular set of spatial features, the disappearance of which come to be constituted as a prime factor in the breakdown of Kabyle strength and unity.

However, these village spaces are not simply symbolic registers of social memory and politicized nostalgia; they are also physical features of the immigrant social landscape. Berber associations, beyond their function as sites for cultural pedagogy, also double as spaces of male sociality, as a trans-village, metropolitan form of the *tajmaat*. They thus build on more localized village assemblies that find themselves reconstructed in Paris. In the outdoor public squares (*places*) on the edges of neighborhoods with prominent Kabyle populations like Belleville and Ménilmontant, crowds of older men (oftentimes not always from the same village) congregate daily and engage in vigorous debates over issues of local and international politics. Kabyle men have likewise established more formal village assemblies in Parisian cafés owned by former residents of their village (Khellil 1979: 121; see Sayad and Dupuy 1995). In their monthly meetings, they make decisions on infrastructural improvements to their natal areas, arrange for the repatriation of their members' corpses, and collect funds to sponsor the migration of family members or otherwise help a member in need (Goodman 2005: 83–89). More recently, the migrant *tajmaat*s have reconstituted themselves as official associations benefiting from French public funding and separate locales. These assemblies operate in parallel with informal *tajmaat*s that have continued to function in Kabylia, in spite of the centralized state administration of Algeria. And, like the Algerian *tajmaat*s, the Parisian village assemblies have become increasingly politicized in the wake of the growing street violence in Kabylia, particularly following the assassinations of political singer Lounès Matoub in 1998 and high school student Mohamed Guermeh in 2001. Like the cultural associations, the migrant *tajmaat*s thus exist as nodes in the enactment of a particular form of Kabyle social organization.

As the physical space of the migrant village assembly is synecdochally linked to rooted notions of Kabyle culture, so too is the concrete form of diasporic Kabyle lived space. As Joëlle Bahloul (1992) has demonstrated, domestic architecture serves as a privileged locus for social memory and nostalgia for Algerian emigrants resident in France. In general nostalgia is certainly a central feature of any "diasporic imaginary" (Axel 2002), with the home and the body tending to function as particularly charged sites in the cultural politics of diasporic groups. In the Kabyle case the domestic practices of nostalgia take on increasing importance given the centrality of housing and urban planning to French and Algerian public discourses on national "integration" (see de Rudder 1992; Silverstein 2004: chapter 3).

In the first place, in spite of the dramatic demographic dwindling of Kabyle villages since independence, emigrants continue to finance the construction of new homes in Kabylia with their remittance monies. On the one hand, such construction signals a continued "myth of return" upheld by the older generation of emigrants: an attempt to maintain concrete connections with the villages they had left in preparation for an anticipated, if permanently deferred, repatriation (cf. Sayad 1998; Zehraoui 1994). On the other hand, these new homes function as potent forms of symbolic capital that index the success of the emigrants to their natal communities. Such signs of a successful migration remain particularly important in ongoing evaluations of family honor (*nnif*) in which non-emigrant kin are engaged. Since the 1960s, these new constructions have almost always incorporated prefabricated materials, electrical conveniences, and "European" architectural styles. Rather than a purely economic calculation, this tendency derives from the symbolic capital that is accorded to Western materiality in these relatively impoverished contexts. Thus the practice of home construction reinscribes a particular modality of patrilineal village organization and sociality, though in an avowedly "modern" presentation that marks a revaluation of economic and symbolic capital.

If Kabyle emigrants have exported European symbolic forms of value to their natal villages, they have likewise imported various aspects of village domestic sociality and architecture into their living spaces in France. Since at least the 1910s, they have filled their French domiciles—even when such accommodation amounted to temporary shanties (*bidonvilles*), immigrant foyers, or employer-provided housing—with oriental rugs and brass tea sets brought over from Algeria or purchased in the multiple North African shops (*épiceries*) that dot the Parisian landscape. Today a number of members of the younger generation have translated this into a veritable fetish of the physical accoutrements of the *akham*. Several active members in Berber associations whose homes I visited in the mid-1990s proudly displayed sheepskins, inlaid *sendouk*s (bridal chests), hand-made *abernu*s (robes), and clay *tasirt*s (hand mills) they had brought back from Kabylia on family visits.

Another Kabyle architect friend, Mohand, a devotee of Bourdieu who had just begun a university degree in ethnology, had explicitly attempted to transform his Parisian home into a miniature *akham*. On one of the walls of his thirty-square-meter studio apartment, he had built a small, lofted *takhana* (mezzanine) on which he displayed scale models of various types of *ikoufen* (storage jars). Next to the *takhana* sat a full-size *achemoukh* (water jug), underlining the iconic representation of the miniatures. He completed the spatial overdetermination by featuring on his coffee table a large-format picture book of old photos of "traditional" Kabyle houses, simply titled *Axxam* (Abouda 1985). While their placement in the house followed the spatial layout of the *akham* as described by Bourdieu and others, these objects had been largely stripped from the symbolic repertoire of oppositions that motivated their particular functioning in Kabylia. Rather, their signification had been telescoped, with each individual object serving as a synecdoche for the studio-*akham* of which it was a part, and the studio-*akham* standing in for Kabyle cultural integrality as a whole. While perhaps an extreme case, Mohand's renovations highlight the salience of domesticity in activists' structural nostalgia for an enracinated, objectified culture.

Conclusion

In this way, rooting and uprooting, as modes of Kabyle historicity, have been directly incorporated into the contemporary Berber cultural movement's politicized nostalgia for an essential, cultural "time before time." As overseas Kabyles incorporate aspects of idealized village public and domestic structures into their everyday lives in (sub)urban France, they objectify their culture as a scarce and endangered resource to be preserved if not revivified. Bourdieu's early writings, based primarily on interviews with displaced villagers engaged in their own forms of memory-making and nascent structural nostalgia, share in both the politics of rehabilitation and the objectifying arboreal tropes of later culturalist politics, and thus find themselves open to appropriation. This is not in and of itself surprising; sources of far less intellectual merit and far more questionable (colonialist) politics have been similarly co-opted into contemporary Berberist autoethnographic practices of authenticity. What is more noteworthy, perhaps, is the *longue durée* of arboreal metaphors or rooting and uprooting as salient tropes of cultural anxiety. In this sense the *akham* becomes a synecdoche not only for a distinctive Kabyle "tradition," but also for a set of anxieties about the future of a Kabyle *ethnos* in a world of nation-states and of commensurable cosmopolitanisms.

Notes

Research for this essay was generously funded by the National Science Foundation and the United States Institute of Peace. I thank Genevieve Bell, Dale Eickleman, Jane Goodman, Abdellah Hammoudi, Michael Herzfeld, Jeremy Lane, Stefania Pandolfo, Loïc Wacquant, and Tassadit Yacine for comments on various drafts. An earlier version of the essay was published in *Ethnography* 5 (4): 553–78. The author thanks Sage Publications for permission to reprint.

1. On the modernity of nostalgia, see Ivy (1995). For a discussion of the work of rooting and nostalgia in the parallel case of Ashelhi Moroccan discourse, see Hoffman (2002). Camille Lacoste-Dujardin (1997: 274, cited in Lane 2000: 135) wrote in reference to the 1970s when Bourdieu's essays on the "Kabyle House" appeared: "One looks in vain for one of those famous 'Kabyle houses' where one would be hard pressed to find the 'world reversed' that Pierre Bourdieu wanted to see there."

2. Throughout the text, I employ Bourdieu's transliterations of Kabyle terms

when referencing his categories. Otherwise, I will follow the accepted, standardized conventions as developed by colonial missionaries and postcolonial Kabyle linguists. For a longer discussion of these conventions, see Chaker (1984) and Goodman (this volume).

3. See Stoler (1997: 224–25) for a discussion of colonial representations and legal categorizations of *métis* children as rootless, as potential subversives without a natural *patrie*.

4. Mauco wrote that "the nationalities where criminality is the highest are those that most suffered from uprooting (*déracinement*) and whose adaptation is most difficult because of highly accentuated ethnic and civilizational differences" (1932: 269). See Noiriel (1988: 125–87) for an extended discussion of this period in French immigration discourse.

5. Likewise, a number of works within refugee and migration studies have appeared in the wake of Bourdieu and Sayad that both regarded the moment of migration as one of violent rupture and also adopted a similar, naturalizing "root" idiom to understand the precontact cultures—a tendency that was reflected in their very titles (see Keller 1975; Nann 1982; and Zwingmann and Pfister-Ammende 1973). For a recent example see André Jacques's 1985 study of refugees, *Les Déracinés*.

6. Maurras claimed that "*déracinés, déracineurs, déracinement*, the same image more or less modified, passed into the language of journalism and [political] debate" (1898: 26). The language of rootedness and rootlessness is maintained within French neonationalist discourse, particularly in the antimodernist, anti-immigrant rhetoric of Jean-Marie Le Pen's *Front National* (Holmes 2000: 88; Taguieff 1994).

7. I am grateful to Jeremy Lane for pointing me to this genealogical thread. Note that the questions of *habitus* and education implicit in Bourdieu's early writings about Kabylia would be later taken up in Bourdieu's work on French academic institutions and class reproduction. Bourdieu (1987: 33) himself acknowledged this debt.

8. I am indebted to Tassadit Yacine (personal communication, 19 February 2004) for indicating this connection.

9. Fanny Colonna (1978) details the afterlives of the concept of *déracinement* in postcolonial Algeria, as it became a hegemonic justification for the redistribution and collectivization of agricultural land during the Agrarian Revolution of the early 1970s. Colonna (this volume) further discusses the lingering ethnographic effects of Bourdieu's focus on violence, domination, and deprivation (his *misérabilisme*) in these early studies, insofar as it led him to bracket issues of everyday accommodation and pay less attention to those in-between figures

(including Sayad) whose relationship to structures of domination had not been solely one of victimization.

10. In later works (esp. 1990: 261; and 2000a: 64) Bourdieu emphasized, to a greater extent than in his earlier work, the flexibility and indeterminacy of *habitus* and the symbolic repertoires that underwrite it. His earlier work, by contrast, was greatly influenced by Durkheim's writings on "mechanical solidarity" (1893) of which the Kabyles—via Emile Masqueray's classic study (1886)—were cited as a cardinal example.

11. See also Bourdieu (2000b: 28–38) for an illustration of this transformation in economic *habitus* as described through the exegesis of one particularly well-placed "folk economist," a Kabyle cook in 1962 Algiers.

12. Bourdieu similarly maps a "pre-perceptive" temporal consciousness onto this cyclical temporal structure, contrasting the *bou niya*'s sense of "the forthcoming" (*l'à venir*)—a term he borrows from Husserl—with Western understandings of an active and agentive, if impersonal, "future" (Bourdieu 1963a: 61–62; see Lane 2000: 22–32).

13. Many thanks to Stefania Pandolfo for reminding me of this important point. Colonna (this volume) and Hammoudi (this volume) explore the ethnographic effects of such a focus on the political and phenomenological field of domination—a conscious philosophical choice undertaken by Bourdieu in order to intercede in French academic debates.

14. For a further discussion of the *akham* in the contemporary Kabyle setting, see Goodman (2005: 77–83).

15. These oppositions in large part derive from Bourdieu's reading of the phenomenological essay by Bachelard (1957) on the poetics of domestic space, including Bachelard's emphasis on inversions (Lane 2000: 98–99). De Certeau comments with relation to the house in Bourdieu's schema: "Through the practices that articulate [the dwelling's] interior space, it inverts the strategies of public space and silently *organizes* the language (a vocabulary, proverbs, etc.). The inversion of the public order and the generation of discourse: these two characteristics make the Kabylian dwelling the inverse of the French *school*, in which Bourdieu . . . sees nothing but the 'reproduction' of social hierarchies and the repetition of their ideologies" (1984: 52).

16. In his later writing, Bourdieu (1990: 192) discussed the centrality of this domestic competition.

17. Bourdieu (1963b, 1979b) had earlier studied similar processes of spatio-symbolic investment and "disenchantment" in the public housing projects of late colonial Algeria. See also the incisive analysis of these structures by architectural historian Zeynep Çelik (1997: 113–79). On the *café arabe* as an important

social institution that transcended Kabyle decolonization and emigration, see Sayad and Dupuy (1995).

18. While the Berber cultural movement today is strongly transnational, with a multiplicity of cultural associations and political parties throughout Algeria and Morocco formed in the wake of the 1980 "Berber Spring" of student demonstrations in Kabylia, France remains a key site of cultural activism. A large number of Kabyle militants, artists, and intellectuals have expatriated themselves to France, fleeing the Algerian civil war that claimed over one hundred thousand lives between 1992 and 1999. Moreover, the World Amazigh Congress, the primary international movement of Berber cultural activism, was founded and remains headquartered in Paris. For a detailed history of the Berber cultural movement in all its vagaries, see Chaker (1990); Maddy-Weitzman (2001); and Silverstein (2003).

19. "Hommage à Pierre Bourdieu par Mabrouk Ferkal: L'ami de la Kabylie vient de mourir." (27 January 2002) www.kabyle.com. Accessed on 20 May 2003. The communiqué was recirculated on a number of websites, garnering many gushing responses by subscribers who shared their memories of and appreciation for Bourdieu.

20. For fuller ethnographic studies of this "community," see Direche-Slimani (1992); Goodman (2005); Khellil (1979); Sayad (1977, 2000); and Silverstein (2004).

21. For in-depth ethnological and sociological descriptions of the working-class suburbs (banlieues), see Lepoutre (1997); Petonnet (1982); and Wihtol de Wenden and Daoud (1993).

22. "Beur" was a term employed by young French North Africans to refer to themselves. It derives from a syllabic inversion of "Arabe" according to the rules of the street language game, verlan (itself the syllabic inversion of "inverse" (l'envers)). Contemporary Berber activists likewise claim that the ethnonym derives from "Berbères d'Europe," and indeed a large number of those active in Beur associations during the 1980s self-identified as Kabyle. In recent years, "Beur" as a term of address or reference has been largely rejected by the younger generation. For wider discussions of the Beur Movement, see Bouamama et al. (1994); Boubekeur and Abdallah (1993); Hargreaves (1995); and Jazouli (1992).

23. For instance, Djura (1993: 25–27), a singer and author born in Kabylia but raised in France, uses the language of déracinement to talk of being "cut from her roots" of Frenchness and Algerianness. Through "nostalgia" for her natal village and her grandmother as repeatedly expressed in her songs, she is able to reattach herself to a "new filiation"—to generations of Kabyle women forced into patriarchal submission.

24. Note the inability of cultural, neighborhood, or religious associations to intercede to quell the October–November 2005 youth street violence in outer-city housing projects across France.

25. The text is framed by the arrival and departure of the son of a Kabyle emigrant to Paris, who comes to learn about the village just as the second-generation immigrant students. The textbook is actually a reissue of a missionary instruction manual originally published in 1957, revised to take into account new developments in the standardization of the language in order to reach a "middle-ground Kabyle" (*kabyle moyen*) understandable across different parts of the region (Chaker 1987: 6).

Works Cited

Abouda, Mohand. 1985. *Axxam (Maisons kabyles): Espaces et fresques murales.* Goussainville: M. Abouda.

Aïchoune, Farid, ed. 1985. *La Beur génération.* Paris: Sans Frontières/ Arcantère.

Apter, Emily. 1999. Uprooted Subjects. In *Continental Drift.* pp. 25–38. Chicago: University of Chicago Press.

Axel, Brian. 2002. The Diasporic Imaginary. *Public Culture* 14 (2): 411–28.

Bachelard, Gaston. 1957. *La Poétique de l'espace.* Paris: Presses Universitaires de France.

Bahloul, Joëlle. 1992. *La Maison de la mémoire.* Paris: Editions Anne-Marie Métailié.

Barrès, Maurice. 1897. *Les Déracinés.* Paris: Bibliothèque-Charpentier.

Benmatti, N. A. 1982. *L'Habitat du tiers monde. Cas de l'Algérie.* Algiers: SNED.

Bodnar, John. 1985. *The Transplanted.* Bloomington: Indiana University Press.

Bouamama, Saïd, Hadjila Sad-Saoud and Mokhtar Djerdoubi. 1994. *Contribution à la mémoire des banlieues.* Paris: Editions du Volga.

Boubekeur, Ahmed and Mogniss H. Abdallah. 1993. *Douce France. La Saga du Mouvement Beur.* Paris: Im'media.

Bouquet, Mary. 1996. Family Trees and Their Affinities: The Visual Imperative of the Genealogical Diagram. *Journal of the Royal Anthropological Institute* 2: 43–66.

Bourdieu, Pierre. 1963a. The Attitude of the Algerian Peasant Toward Time. In *Mediterranean Countrymen,* ed. Julian Pitt-Rivers. pp. 55–72. Paris: Mouton.

———. 1963b. Etude sociologique. In *Travail et travailleurs en Algérie*, ed. Pierre Bourdieu, Alain Darbel, Jean-Pierre Rivet, and Claude Seibel. pp. 253–562. Paris: Mouton.

———. 1967. Postface. In *Architecture gothique et pensée scholastique*, Erwin Panofsky, trans. Pierre Bourdieu. pp. 136–167. Paris: Minuit.

———. 1972. Les stratégies matrimoniales dans le système de reproduction. *Annales* 27: 1105–27.

———. 1977 (1972). *Outline of a Theory of Practice*. Cambridge: Cambridge University Press.

———. 1979a (1970). The Kabyle House or the World Reversed. In *Algeria 1960*. pp. 133–53. Cambridge: Cambridge University Press.

———. 1979b. The Disenchantment of the World. In *Algeria 1960*. pp. 1–94. Cambridge: Cambridge University Press.

———. 1987. *Choses dites*. Paris: Minuit.

———. 1990 (1980). *The Logic of Practice*. Stanford: Stanford University Press.

———. 2000a (1997). *Pascalian Meditations*. Stanford: Stanford University Press.

———. 2000b. Making the Economic Habitus: Algerian Workers Revisited. *Ethnography* 1 (1): 17–41.

Bourdieu, Pierre, and Abdelmalek Sayad. 1964. *Le Déracinement. La Crise de l'agriculture traditionelle en Algérie*. Paris: Minuit.

Bourdieu, Pierre and Didier Eribon. 1980. Clou de Djeha: Des contradictions linguistiques léguées par le colonisateur. *Libération*, 19–20 April, 13.

Çelik, Zeynep. 1997. *Urban Forms and Colonial Confrontations. Algiers Under French Rule*. Berkeley: University of California Press.

Chaker, Salem. 1984. *Textes en linguistique berbère*. Paris: CNRS.

———. 1987. Preface. In *Tizi-Wwuccen. Méthode de langue berbère (taqbaylit)*. pp. 5–7. Aix-en-Provence: Edisud.

———. 1990. *Imazighen ass-a (Berbères dans le Maghreb contemporain)*. Algiers: Editions Bouchene.

Colonna Fanny. 1978. *Le Déracinement comme concept et comme politique. Questions de sciences sociales*. Algiers: ONRS.

Comaroff, Jean. 1985. *Body of Power, Spirit of Resistance*. Chicago: University of Chicago Press.

Darian-Smith, Eve. 1999. *Bridging Divides: The Channel Tunnel and English Legal Identity in the New Europe*. Berkeley: University of California Press.

de Certeau, Michel. 1984. *The Practice of Everyday Life*. Berkeley: University of California Press.

de Rudder, Véronique. 1992. Immigrant Housing and Integration in French Cities. In *Immigrants in two Democracies: French and American Experience*, ed. Donald L. Horowitz and Gérard Noiriel, pp. 247–67. New York: New York University Press.

Direche-Slimani, Karima. 1992. *Histoire de l'émigration kabyle en France au XXe siècle: Réalités culturelles et réappropriations identitaires*. Diplôme de troisième cycle, dirigé par Salem Chaker. Aix-en-Provence: Université de Provence-Aix-Marseille I.

Djura. 1993. *La Saison des narcisses*. Paris: Michel Lafon.

Duret, Pascal. 1996. *Anthropologie de la fraternité dans les cités*. Paris: Presses Universitaires de France.

Durkheim, Emile. 1893. *De la division du travail social. Etude sur l'organisation des sociétés supérieures*. Paris: F. Alcan.

Eickelman, Dale. 1977. Time in a Complex Society: A Moroccan Example. *Ethnology* 16 (1): 39–55.

Ford, Caroline. 1991. *Creating the Nation in Provincial France*. Princeton: Princeton University Press.

Free, Anthony. 1996. The Anthropology of Pierre Bourdieu: A Reconsideration. *Critique of Anthropology* 16 (4): 395–416.

Goodman, Jane. 2005. *Berber Culture on the World Stage: From Village to Video*. Bloomington: Indiana University Press.

Handlin, Oscar. 1951. *The Uprooted*. New York: Grosset and Dunlap.

Hargreaves, Alec. 1995. *Immigration, "Race," and Ethnicity in Contemporary France*. New York: Routledge.

Herzfeld, Michael. 1987. *Anthropology through the Looking Glass*. Cambridge: Cambridge University Press.

———. 1997. *Cultural Intimacy*. London: Routledge.

Hoffman, Katherine. 2002. Moving and Dwelling: Building the Moroccan Ashelhi Homeland. *American Ethnologist* 29(4): 928–62.

Holmes, Douglas R. 2000. *Integral Europe: Fast-Capitalism, Multiculturalism, Neofascism*. Princeton: Princeton University Press.

Iguedelane, El-Hadi. 1996. *Anthropologie de l'espace kabyle. Le village de Tizouyar*. Diplôme d'étude approfondie en anthropologie sociale et ethnologie, dirigé par Tassadit Yacine. Paris: Ecole des Hautes Etudes en Sciences Sociales.

Ivy, Marilyn. 1995. *Discourses of the Vanishing: Modernity, Phantasm, Japan*. Chicago: University of Chicago Press.

Jacques, André. 1985. *Les Déracinés. Réfugiés et migrants dans le monde*. Paris: La Découverte.

Jazouli, Adil. 1992. *Les Années banlieues*. Paris: Seuil.

Keller, Stephen L. 1975. *Uprooting and Social Change: The Role of Refugees in Development*. Delhi: Manshar.

Khellil, Mohand. 1979. *L'Exil kabyle*. Paris: Harmattan.

―――. 1984. *La Kabylie ou l'ancêtre sacrifié*. Paris: Harmattan.

Lacoste-Dujardin, Camille. 1976. A propos de Pierre Bourdieu et de l'*Esquisse d'une théorie de la pratique*. *Hérodote* 2: 102–116.

―――. 1997. *Opération 'Oiseau bleu': Des Kabyles, des ethnologues et la guerre en Algérie*. Paris: La Découverte.

Lane, Jeremy F. 2000. *Pierre Bourdieu: A Critical Introduction*. London: Pluto.

―――. 2005. *Jazz as Habitus*: Discourses of Class and Ethnicity in Hugues Panassié's *Le Jazz Hot* (1934). *Nottingham French Studies* 44 (3): 40–53.

Lepoutre, David. 1997. *Coeur de banlieue: Codes, rites et langages*. Paris: O. Jacob.

Linke, Uli. 1999. *German Bodies: Race and Representation after Hitler*. London: Routledge.

Maddy-Weitzman, Bruce. 2001. Contested Identities: Berbers, "Berberism" and the State in North Africa. *Journal of North African Studies* 6 (3): 23–47.

Malkki, Liisa. 1992. National Geographic: The Rooting of Peoples and the Territorialization of National Identity among Scholars and Refugees. *Cultural Anthropology* 7 (1): 24–44.

Maritain, Jean. 1930 (1920). *Art and Scholasticism*. New York: Charles Scribner's Sons.

Masqueray, Emile. 1886. *Formation des cités chez les populations sédentaires de l'Algérie*. Paris: Ernst Leroux.

Mauco, Georges. 1932. *Les Etrangers en France*. Paris: A. Colin.

Maurras, Charles. 1898. *L'Idée de la décentralisation*. Paris: Revue encyclopédique.

Mitchell, Timothy. 1988. *Colonising Egypt*. Berkeley: University of California Press.

Nann, Richard C. 1982. *Uprooting and Surviving: Adaptation and Resettlement of Migrant Females and Children*. Dordecht: D. Reidel.

Noiriel, Gérard. 1988. *Le Creuset français*. Paris: Seuil.

Parti Socialiste. 1981. *La France au pluriel*. Paris: Editions Entente.

Petonnet, Colette. 1982. *Ethnologie des banlieues*. Paris: Galilée.

Reed-Danahay, Deborah. 1995. The Kabyle and the French: Occidentalism in Bourdieu's "Theory of Practice." In *Occidentalism: Images of the West*, ed. James G. Carrier, pp. 61–84. Oxford: Clarendon Press.

Sayad, Abdelmalek. 1977. Les trois "âges" de l'émigration algérienne en France. *Actes de la Recherche en Sciences Sociales* 15: 59–79.

————. 1998. Le retour, élément constitutif de la condition de l'immigré. *Migrations Sociétés* 57 (May–June): 9–45.

————. 1999. *La Double absence. Des illusions de l'émigré aux souffrances de l'immigré.* Paris: Seuil.

————. 2000. El Ghorba: From Original Sin to Collective Lie. *Ethnography* 1 (2): 147–71.

Sayad, Abdelmalek and Eliane Dupuy. 1995. *Un Nanterre algérien, terre de bidonvilles.* Paris: Autrement.

Silverstein, Paul A. 2003. Martyrs and Patriots: Ethnic, National, and Transnational Dimensions of Kabyle Politics. *Journal of North African Studies* 8 (1): 87–111.

————. 2004. *Algeria in France: Race, Nation, Trans-Politics.* Bloomington: Indiana University Press.

Sombart, Werner. 1915. *The Quintessence of Capitalism: A Study of the History and Psychology of the Modern Business Man.* London: Unwin.

Stoler, Ann Laura. 1997. Sexual Affronts and Racial Categories: European Identities and the Cultural Politics of Exclusion in Colonial Southeast Asia. In *Tensions of Empire: Colonial Cultures in a Bourgeois World*, ed. Frederick Cooper and Anne Laura Stoler. pp. 198–237. Berkeley: University of California Press.

Taguieff, Pierre-André. 1994. The Doctrine of the National Front in France (1972–1989). *New Political Science* 16/17: 29–70.

Tönnies, Ferdinand. 1887. *Gemeinschaft und Gesellschaft. Abhandlung des Communismus und des Socialismus als empirischer Culturformen.* Leipzig: Fues's Verlag.

Weber, Max. 1924. *Gesammelte Aufsätze zur Sozial- und Wirtschaftsgeschichte.* Tübingen: Mohr.

Weil, Simone. 1949. *L'Enracinement. Prélude à une déclaration des devoirs envers l'être humain.* Paris: Gallimard.

Wihtol de Wenden, Catherine and Zakya Daoud. 1993. *Banlieues . . . intégration ou explosion.* Special edition of *Panoramiques.* II (12).

Zehraoui, Ahsène. 1994. *L'Immigration: de l'homme seul à la famille.* Paris: CIEMI/Harmattan.

Zwingmann, Charles. and Maria Pfister-Ammende. 1973. *Uprooting and After.* New York: Springer-Verlag.

FIVE

Phenomenology and Ethnography

On Kabyle *Habitus* in the Work
of Pierre Bourdieu

ABDELLAH HAMMOUDI

Translated by Tristan Jean

Introduction

Among Bourdieu's contributions to the social sciences, the concept of *habitus* is certainly the most widely discussed, even—I would say—routine-ized. However, there is an angle from which *habitus* has never truly been reconsidered: the angle of ethnographic practice. The absence of discussion on this point is all the more surprising since—as it is well known—Bourdieu elaborated the essentials of his views on *practice*—"fields," "*habitus*," "temporality," and "symbolic capital"—on the basis of his Kabyle ethnology.

By following the development of the notion of *habitus* in Bourdieu's ethnological work, I want to reflect on his ethnographic approach and its epistemological underpinnings.[1] It is not my purpose to deny that Bourdieu's studies on Algeria represented a breakthrough, nor to minimize the productive character of his conceptual elaboration regarding the interpretation of Maghrebi societies and their transformations (Hammoudi 2000a). Nonetheless, a close look at his method opens the question of the fit between his ethnography on the one hand, and his theoretical project on the other.

During the course of Bourdieu's works on Algeria, the concept of *habitus* comes to supplant that of *tradition*. This, however, raises the question of whether the former retains some of the limitations of the latter. And indeed, Kabyle tradition, as Bourdieu presents it, appears monolithic, static, and limited to a restricted space: that of a Kabylia whose contours and physiognomy were constrained by colonial definitions. So much so that, in the case at hand, a (colonial) discursive *tradition*, it would seem, had instilled a certain Kabyle *tradition*. This is not all that surprising; indeed, whether in the Maghreb or elsewhere, dominant discourses granted specific and well-designed *traditions* to dominated societies.

Having been an assiduous reader of Max Weber, Bourdieu surprisingly writes as if traditions were only called into question with the development of a rationality arriving from elsewhere: in this case, a modern, capitalist one imposed by colonial domination. Thus, *tradition* and *habitus*, in this scheme, leave little room for study of the use of reason in social practices anterior to colonization—an assumption which is surely debatable. Similarly, they not only marginalize internal contradictions but also the relative freedom that men and women in their action exercise with regard to normative systems. Returning once more to Max Weber, it is well known that charismatic movements frequently challenge traditions and create new ones, as has been frequently the case also in the Maghreb. Finally, it is entirely possible to conform to a tradition for some rational motive.

These considerations spur us to reflect on the question of ethnography, on the research practices and human interactions which lie beneath Bourdieu's *theory of practice*. Pierre Bourdieu left few traces of the concrete circumstances surrounding his research activities in Kabyle villages between 1958 and 1961, during the height of the Algerian war; neither did he write much on his own ethnographic practice or on the implications of his own presence in Kabylia. Thus, one can get an idea of his ethnographic practice and its consequences only from an analysis of his writings (as has been done by Hammoudi 2000a; Bourdieu and Wacquant 1992: 204; Dortier 2002: 7, 9).[2] A close look at Bourdieu's writings shows one such consequence, one significant relation between ethnographic practice and theory that can be summarized as follows: Bourdieu's ethnographic practice failed to register the tensions, contradictions, and debate within the so-called "traditional society." For, having uncritically borrowed much from colonial ethnography, Bourdieu's theoretical innovations left intact many of the simplifying schemata of his predecessors.

Moreover, the sort of ethnography that Bourdieu took for granted was, in fact, hardly adequate for his project. For example, it worked along an old division of labor between ethnology and Orientalism. According to this disciplinary order, ethnologists of Kabylia learned and used the oral vernacular for their inquiries, while Orientalists specialized in the written language. In this case, ethnologists learned to speak Berber with their informants, while Orientalists learned classical Arabic. This dichotomy occulted the fact that Kabyles, like many other peoples, spoke and/or wrote about themselves, others, and about the world not only in Berber, but in other languages as well: for example, in colloquial Arabic, classical Arabic, and French. Obviously, not all of them did. But a number of them did so—still do—and from a multiplicity of spaces and cultural settings: Kabylia, Algeria, other places in the Maghreb and France (among others).

The problems multiply when one considers, from this complex perspective, the notions of *field*, *strategy*, and *temporality*, all of which are related to *habitus*, and crucial regarding Bourdieu's objections to the structuralism of Lévi-Strauss; for one can no longer say for sure what is a matter of a *habitus* of strategies and what would be better accounted for by pragmatics more or less consciously deployed.

Under such conditions, it becomes difficult to determine how time plays out (*comment joue le temps*) versus how one plays with time (*comment l'on joue le temps*). For that, it would have been necessary for Bourdieu to call upon a *process-based* ethnography; it would have been necessary, in other words, to follow actions as they occur, or, in the case of past actions, to give oneself the means to imagine them in the process of occurring through an analysis of their available traces, whether they be written, oral, or archaeological. However, Bourdieu's ethnography is composed of bits and pieces arranged in order to create illustrative syntheses, with an almost total absence of the use of written materials (in Tamazight, Arabic, or French), and especially material written by Algerians themselves. Moreover, Bourdieu paid little attention to the works of the great specialists in written material (such as Jacques Berque, among others).

Finally, in cases where dynamic processes unfold with a certain degree of complexity, Bourdieu's ethnography reveals its limits. These limits appear clearly linked to its philosophical foundations, most clearly regarding the space/time relation as it works contextually in life and action. On this subject, Bourdieu has made clear his debt to the thought of Merleau-Ponty (Héran 1987).[3] However, if one returns to Merleau-Ponty's reflections on the dynamic constitution of the fields of action as a function of spatial-temporal relations, one can sketch a very different Kabylia and "Kabyle tradition," with much less static borders than those presented in Bourdieu's influential works. It appears that, despite being the sociologist who best expressed the need for a "double break"—with, on the one hand, the "indigenous representation of experience" and, on the other hand, the researcher's own presuppositions and the implications of his own position as a researcher (Bourdieu 1977: 1–4)—Bourdieu nonetheless remained bound by the French ethnological tradition. Overall, his ethnographic practice seems to rest upon an overly rigid and static variant of Merleau-Ponty's *existential* phenomenology.

The Ancestors of *Habitus*: Kabyle Tradition and Ethnographic Tradition

The lack of attention to Kabyle *habitus* and to the ethnography at its base in the large body of literature on French and European social theory is an interesting fact in itself. This is not the place to treat this question or to trace the rich history of scholarly and ordinary uses of the words *habitude* and *habitus* (Héran 1987). Suffice it to note that anthropologists who took a critical interest in Bourdieu's ideas have not taken much of an interest in the ethnography of *habitus*, instead contenting themselves either with reducing them to their deterministic aspect and/or pushing them toward other notions such as the "implicit" character of ideology (for example, Ortner 1984; Comaroff 1985: 5, 54, 125, 263).

In *Sociologie de l'Algérie* (translated as *The Algerians* [1962]), his first work, dating from 1958, Bourdieu gives us an image of a Kabyle (and more generally Algerian) social organization that clearly departs from an earlier model of mechanical solidarity. His descriptions are at variance with the segmentary model in which integration would take place by means of the opposition and complementarity of groups of the same size and at the same level (extended family, lineage, clan, tribe, etc.). Bourdieu observes that there are levels of segmentation (i.e., groups) between the family and the clan, whose activation in terms of solidarity and opposition remains virtual, depending on circumstances. He adds that alongside the principle of integration through kinship, another principle functions: the principle of ancestrality (*tadjadit*). Thus, if genealogy determines loyalties and alignments, ancestrality establishes a more general cultural identity that is not incompatible with the mobility of the extended families between clans (Bourdieu 1962: 101).[4] These fluctuations, which Bourdieu notes in Kabylia, have been observed elsewhere in the Maghreb (Berque 1954: 261–71; Hammoudi 1974, 2000a: 272–73). This raises serious objections to the segmentary model of perfect equilibrium and universal taxonomy. Subsequent research shows that such simplification and rationalization is due to the work of colonial administrators who are mindful of fixing territories and populations—in other words, of imposing the new order of colonial modernity (Hammoudi 2000a).

Bourdieu does not deny that the model—up to a point—may have been inspired by an *indigenous* theory of solidarity, but he rightly proposes that such a folk theory be interpreted rather as a rule of a game whose dynamics frequently modify its meaning (*sens*). Thus, for example, there is indeed a tendency for groups to oscillate between the fission and fusion of genealogical segments yet not all the families of a complex clan will invariably mobilize in the same manner or at the same moment when conflict arises. Each individual does indeed act according to *tradition*, but this tradition contains more than one criterion for self-identification and group solidarity: these include solidarity through the agnatic line, ancestrality, and division of groups into two opposing lines.

Bourdieu remains silent on other social organizations such as the religious brotherhoods. He also neglects Kabyles' relations with central powers, which would have added to the complexity he had set out to account for. Most importantly, though, a tension remains between, on the one hand, his description of the dynamics of group solidarity and, on the other hand, the notions that Bourdieu calls upon to interpret such dynamics. This is particularly striking regarding norms in their relation with action. Bourdieu's vision is shadowed by an image of traditional society as self-sufficient, localized, and homogenous. According to him, the molding of each generation according to a purely inherited wisdom is such that individuality is entirely absorbed by social role, i.e., "a being for others" (*être pour autrui*) and through others (*être par autrui*). For him, total conformity is what Kabyle society demanded of its members. (Bourdieu 1962: 96–97).

At this point, *habitus* has not yet appeared in Bourdieu's writing. He relies on notions such as *tradition, customs, culture,* and *ethos,* which are still influenced by a deterministic epistemology. Unlike the change in Bourdieu's thinking that came with *habitus* (a notion which marks a passage to a middle ground between determination and creativity), custom and education are still viewed by him as static. According to him, they work "apparently to guard against, or even to forbid, any improvisation, or at least to impose an impersonal form on thought and personal feeling" (1962: 95).[5] Individual differences are either denied, or else referred to as variations from the same model. This is, for example, what happens when Bourdieu reflects on social morphology. He notes differences between Kabyles, Shawiya, and Ibadites, only to contend that these differences result from transformations conforming to the Saussurian principle of assimilation/dissimilation (1962: 90). Each group would seem to have developed a combination of identical attributes with variations affecting some disposition and/or valence. Following Lévi-Strauss, Bourdieu assumes that historical transformations are obviated by logical permutations. Finally, tradition appears as a set of "psychological montages" which operate in each individual to insure the permanence and reproduction of tradition (1962: 95).

While *Sociologie de l'Algérie* is primarily an ethnological text, Bourdieu's subsequent works make use of techniques that belong more in the domain of sociology: questionnaires, directed interviews, samplings, intensive use of statistics, correlations (*intersections des variables*), etc. One must keep in mind that Bourdieu for the most part disregarded compartmental academic divisions. However, this disregard, which explains in part the success of his research, seems to have also problematically affected his approach to social change in Algeria. When he studied change Bourdieu worked as a sociologist, and he worked as an ethnologist when he studied tradition. Taking this methodological division for granted, Bourdieu leaves intact a model of *traditional* society whose features he constructed by selecting uncritically many elements from a vast body of colonial ethnography to which he added his own observations. So, instead of comparing two dynamics—an old one and a new one—Bourdieu employs the classic schema of a passage from a (static) tradition to a (dynamic) modernization. To be sure, unlike the theories of modernization prevalent in the 1960s, Bourdieu describes in detail the role of colonial domination in the process of change. Nonetheless, he did not pay attention to the dynamics of tradition.

Travail et travailleurs en Algérie was published in 1963. The work analyzes Algerian society's responses to its contact with industrial society, which imposed itself in the harsh context of colonialism. The work's focus is on the peasantry, which had been devastated by the loss of land—its means of subsistence—to the French colonists, and forced into wage labor, unemployment, or emigration. Having depicted a peasant acting according to *tradition*, Bourdieu and his collaborators attempted to explain how peasants succeed or fail to adapt to the cultural model of capitalism. To do this, they chose to center their observations on notions of time and how people use their time. Adaptation to capitalism was to be measured by the degree to which peasants learned and accepted the practice of a calculated time allocation for each task. The level of adaptation thus measured

206

was correlated with class position (Bourdieu et al. 1963: part II, chapters 1–2).

Bourdieu took for granted that the concept of social class was pertinent to this situation. He describes three modes of change. First, there is the partially successful adaptation of the peasant who acquires the aptitude to calculate time spent working and to compare it with the gain derived from it (though always in a risk-averse manner). A second path is followed by those who, unable to cope, fall back on haphazard styles of action and magical practices. Finally, a third option is survival by clinging to a second-order traditionalism. Here, peasants declare their attachment to an unchanged discourse regarding communal land ownership, traditional patterns of communal family consumption, and values, all the while disregarding the deep transformation that had affected their social and legal relationship to land. This is tradition, for lack of an alternative: a "tradition of despair" (Bourdieu and Sayad 1964: 20).

As noted, these three modes of adaptation are correlated with class conditions. "Classes" are represented by statistical aggregates established on the basis of income levels (including property), as well as family members' attitudes toward work seen as a function of their income levels and consumption choices. The three modes of adaptation and response described above thus correlate, respectively, to the relatively high-income propertied class, the peasant classes, and, finally, those peasants and artisans of modest means. Given the great material and social changes that they had recently experienced, the two latter groups' perceptions of future possibilities prohibit any hope of integration in the new system.

However, such correlations remain problematic because they are based on an undiscussed premise: the homogeneity of the culture, its ethos, and its tradition (Bourdieu et al. 1963: 350, 361, 319). This is

207

all the more surprising in that Bourdieu retained cultural homogeneity, class differentiation, and change side-by-side. Thus, studying social transformation, Bourdieu subsumed what he saw as an undifferentiated cultural economy under the effects of a differentiated material economy. From this perspective Bourdieu treated magical practices and second-order traditionalism as nothing more than a reaction of impotence, whereas it would have been equally plausible to see in them a form of protest, a taking of position, and perhaps even the outline of a revolt against a system that cannot itself be reduced to the simple passage from one structure to another. In brief, such a situation could also have been expressed, and perhaps in a better way, in terms of a transformation (*mutation*), with an elaboration of this concept so as to portray the multidirectionalities inherent to all transformations.

Moreover, Bourdieu's correlations between degrees of adaptation and class position are meant to give an account of the changes that had profoundly modified cultural attitudes. However, the correlations systematically ignore ambivalent and atypical individuals, and the relationship between these degrees of adaptation (as they are measured) and the systems of ideas in question is not clearly established. Finally, Bourdieu's statistical correlations give a static picture of change itself—for they merely measure a distribution of responses in the moment, instantaneously. They do not allow one to consistently chart attitudes in the course of their formation, or for a sufficient amount of time thereafter. For that, it would have been necessary for Bourdieu to take a greater interest in the sinuous paths of his interlocutors' lives, which in every case resist simple correlations.

In these studies, which constitute a remarkable testimony to some crucial aspects of the upheavals and aspirations of Algerian society in the 1960s, Bourdieu extends his vocabulary to include expressions such as *system of attitudes, ideology, norms and values, modes of behavior*, and *deep structures*. Above all, he introduces the notion of *aptitude*, which evokes a sort of competence close to that of *habitus*. Such terminological developments, which denote an evolution in Bourdieu's thinking, do not, however, modify his general approach. Furthermore, the sociologist elaborates his knowledge through what I would call a synchronic empiricism, an approach that resembles the one followed by colonial ethnographers who tended to fix Kabylia within rigid spatial and temporal limits.

Bourdieu first uses the word *habitus* in 1962 in his work on Béarn (France). The word and the notion appeared shortly afterward in his Algerian studies, specifically in *Le Déracinement* (Bourdieu and Sayad 1964: 14, 152–53, 163).[6] Although the concept had not yet fully matured, it already signified a dynamic corporeality.

In fact, *habitus* appears as the concrete sense of one's demeanor, gait, and assumption of selfhood in a specific milieu; it is a way of behaving and moving with ease due to embodied perceptions of spatiotemporal coordinates, and of becoming one *(faire corps)* with them. The relation of *habitus* to norms and values, though, is not clarified, except insofar as Bourdieu and Sayad understand norms and values as the explicit reinforcement of implicit (embodied) positions; from this point of view, norms are to "habitus of the body" *(habitus corporel)* what ethics is to ethos. Bourdieu and Sayad do, however, note the profound disorganization of "embodied implicit" behaviors that affects peasants displaced and forcibly relocated by the French colonial army:

Because the familiar world is, for him, the world of his birth, because his entire *habitus* of the body, his entire *habitus corporel*

[my emphasis] is tailored to the space of his customary movements, the uprooted (*déraciné*) peasant is struck in the depths of
his being, so deeply that he cannot formulate his disarray, much
less define a reason for it. (Bourdieu and Sayad 1964: 152)[7]

These observations testify to the interest that Bourdieu and his
collaborators have for the real and situated activities of Algerians,
whether they be actions that obey the rules of simple (social) reproduction, or those in which a spirit of calculation and goals of
accumulation intervene. But this is the first place in Bourdieu's writing where one sees concrete activities, the implicit meaning (*sens*)
of norms, and *habitus*—considered as the tradition of a person tailored to his environment by the prolonged exercise of the body—
linked in this way. The resulting behaviors are not the reflection of
a fundamental personality whose traits are abstractly assembled by
the anthropologist, nor do they derive from the universal cognitive
structures directly apprehended by a coextensive human mind (as
in Lévi-Strauss's structuralism); neither still do they concern a set of
separable symbols (as in Geertz's symbolic anthropology).

At any rate, Bourdieu understands the diversity of reactions to the
impact of colonial capitalism as correlating to social stratification,
yet he reduces these differences to a function of the space opened by
the erosion of tradition under the impact of colonization. Bourdieu
does not imagine that diversity of response, debate, and discord did
not exist in the so-called traditional society. But, at this point, he still
believes in "psychological montages" that determine action and reaction identically in all members of the Kabyle society, a mechanism
that is averse to improvisation and innovation. He admits and tries
to account for variations in social morphology, but admits none in
the "psychological montages." In other words, he had not yet tried

to grapple with the manifestation of the social in the individual and vice versa. It will be the task of the theory of *habitus* to account for the emergence of individual singularities that are acceptable, or at least defensible, within the frames of common sense.

The Theory of *Habitus* and the Authority of "Kabyle Ethnology"

Let us now consider Bourdieu's theory of *habitus* in its most systematic and complete form. Through a close analysis of the principal formulations of the concept, along with some of their variants, one can follow the effects of an already-noted set of tensions, which function both as an antidote to paralyzing dichotomies and as the trace of their persistence: freedom/determinism, subjectivism/objectivism, collectivity/individuality, and conformism/singularity, among others. Determined to find the social in the individual, Bourdieu missed the symbolic productions of these tensions: namely, communicative configurations that can be reduced neither to sets of practices in approximate congruence, nor to cognitive systems, and still less to social structures.

Bourdieu enriches his use of the notion of *habitus* in dialogue with the work of Panofsky, which he translated in 1967 and for which he wrote an afterword. In this text he affirmed that *habitus* is what makes the "creator—artist, thinker—participate in the collectivity of his time and that which orients and directs, unbeknownst to him, his acts of creation which appear the most unique" (1967: 142). Here, *habitus* is practically a synonym for culture, as he had used the latter in his anthropology of Algerian society. Both occupy the semantic field of aptitudes and implicit, inculcated forms of know-how (*savoir-faire*).

Bourdieu developed the theory of *habitus* most fully in *Outline of a Theory of Practice*, which he later further elaborated in *The Logic of Practice*, two great syntheses which drew upon his Kabyle ethnography. Even more significantly for our purpose, the main theoretical discussion in the *Outline* was preceded by the well-known "Three Studies of Kabyle Ethnology" (*Trois études d'ethnologie kabyle*).

Bourdieu's approach is now centered on the agent (Bourdieu prefers this word to *actor*) and his activity, which is considered as sets of practices regulated by principles and forms of action shared by the members of the group. The goals of these actions are configured by prior experience and a *practical sense*, which takes into account the agent's perceptions of socially perceived and sanctioned regularities. *Habitus* is the capacity acquired by the agent to pursue these goals by producing a coordinated set of moves specially tailored to meet them. It is not a matter of either determination or conscious decision, since *habitus* is an unconscious principle that regulates practices according to particular objectives:

> The structures constitutive of a particular type of environment (e.g., the material conditions of existence characteristic of a class condition) produce *habitus*, systems of durable, transposable dispositions, structured structures predisposed to function as structuring structures, that is, as principles of the generation and structuring of practices and representations which can be objectively 'regulated' and 'regular' without in any way being the product of obedience to rules, objectively adapted to their goals without presupposing a conscious aiming at ends or an express mastery of the operations necessary to attain them and, being all of this, collectively orchestrated without being the product of the orchestrating action of a conductor. (Bourdieu 1977: 72)

Bourdieu gives as an example the conditions of existence of a social class. But it is evident that what he says about class holds true for every group *habitus*, and that his model is not one that opposes an individual to society or, inversely, a society to the individual. Old dualisms are both taken up again and short-circuited, the new point of departure being a type of environment that presents itself in the form of socially-structured regularities, and which is available to empirical apprehension. This bypasses the individual/society dichotomy and its various abstract projections, since *habitus* is precisely a principle acquired by everyone, which is formed in and through the life experiences of different groups, and which, in turn, gives form and structure to individual representations and practices. The interiorization of practices and representations by groups of subjects under the same conditions is at the origin of the observable similarities in their actions and of the compatibilities that can be noted between these actions. According to this approach, what is at issue is neither abstract concepts anticipating empirical incarnations nor individuated rational choices whose statistical aggregation delineates laws of action. Such approaches would dissolve the very lived milieu the sociologist seeks to understand. Rather, social life exists in concrete and ordered activities that play out along broad lines, which organize a social field of action, and agentive moves that are inseparable from them.

Thus, Bourdieu proposes a sociology attuned to the ways in which agents put to work (*mise en œuvre*) perceived social exigencies in order to achieve their goals. This evacuates the notion of the self-determining Sartrian subject thrown against the conditions of existence and against other people. It also evacuates interpretations of human action as determined by cognitive structures or as attuned to networks of symbols through which consciousness projects itself. In Bourdieu's formulation, structures and symbolic formations cannot be detached from life such as it is lived—with its stakes, its strategies

and tactics, its gains and losses of material and/or symbolic capital—
and finally, its situations of domination and submission.

Habitus is the product and the producer of real and concrete configurations in which individuals acquire "durable dispositions" that
allow them to act correctly in situations as they present themselves.
These dispositions include principles of transformation capable of
responding to changes in the situations themselves. A degree of organization and coherence is thus given to action because *habitus* is
systematic. At this point, Bourdieu felt he had to justify the word
disposition by stating that it expresses first of all "the result of an
organizing action"—in a sense close to that of *structure*—and that
it also "designates a *way of being*, a *habitual state* (especially of the
body)." Bourdieu further specifies this "state" through terms like
predisposition, tendency, propensity, and *inclination* (Bourdieu 1977:
214n.1). *Habitus* thus seems to arise from the varied circumstances
of sociality and culture—morphologies, institutions, norms, ethos,
etc.—whereas other approaches are based in psychic and cognitive
faculties.

Actions and reactions regulated by *habitus* are done so play-by-play
(*coup par coup*); they are made up of tested formulae that respond in
the immediacy of the moment. It is not a matter of a future conceived
of as an open-ended interval of time in which foreseeable events
will happen, and whose nature and risks one will try to anticipate.
Rather it is a coming future, proximate and preformed by a shared
past. For *habitus* is impersonal. Being a principle of generation and
structuration of practices and representations, which are "collectively
orchestrated without being the product of the orchestrating action of
a conductor," it belongs to no one. It is both mine and also belongs to
everyone. It resembles the Kantian categorical imperative in the sense
that it transcends individual consciousnesses, yet its power remains

unconscious. Bourdieu's agent resembles a transcendental subject, but one that is only seen at work and through concrete practices, including the generative practices of representations. Moreover, given its formation, *habitus* is at the basis of behaviors that tend to reproduce observed regularities, insofar as it presided over the generation of such behaviors over time.

From this point of view one must insist on the fact that the adoption of practices adjusted to specific situations does not result from something like calculation of statistical probability; for in this case, the chances of success of a given action cannot be evaluated ahead of time as they could be in situations in which the factors in play would be under one's control. Rather, the chances of success are apprehended through formulae of a commonly held, semi-formalized wisdom (*sagesse*), correlating to an ethos. For all agents fashioned by the regularities of conduct within a specific form of life, *habitus* works as an immanent law for the selection of *reasonable* acts, and for the exclusion of *mad* ones (*folies*). "History made into nature," *habitus* changes the possible into desire: i.e., that which is both desirable and susceptible of being effectively attained (Bourdieu 1977: 76–80).

Thus, barring a radical rupture of the sort produced by colonial contact in Algeria and elsewhere, *habitus* allows one to resolve new problems by means of an analogical "transfer" (*transfert analogique*) of schemata of judgment and action. Practice, moreover, not only unfolds in concrete conjunctures, but also and above all by the mastered exercise of these analogical transfers. In this way it both conserves its autonomy and shows itself to be simultaneously ready to deal with the difficulties brought about by new situations. Finally, *habitus* does not exclude diversity any more than it does initiative. For it makes possible the improvisation which Bourdieu frequently describes using the metaphor of the game and the player, in the fields of sports, music, or speech (*la parole*). However, these variations occur along the lines of a worldview and, as such, are transposable. This accounts for the existence of differences, which, notwithstanding exceptional cases and suppressed or marginalized deviance, are compatible with common sense:

> *Habitus* could be considered as a subjective but not individual system of internalized structures, schemes of perception, conception, and action common to all members of the same group or class and constituting the precondition for all objectification and apperception: and the objective coordination of practices and the sharing of a world-view could be founded on the perfect impersonality and interchangeability of singular practices and views. (Bourdieu 1977: 86)

Everyone can recognize himself in his practices, and, as such, there is no need to posit a self-transparent, deliberating consciousness. Moreover, *habitus*—the system of internalized structures—is formed through education and socialization, both in the memorization of explicit wisdom that reinforces the group's ethos, and in the education of the body in behavioral schemes. The body's *hexis* and the geometrical body evolve according to a law that is immanent to them in both present and future situations, inasmuch as they are configured within a horizon of practical intention. From this point of view *habitus* can neither be confused with exterior factors that would condition existence nor with models drawn from already-accomplished actions. Thus, for example, rites and myths cannot be reduced to the schematas that structural anthropology develops by separating them into series of already-accomplished actions whose meanings (*sens*) are classed in tables according to the logic of identities and differences. On the contrary, it is necessary to approach rites and myths in the way they play out in time, as institutions of common sense. Bourdieu thus proposes going beyond an analysis of the *opus operatum*—which is to say an analysis of the accomplished action. Instead, he proposes that one study the manner in which actions operate so as to bring to light the effects of time and strategies of action. For him, such an approach eliminates any sense of determinism by transcendental, material, or symbolic factors.

In *The Logic of Practice* Bourdieu takes up the definition of *habitus* in similar terms, all the while considerably broadening his reflections. More particularly, he proceeds to a close analysis of (analogical) transfers, substitutions, and conversions (both total and partial) of embodied schemes and representations. Thanks to a homologating *habitus*, these transfers operate when an agent passes from one domain of activity—from one aspect of life—to another. They chart the logic of practices especially as to how to operate certain conversions of factors from one domain to the other. Examples include questions of land tenure as they relate to marriage and kinship; custom as it relates to and regulates exchanges of gifts and blows, or knowledge linked to the temporal organization of activities; and rituals which give structure and rhythm to the totality of life in *traditional society*. Unlike societies linked to the marketplace, traditional society maintains social ties, according to Bourdieu, by multiplying opportunities for social interaction across a rich calendar of celebrations and rituals.

What governs the formation of identities, differences, and their hierarchies, according to Bourdieu, is analogy—the "principle of production" of mastered practice. It is the result of a forgotten history, of a memory that manifests itself as an ability to actively respond to conjunctures in which situations do not recur identically. *Habitus* is this principle immanent to "general, fuzzy analogies" (*analogies globales, floues*) (Bourdieu 1990: 86–87), which are perfectly useful for the orientation of behavior and practice. Bourdieu thus proposes to replace the structuralist logic of cognitive analogies with the work of practical schemes that structure the field of lived action (and that can in no way be equated simply with the life of the mind).

> Thus one has to move from ergon to energeia (in accordance with the opposition established by Wilhelm von Humboldt), from objects or actions to the principle of their production, or, more precisely, from the fait accompli and dead letter of already effected analogy or metaphor (a : b :: c : d) that objectivist hermeneutics considers, to analogical practice understood as a transfer of schemes that *habitus* performs on the basis of acquired equivalences, facilitating the substitutability of one reaction for another and enabling the agent to master all problems of a similar form that may arise in new situations, by a kind of practical generalization. (Bourdieu 1990: 94)

The advantage of such an approach is that it opens up an immense research project (*chantier*) for the investigation of various specific *habitus* and the comparison of particular histories without falling prey to abstract universalisms, which bracket differences and relations of domination. Consequently, Bourdieu brought to the fore these differences and relations of domination between men and women,[8] *traditional* societies and colonial capitalist ones, Europeans and Algerians, peasants and entrepreneurs. In each case, the research aim is to shed light on the various combinations of the limited number of schemes of perception, judgment, and action, which form *habitus*. Emphatically, such an approach does not ignore the undeniable existence of heterogeneity and differences in choices of action. On the contrary, Bourdieu speaks of innovation and improvisation as compatible in practice, always in a logic of an approximation (*à peu pres*), for "each individual system of dispositions," he writes, "is a structural variant of the others" (1990: 60).

Furthermore, those combinations function in time. In all non-market exchanges (of gifts, words, friendship, mutual assistance, or blows struck during a conflict) the time interval between moments of exchange introduces a characteristic fuzziness to the actions, as well as what one might call an ambiguity of motives (Bourdieu 1990: 106–7). This results, according to Bourdieu, in the nonrecognition of the conditions that form *habitus*. *Habitus*, then, is a generating principle that tends to reproduce the conditions that produced it in misrecognized forms by "inserting them into the structure of a system of symbolic relationships" (Bourdieu 1990: 95). This process escapes the consciousness of agents, for, due to its practical character, it cannot be apperceived through reflexive distance. In these conditions, *habitus*, like a second nature, can "generate all the 'reasonable,' 'common-sense' behaviors" within the limits of objective regularities, which is to say "conditionings" (*conditionnements*) associated with a "particular class of conditions of existence" (Bourdieu 1990: 55, 53). Additionally, the sides that agents may take on one or another occasion are hardly foreseeable in advance or *a priori*, and the unfolding of their actions, although irreversible, can change direction. In Kabyle society—which Bourdieu always invokes as the example of traditionalist society—as elsewhere, actions take place in time and, according to variable strategies, either fulfill or fail to achieve socially acceptable goals.

Philosophical Transpositions and the Ethnography of Kabylia

It is well known that Bourdieu went to Algeria after extended philosophical training. His theoretical reflections are informed by his ethnography, and both of them—in their developments, critiques, and transpositions—draw on a philosophical basis. *Habitus*, in its more precise and refined form, in which it serves as an alternative to the concepts of culture and structure, results partly from a transposition of phenomenology such as it was reworked by Merleau-Ponty, to whom Bourdieu acknowledges a particular debt. Some of Bourdieu's disciples insist that Bourdieu was not only strongly inspired by Merleau-Ponty but surpassed him, since the latter's phenomenology could not be translated into a research program in the human sciences. Others, on the contrary, stress Bourdieu's use of the teachings of Merleau-Ponty on the primacy of one's pre-reflexive and corporeal relationship to the world (an approach that breaks with the prior emphasis on the subject/object relationship as affirmed by idealism and empiricism). The philosopher insisted particularly upon the idea of an embodied, practical intentionality that is anterior to the construction of things as objects of pure knowledge.[9]

Upon closer inspection, however, Bourdieu's transposition of Merleau-Ponty's phenomenology led to results that were, at the very least, ambivalent. To be sure, Merleau-Ponty's reflections on the lived world, embodiment, habit (*habitude*) (Héran 1987: 403–5), and on the perception of one's environment are not unconnected to Bourdieu's notions of *habitus* and *field* (*champ*), the latter being the scene of the deployment of the former. However, the way in which Bourdieu develops these concepts limits the pertinence of phenomenology for ethnography. In particular, *habitus* appears more rigid, and *field* more static and fixed than it would appear in an approach closer to Merleau-Ponty's phenomenological description. Bourdieu's Kabylia and Kabyle tradition appear as excessively closed off and homogeneous, with boundedness and homogeneity being coterminous. And what is missing in the constitution and playing out of *habitus* thus understood are the relations of tension and accommodation between pre-reflexive and reflexive consciousness, the latter being practically absent from Bourdieu's theory and ethnography of tradition.

Bourdieu duly emphasizes bodily postures and the inscription of practice in and by the body as the mode through which tradition is learned and put into practice. This operates in a general sense, for even in Bourdieu's most deterministic formulation one's relationship to the world comes off as a consequence of a corporeal montage (*montage corporel*): it is not a matter of a series of stimuli and responses activated by purely biological mechanisms, nor is it a question of a set of (psychic) associations spurred by the centralized actions of an ego (all the while operating as if the ego did not exist). This embodiment (*corporéité*)—intrinsic, from every perspective, to a subject who is always already in the world—can even be found in Bourdieu's analysis of the Kabyle house, despite the fact that his analysis relies on a structuralist methodology (see Silverstein, this volume). For, in a purely structuralist vision, analogies and their inversions, as well as differences and complementarities, are the work of the mind, whereas Bourdieu links them to the half-rotation (*demi-rotation*) of the body in the physical space of the house. But, if the author is to be believed, this study dates from 1963–64, which is to say the period when he had already introduced the notion of *habitus*.[10]

As theories of *habitus* and *field* became more systematic, the transposition of phenomenology and the difficulties it entailed appeared with more clarity. Merleau-Ponty had in fact given a new direction to the Husserlian *Lebenswelt* by positing the body as the principle of perception, of the self's apperception of the world, and of its social relationships with others. For Merleau-Ponty, the *lived world* is not primarily reflected at the level of an interior intellect; rather, it is immanent to the practical intentions of the subject, and, before any reflexive consciousness, a pre-reflexive consciousness is at work. In this way we are always ahead of our capacity for reflection, already projected in and toward that which we can accomplish. It is this willpower (*pouvoir de volonté*)—instead of the Cartesian *cogito*—which, according to Merleau-Ponty, best defines the human subject; it is the center of acts which are nonetheless always decentered in relation to it. In brief, the world—life in its concrete and corporeal sense—organizes itself according to a particular mode of general coordination and configuration, at the base of which is, first of all, a capacity for doing (*un pouvoir faire*).[11]

Unlike his later sociological works that treat questions of the *habitus* of social class, Bourdieu's Kabyle ethnology takes only group *habitus* into consideration. The question of class does not enter into consideration in the Kabyle ethnology, despite the fact that one's primary *habitus*—that which is formed by socialization during one's earliest education—operates similarly in both cases, producing forms of action in which the possible assumes in practice the characteristics of the desirable, and where transposition is regulated according to compatible criteria of judgment. Bourdieu is aware of differences in rank, wealth, and status in Kabyle society, but this differentiation inscribes itself, according to him, in a common sense, which defines appropriate actions for different situations. In brief, it is a competence that is more or less well acquired through the inculcation in individuals of practices emerging from a homogeneous tradition.

The image that Bourdieu gives of traditional society, with its psychological montages and its absolute conformity to customs, is hardly called into question when he insists on fluidity and variations within the limits of the rules of the game (for example, in his interpretation of practices linked to honor or to marriage). What is more, the flexibility of such limits eludes his attention due to the fact that variabilities in practice and in the meaning of the rules are foreclosed by Bourdieu's image of Kabylia as a virtually closed society. Seen in this way, one must reconsider notions of the feel (*sens*) for the game (paying particular attention to the limits of certainty available in all decisions relating to an action or a strategy) as well as the notion of *field*, in which these games take place, and which they in turn define and redefine. Such a reconsideration would allow one to really conceive of Kabylia as a *field* on the model of a playing field, and to pursue such an analogy to its conclusion, which Bourdieu does not do. In a well-known description, Merleau-Ponty shows that the configuration of the playing field is modified as a result of changes in the players and of the incessant shifts in their perspectives. In other words, if in fact Bourdieu was inspired by the renowned philosopher's phenomenology of *field* and *game*, one must conclude that Bourdieu injected a new type of determinism into it, thus depriving Kabyles, and probably all subjects in general, of an operative reflexivity, as well as of the reflexive distance that they could possibly take with regard to practice. Before going any further in this discussion, let me quote Merleau-Ponty's description:

> For the player in action the football[12] field is not an "object," that is, the ideal term which can give rise to an indefinite multiplicity of perspectival views and remain equivalent under its apparent transformations. It is pervaded with lines of force (the "yard lines," those which demarcate the "penalty area") and articulated in sectors (for example, the "openings" between the adversaries) which call for a certain mode of action and which initiate and guide the action as if the player were unaware of it. The field itself is not given to him, but present as the immanent term of his practical intentions; the player becomes one with it

and feels the direction of the "goal," for example, just as immediately as the vertical and the horizontal planes of his own body. It would not be sufficient to say that consciousness inhabits this milieu. At this moment consciousness is nothing other than the dialectic of milieu and action. Each maneuver undertaken by the player modifies the character of the field and establishes in it new lines of force in which the action in turn unfolds and is accomplished, again altering the phenomenal field. (Merleau-Ponty 1963: 168–69; cf. Bourdieu and Wacquant 1992: 21, 28, 31–32, 53–54, 122, 128; Pinto 1998: 54)[13]

Bourdieu uses the notion of the feel (*sens*) for the game to introduce the idea of improvisation within practical schemas. According to him, *habitus*, being itself a structuring of criteria belonging to the phenomenal world, allows one to make the right move without conscious calculation: *invention without intention*. A player performs more and more sophisticated moves through extensive training, which produces an increasingly refined sense of the rules. For Bourdieu, however, all these possible moves (whether in games of honor or in matrimonial alliances) are limited by social usages (*usages sociaux*) and by the agents' knowledge of such usages. Although no event occasioned in this dynamic ever resembles another event, all events that occur in *traditional society* do, however, reproduce the same game. In all contexts, *habitus* leads to what one might call reproduction.

While Merleau-Ponty describes a game that ceaselessly modifies itself according to the maneuvers that change the perceived dimensions of the playing field, Bourdieu posits that a limit is marked by social utility, which outlines a tradition that has remained more or less *intact*. In any case the anthropologist will seek out this tradition in communities he believes to have preserved it. This is a surprising approach for a researcher, like Bourdieu, who arrived in a society devastated by colonization and an ongoing war of liberation. In his work, Bourdieu cites many examples of violations of norms and of refusals to play the game (or, at the least, of a lack of the feel for the game), including examples of failures to reciprocate gifts, failures to extend proper generosity, and failures to meet certain requirements of honor. These examples, though, are themselves drained of their import through Bourdieu's recurrent usage of them to emphasize the vigor of traditionalist reactions.

Compared to the phenomenology of the playing field during the game such as it appears in Merleau-Ponty's text, the *practice* of the game as presented by Bourdieu, with its social environment structured by *habitus*, appears quite static, and, what is more, is incongruous with the upheavals that he himself describes in his numerous works of Algerian sociology.

It must finally be noted that Merleau-Ponty himself adopts the perspective of a soccer player engaged in a game in which he is, of course, constantly interacting with other players. The essential point here is that in his description, and regardless of whatever takes place between the observation of the game and the writing of the text, the philosopher puts himself in the situation of a game as it was happening, as it was being produced. In other words, he evokes action as an unfolding event. Such an approach is nowhere to be found in Bourdieu's Kabyle ethnography. I will return to this point later, with regard to the phenomenal field; for now, let us return to Bourdieu's *choice* of Kabylia as a field of research. In fact this choice, as well as the problems it entailed, seems to have played a much more decisive role for the development of the theory of *habitus* than that of phenomenology's alleged failure in translating itself into a research program (Pinto 1998: 54).

For a young man and a former student of the Ecole Normale at odds with his profession (*en rupture de banc*), chance no doubt played an important role in the choice of Algeria and Kabylia. Yet, once that choice was made, it seems to have been reinforced by a certain elective affinity between this brilliant intellectual originating from the marginalized peasantry of France and the dominated people of Algeria (see Reed-Danahay, this volume). Bourdieu himself evoked this parallel at a later point in his career (Bourdieu 1976, 1990: 2–3, 15–18, 20–21). It is also noteworthy that his work on Béarn and Algeria overlapped in time and shared common theoretical influences and orientations. Despite all this, though, when viewed in a different light, his career seems nonetheless to follow a well-established tradition from the very beginning, insofar as Kabylia had previously been canonized as a privileged field of inquiry by the Durkheimian school. In this way, one can say that as much as the departure of Bourdieu and others of his generation for Algiers was an event, Kabylia had maintained a fixed position in well-defined academic debates into which new researchers had to find their own points of entry.

Whatever professional assurance Bourdieu's choice of Kabylia could have secured does not, however, suffice to explain it. A certain number of research questions considered as being key at the time also probably oriented the young sociologist-anthropologist. In fact, the institutions of learning and research in which Bourdieu's generation enrolled were rapidly changing, and the questions that then interested researchers principally concerned the status of consciousness in the production of knowledge and the determination of action. In these debates, where philosophy had the last word, the future of industrialized societies—societies physically and morally ravaged by two world wars—was at stake. The development of extermination instruments and their unprecedented levels of implementation in

World War II contradicted humanist professions of faith (Poster 1975: 139, 174–79, 187–93, 201; Bourdieu and Wacquant 1992; Pinto 1998). The confrontation of theories concerning the destiny of these societies, as well as their relations with the non-European societies over which they had established domination, took an even sharper turn in the context of the Algerian war and its political debates, all of which reinvigorated crucial questions concerning the conditions of human knowledge. On the one hand, philosophers challenged Bergsonian intuitionism with its transcendental categories that determine the object of knowledge and the imperatives for action; on the other hand, it was realized that social action did not always conform to this logic. Something else was at work prior to or alongside these philosophical constructions. Human action and history unfolded in ways that did not conform to the image of a rational consciousness transparent to itself. Some philosophers hoped to deduce the impersonal laws governing these processes. They invoked class economies (*économies de classe*), libidinal economies, or logical ones (*logiques d'action*) to uncover the articulated sets of constraints defining the purview of individual wills. Or yet still, others dedicated themselves to an archaeology of human institutions, founded on the principles of a structural economy of the human mind or (from a basis in existential phenomenology) attempted to elucidate major paradoxes and antinomies of the lived world.

When Bourdieu began his career, what was at stake in the opposition between the study of libidinal, intellectual, and material economies, and phenomenological discourse was the relationship between academic power and social mobilization. It was a moment characterized, among other things, by the transformation, broadening, and diversification of institutions of higher learning and research, thus opening the door to new academic entrepreneurs, among

227

whom Bourdieu was without a doubt one of the most determined and active.[14]

In this context where Bourdieu progressively acquired both his vocabulary and analytical instruments, a problematic arose which became increasingly difficult to parse: in becoming his/her own object of study, was woman or man once more caught up in the primary subject/object dichotomy from which all other oppositions flowed? The structuralism of Lévi-Strauss offered a solution to this aporia, or, at the least, a means of obviating it. The solution followed the example of the synthesis of the signifier and the signified in and through the sign, which was conceived of as a product of the human mind in the manner of an *Aufhebung* from which communication, knowledge, and human institutions had derived, and through which they had been organized into viable systems. Bourdieu applied structuralism to Kabylia very early on (Bourdieu 1962: 90–91, 110–11). As already noted, according to him, the diverse ethnic and tribal groups of Algeria constituted variants of a common base (*fond commun*), each group defining itself through assimilation and dissimilation (or, as Lévi-Strauss wrote, an optimal diversity compatible with social cohesion). However, each variant, like Kabyle society or culture, is a system of choices made by no one, but which serves to constitute identities and perpetuate groups. Bourdieu, in places, deployed such structuralist formulations, while, elsewhere, he called upon notions such as the *spirit* (*esprit*) *of a civilization, ethos*, or the deep *intention* of a culture.

The coexistence of such terminologies with those that draw on structuralism indicates the existence in Bourdieu's work of a theoretical space in which structure, the unconscious, and the lived pre-reflexive of Merleau-Ponty cohabit. This cohabitation may have been encouraged by the generous reception which Merleau-Ponty accorded to the work of Lévi-Strauss, and by the well-known influence of Merleau-Ponty on the latter's career.[15] In any case, and at least in the beginning, Bourdieu brought together (*bricole*) Merleau-Pontian phenomenology and a structuralism he would later abandon, transposing the phenomenal field and the *Lebenswelt* with the feel for the game (*le sens du jeu*) and its conditions, the agent, and action in the world (which is not primarily the cognitive world *[le monde pensé]*). It is a global, all-encompassing world insofar as it is immanent to the designs of an operative and always incarnated consciousness—an ego positioned as active body engaged with the world.

It is obvious that the idea of the phenomenal field is not the same as the theory of fields, of their interests, and of their rules of functioning, which Bourdieu would later elaborate on and illustrate in a powerful body of work. But it would be difficult not to see that the theory of fields owes something to the theory of phenomenal fields, where agents, always in concrete situations, occupy the center of analysis. Yet it appears that in his works about tradition, the lived experience (*le vécu*) of these agents had little influence, whereas in his works dealing with the modernity imposed by the colonists, this lived experience informs a greater part of the social world described, even in his most objectivist analyses (Bourdieu 1961, 1962: chap. 6; 1979: chapters 1–2, conclusion; Bourdieu et al. 1963; Bourdieu and Sayad 1964).

In any case, Bourdieu's approach neglected the layering of experiences and the collisions of the pre-reflexive and the reflexive inherent to tradition itself, a phenomenon well described at the time by Jacques Berque (1955, 1962, 1978).

Phenomenal Field, Ethnography, and Disciplinary Division of Labor

Let us now turn to the question of Kabylia considered as a phenomenal field. This will shed some light on the layering of experience and the collision between the reflexive and the pre-reflexive, and will broaden the discussion of ethnography. One possible translation of the phenomenal field into an ethnographic program would require a reconsideration of the metaphor of the playing field and the game. The soccer playing field has agreed-upon, materially marked boundaries, which is not always the case in the ethnographic field (*terrain*). Of course, it is well known that defining the units of ethnographic study has always been problematic: borders are contested, and informants' comings and goings do not resemble the entries and exits of players during the course of a match. Finally, in the case of social formations, the concept of a rule covers both the regularity of a fact's occurrence and the inference of the rule by the participants (as well as by the anthropologist). Unlike the rules of soccer, rules in social formations do not always imply the existence or activity of an authority charged with establishing the rules and making sure that they are respected. At the same time, changes to the phenomenal field in the course of the actions and reactions of the actors is a general condition which one must keep in mind when approaching the study of any social formation as a phenomenal field. In this regard, Kabylia is no different than other regions of the Maghreb or of the world as a whole. Bourdieu's approach, however, misses this dynamic, and, on this point, its problems stem from both the style of ethnography he practiced and the extant disciplinary division of labor between ethnology and Orientalism. The borders between these domains were rarely crossed, with Bourdieu's work being no exception.

Once he introduced the concept of *habitus*, Bourdieu slowly abandoned that of *tradition*. Even the use of the term becomes rare and, significantly, it no longer appears in the indexes of the theoretical works based on the Maghrebi ethnography. These synthetic texts depart from the structural–functionalist approaches that were being applied to societies of the Maghreb at about the same time as Bourdieu was himself writing on Algeria. His method, refusing the delimitations and divisions of colonial social science (except the division between ethnology/sociology and Orientalism), assumed a perspective of proximity and dialogue with Algerians, and Bourdieu's anticolonialist positions are well known. Nevertheless, in his writings, Kabylia appears as an agglomeration of certain traits that obscure others. The agents do indeed make choices, but one sees neither the processes nor lines of fragmentation that modify the meanings of these choices in a lived tradition. Without doubt, the problem was a matter of ethnographic practice.

First of all, Bourdieu seems to have used only two languages to describe Kabylia: Kabyle and French—which is to say, an oral, Berber language (which had, nonetheless, a few texts written in Arabic characters, and a larger number inscribed with the Latin alphabet, thanks to colonial writers), and a scientific language. These hierarchical uses of Berber and French, or of spoken Arabic and French, dominated the ethnography of the Maghreb at the time (with only a few exceptions, notably those of Edmond Doutté and Jacques Berque). In the majority of cases, as with Bourdieu, there was one language of scientific practice and another that is merely used *in practice*.

However, seen as a phenomenal field, and without denying either the primacy of Kabyle or the importance of French, the Kabylia of Bourdieu's time was a society in which at least three languages, if not four (if one considers some form of spoken Arabic) were at play. One had to draw on all these languages locally, in cities, in the French army, and during voyages and migrations. The hierarchy of these eminently spatial and temporal language forms was based on differences in symbolic capital, but this hierarchy was itself only partial, given the amount of play between languages.

231

It is also worth noting that in Kabylia, as elsewhere in the Maghreb, mosques, Qur'anic schools, and (networks of) religious brotherhoods were numerous. To take only one example, the Rahmaniyya *zawiya* was known for its influence in the country. Its founder was Kabyle, trained in Islamic learning in eighteenth-century Algeria and in the famous Al-Azhar school in Cairo. Even today, the written poetry and commentary that initiates to the Rahmaniyya path (*tariqa*) have to learn in Arabic is maintained. Considering the rigor of this discipline that works through the body, the heart, and the mind, one should conclude that a Sufi *habitus* is very different from an everyday *habitus*, the contact between the two having always resulted in some tension. Finally, not far from the villages Bourdieu visited, is another village (At Yenni) which houses a *zawiya* where the writer and anthropologist Mouloud Mammeri and the Islamic scholar Mohamed Arkoun were born (Hanoteau and Letourneux 1873: tome 2, chapters 11–13; Rinn 1884: 530; Robin 1901: 77; Mérad 1967: 59–60, 50n5; cf. de Neveu 1845: chapter 4; Mahé 2001: 46).[16] This was a well-known school of religious science that trained *tolbas* and jurists. One of Mammeri's relatives was, at the beginning of the twentieth century, a fqih and the tutor to the future King Mohamed V.

Tamazight (Berber language) remains, of course, the privileged means of interaction with the lives and imaginations of Kabyles. However, here as elsewhere, Islam had established Arabic as the language of access to the Qur'an and its interpretations and as the language of the canonical five daily prayers. Thus, the Kabylia that Bourdieu demarcated as an object of study was impoverished as a phenomenal cultural field and stripped of its living complexity. This is so not only because of the small importance which Bourdieu accorded to Kabylia's Islamic elements but also because of the fact that, like all regions and social formations, its reality and its limits ought to remain, for the scholar, open-ended questions with no predetermined answers. This is so not only because its languages are not limited to the one most frequently spoken locally, but also because its "tradition" is in fact composed of several traditions. Bourdieu, like many others, notes that there are tensions between Qur'anic law and the customary laws of Kabyle communities, in particular regarding issues of inheritance and rules of succession. In these conditions, it is hard to imagine the participants in a dispute automatically applying one or another legal system without any hesitation as to which system should be used. These differences, and the necessity of reconciling them, have given rise to a rich literature, which has not stopped developing since the first centuries of Islamization, and it is very likely that these efforts will continue in the languages spoken and written by the inhabitants of the Maghreb.

Bourdieu reserves a limited place in his writings for Islam, which he discusses in his first work only to forget about it afterward. He does indeed note that everywhere in North Africa, "It is the atmosphere of Islam which pervades all of life, not only religious or intellectual life, but private, social and professional life" (1962: 108). He remarks that, like every religion, Islam presents several possible profiles, and that, in the end, the profile adopted by a given traditional society is that which best suits its deep culture (*culture profonde*), whether this be in the economic, social, or juridical realms. Laws and rules, ways of living, rites and celebrations thus constitute the explicit expression of culturally sanctioned behaviors and ethos (Bourdieu 1962: esp. 110–13).[17] However, with the exception of a few well-chosen examples—the prohibition of usury, for instance—Bourdieu analyzed North African religion in terms of "levels" (*niveaux*) (animist, naturist, agrarian, orthopractic, and mystical) in order to illustrate the well-known thesis of structural affinities which denotes "the hierarchical integration in each individual of the different levels, the relative importance of which would vary with his way of life, his education, and his aspirations" (1962: 117). Bourdieu had rediscovered this phenomenon of layering, which had been already noted by Berque in his writings, the publication of which had had a large impact (Berque 1955, 1962, 1978). In Bourdieu's works, unlike those of Berque, this hierarchical integration and its variations bracket particular historical configurations as well as their frequent disintegrations. In other words, it sidelines the dynamics whereby culture functions as a field of competing paradigms, conflicts, and accommodations. It is these dynamics that allow for an understanding of the multiple profiles of a tradition, and their changing arrangements (*mises en œuvre*), including the identity claims they may imply or put forward.

Yet Islam played no further role in Bourdieu's writings after *Sociologie de l'Algérie*. The sense of honor, marriage, and the Kabyle house are described independently of their Islamic context. Rather, if we follow Bourdieu, it all seems like there is another culture at play in *practice*, both in terms of the particular domains of practice and the various schemes that structure ritual and daily life. This turn led Bourdieu to some very significant ethnographic choices: for example, only the agrarian calendar is the object of a detailed ethnographic treatment. This is so much the case that instead of basing his analysis on social levels, the arrangement of which and whose hierarchies change as a function of time, Bourdieu's ethnology emphasizes just one level, without any justification for this emphasis. What is more, his approach privileges individuals, most often older males, in whom decision-making powers are concentrated, and who are engaged in struggles for domination. Therefore, one will never know, for example, how women or young people who wish to engage in Qur'anic studies or in mystical vocations position themselves, let alone other individuals such as clients, dependents, and others. Nor can the reader know which facets of Islam intervene in the self-image the latter categories of individuals might have had of themselves.

Given these differences and, one must add, these contradictions, one can dispute Bourdieu's ideas through his own notion of the fuzziness of practical logics. Kabyle identity, like other identities, defines itself also in the interstices, the in-betweens; its exaltation in the "sense of honor" may be significant in the power play among "big men" without having such significance for other social categories. This is so even as the sense of honor may be presented as the primary or exclusive ethos of the group. Furthermore, it is at the margins that discussion, hesitation, and even transgression occur. For example, mysticism, concentrated in religious brotherhoods, both breaks with and complements the family, the lineage, and the tribe. And, in locations and moments of mysticism, reflection, contemplation, and the questioning of customs do occur.

Bourdieu's ethnography hardly allows him to apprehend these dynamics. For to apprehend them it would have been necessary to proceed in two complementary fashions: first, to take into account the elastic character of the boundaries of Kabylia considered as a phenomenal field; second, to try and follow processes of action as they actually occurred—for example, to observe and describe canonical prayers being pronounced at a mosque, supplicants addressing their pleas to a saint, sacrifices, and other rites and ceremonies (linked to work, harvests, etc.) as they unfolded. Instead, Bourdieu makes use of a corpus of information accumulated since the nineteenth century and up until his arrival in Algeria in the 1950s and he supplements this information with a synchronic ethnography focusing on sites where he believed traditions to have been well preserved.

It is not necessary to dwell on the difficulties of reconstituting *traditional society* on the basis of a tradition that has no doubt never stopped traditionalizing itself in relation (and opposition) to Ottoman powers and in the context of wars against French colonialism. More important to the present discussion is the intertwining of temporalities we can see, for example, in the use of several calendars (the agrarian calendar, the lunar calendar, the Gregorian calendar, and other systems for time reckoning) and in the awareness not only of a local past, but also of a larger one that connects Kabyles to a wider world (Maghreb, Islam) (see Goodman, this volume). Needless to say, these contending calendars and pasts cannot be documented from the same types of sources, oral or written. This play of multiple temporalities includes that, for example, which relates eschatological horizons to individual destinies in the reproduction of family, lineage, or tribal formation. Seen in this light, rituals would still illustrate Bourdieu's concept of individual and group strategy; however, they would retain more of their fuzziness because of the diverse temporalities involved in each set of actions. For this reason, the health of the community and the abundance of the harvest would be but one horizon of meaning, and not the only one—as Bourdieu maintains— for the interpretation of ritual.

At this point, it seems clear that Bourdieu's ethnography consists above all in examples of actions that are tailored to the needs of his argument and cited after the fact; in fables, dictums, and proverbs taken from earlier ethnographic works (see Goodman, this volume); and, lastly, in descriptions of facts detached from their particular, time-stamped occurrences. To be sure, Bourdieu did collect testimonies, particularly during his studies of "labour" in peasant communities, in the context of colonial destructuration and forcible relocation. These testimonies do bring forth Algerian voices that express their concerns in their own words. Nonetheless, these testimonies are reported, as noted above, in a synchronic fashion; and, barring those with intellectuals, these valuable pieces of conversation rarely attain the level of an extended dialogue. In this sense, Bourdieu's ethnography inherits the interests and limitations of the ethnography practiced by his colonial predecessors.

Such an ethnographic practice hardly helps consummate the break with intellectualism, which Bourdieu had called for in decisive terms. The principal difficulty lies in the central distinction that Bourdieu introduces between *opus operatum* and *modus operandi*. For if this distinction allows him to come up with a new principle of interpretation, i.e., the meaning of action in practice, insofar as it would differ from a structural or more generally symbolic approach, it is still insufficiently refined to permit an ethnography guided by "the reality principle" of actions as they unfold, with their rhythms, proliferations, unforeseen consequences, condensations, dispersions, and spatiotemporal mediations.

Likewise, as noted above, such an approach is not sufficiently refined to broach questions concerning the layering and hierarchy of languages of work and communication, or concerning the relations between oral and written registers.[18] As an ethnographer, Bourdieu privileged relations of orality, a stance which, even if it does not deny the existence of writing, nonetheless obfuscated the Kabyles' reliance on written texts (and in particular their relation to the Qur'an and its exegeses) and on writing in important domains of their everyday life. It is intriguing that Bourdieu himself reports that the notion of "destiny" is expressed by the colloquial Arabic *mektoub*—that is, "written"—without drawing any conclusion from this on the subject of Maghrebi writing and textuality.

These linguistic "choices," which are perhaps unconscious and are in any case considered to "go without saying," are not unrelated to Bourdieu's choice of groups in which to seek out schemata of tradition. The groups chosen resided far from the central powers and cities associated with writing. Bourdieu, on this point, worked as if the colonial onslaught had not transformed *his* Kabylia. He also seemed unaware that the social fabric of Kabylia's past had to be analyzed for its internal divisions as well as the latter's articulations with external groups and institutions. It is, for instance, well known that some Kabyle tribes paid taxes and tributes to the regency of Algiers and maintained all sorts of relations with it (in particular to guarantee access to the plains and valleys close to centers of command, or accessible to the armies of the power center), while others frequently supplied the regency of Tunis with guards.

Neglecting the intertwining of temporalities as well as spatialities, Bourdieu's ethnographic approach was not able to grasp the historical connections that archives and written chronicles could have furnished. The stories one can draw from the written sources involve Kabyles in large dramas, which influence local evolution and vice versa. Such connections between the local and the global could not be grasped by the sort of ethnography Bourdieu and many others practiced until recently. There is no need at present to dwell on the treasure trove offered by archives of families and power centers as well as other literatures such as chronicles, historiographies, hagiographies, poetry, and song. It is not, of course, a matter of requiring the ethnographer to master all the languages and proficiencies necessary to engage in these fields of inquiry, but rather of simply requiring that she/he be attentive to the fact that these cultural productions provide a larger, more open, and more flexible—not to mention, richer—image of the times and spaces in which all local traditions are sited.

If Bourdieu limited and, to a certain extent, fixed in place the contours of Kabyle culture, this is due to his training and also to the particular strategies he deployed within the academic division of labor and its attendant power relations. In this regard the rarity of conversations between him and Jacques Berque, to cite only one example, seems particularly symptomatic, even though the latter was Bourdieu's elder, predecessor in North African studies, and colleague at the Collège de France. This lack of dialogue is all the more surprising since Berque's work encompasses both the written and the oral, illuminating the one through the other and always seeking out articulations between local histories and what he calls "great history" (*la grande histoire*), so that he moves in this way from the study of texts to uninterrupted encounters with the men and women who employ these textual references and traditional authorities in daily life. The rarity of interchange between the two men, which may have numerous explanations, doubtless indicates the power of the division of academic labor as well as the options that this division could or could not authorize. By limiting himself to a particular, earlier style of ethnographic practice, Bourdieu, who crossed many borders, was not, however, willing or able to cross this particular disciplinary one. Remaining in the enchanted circle of a dominant epistemic legitimacy, he seems to have opted for objects of study that assured him above all else of a choice position in the philosophical and political debates of the European tradition.

Conclusions

The attention Bourdieu gave, from the very beginning, to the moral and political condition of Algerian society ravaged by colonialism and war, and the emphasis he placed on the logic of practice put him squarely in opposition to the anthropological approaches prevalent at the time. These approaches relied either on segmentary mechanics or the structural logics of institutions, as Bourdieu himself did in his early works. In all these approaches, including Bourdieu's elaboration of *habitus*, however, the forms of consciousness implied by (and in) action were bracketed at the start, and thus impossible to reintroduce in the final description and interpretation. Seen from this angle, the concept of *habitus* reveals as much as it conceals. And, besides its productivity, it shows itself to be at least a partial optical illusion.

Bourdieu was in search of a mediation not premised on the relationship between objects and a transcendental subject. He sought to mediate objectivity and subjectivity without positing a sovereign consciousness as the end result of interpretation. The principle of a double critique of the phenomenological assumptions of the anthropologist and those of the people (the lifeworlds that he studies) was proposed by Bourdieu with the aim of finding a new articulation of the object and subject as a foundation for anthropological knowledge.

Bourdieu's *habitus*—together with the conceptual apparatus he built around the notion of *practice*—was elaborated as a response to this need for a new mediation. The question of its pertinence elicited many different and diverging responses. Regardless, the emphasis on *practice* opened new perspectives; it ushered in a productive critical method, distinct from both mechanistic contextualisms and abstract universalisms. This was a new angle from which important realities, which previous methods occluded or silenced, were revealed. Nonetheless, the new and critical position assumed by Bourdieu proved to be both fecund and limited by his ethnographic practice; his conceptual innovations failed to translate into a matching and operational concept of ethnography. The productivity of his theoretical position suffered from the limits of his method.

And, indeed, Bourdieu's approach sheds a new light on human action, guided by an immanent logic. This immanent practical logic—and not an intellectual, abstract logic projected by the researcher's *habitus*—gives global coherence to common sense in its determination of the possible within a structured perception of a specific environment. This common sense works through the body and its inculcated memory, in tune with local institutions. Bourdieu further notes that the latter are less separated from daily life and ritual in "traditional society" than they are in those societies that have been transformed by capitalism. Finally, we owe to Bourdieu a definitive description and interpretation of the radical transformations under colonialism and its modes of domination, as compared to prior modes of domination.

However, beyond these gains, one is forced to note that Bourdieu was unable to remedy the fixity and strict oppositions inherent in his typologies. This is particularly striking in his search for an immutable tradition, which he thought was to be found in Kabylia, as if the latter had not been affected by historical change. More importantly, Bourdieu uncritically combines oral, local "knowledges" with the ethnographies of his colonial predecessors. He was apparently unaware that the "native point of view," as well as the current ethnographic point of view, presented Kabyle forms of life through lenses of immobility and juxtaposition. By approaching his "Kabyle society" as a sort of open-air museum of tradition, Bourdieu seems to have unwittingly worked within the borders of a well-established ethnographic tradition.

This difficulty gravely affects the concepts that organize his "Kabyle ethnology" (*ethnologie kabyle*). Bourdieu claims existential phenomenology, as it was rethought by Merleau-Ponty, as a special source of influence on his work. And, in point of fact, it would be easy to trace back notions such as "field," "game," "feel for the game," "hexis," "regulated improvisation," and so on, to Merleau-Ponty's ideas. The set of concepts grouped around those of *practice* and *habitus* clearly owes something important to a transposition of the latter's phenomenological reflection. However, upon closer inspection, it is clear that Bourdieu does not employ these concepts in the same way as the phenomenology he invokes. For a Merleau-Pontian description would not have permitted Kabylia to be depicted as having rigid and unchanging cultural frontiers, nor would it have permitted the human agent (Kabyle or other) to be viewed as constantly taken by (and in) the game, without imperfections, skepticism, distance, or cynicism. Likewise, while it would be possible to translate Merleau-Ponty's reflection on the body in terms of *habitus*, the price—as one realizes in reading Bourdieu—is heavy. What is missed is the communicative configurations of the human body, which orient the inculcated structures toward signification. And what gets forgotten is that the human body is able to express itself beyond the "montages."

The horizon of expectation is always elastic and changing; thus, a theory of "tradition" and "*habitus*" cannot be purely based on a notion of formulaic inculcation. Society's true elasticity needs an ethnography capable of following its flexibilities and instabilities, attentive to currents (of action and opinion) as they converge in concordances and coalescences, as well as their possible dispersions, divergences, conflicts, and bifurcations. That is to say, this situation requires an ethnography of repetition, "regulated" improvisation, *and*—simultaneously—an ethnography of chance encounter, of nonpredictable events and situations. Bourdieu, unfortunately, limits himself to descriptions of serial practices, presented in static juxtapositions—a procedure that is in tension with his own insistent claim of the need to be attuned to considerations of "strategy" and "time" when it comes to interpreting action. Bourdieu proceeds in the same manner when he reports his personal observations or quotes his interlocutor, or when he uses the ethnography of his predecessors in

242

a manner that is exclusively geared to reinforcing his own claims. In short, Bourdieu too often *illustrates* his theory rather than *uses* it.

Bourdieu's ethnography appears inadequate to the critical and philosophical foundations he claimed it had. This problem affected the manner in which he conducted his research as well as his thinking. This is particularly salient in terms of his consideration of temporality. Bourdieu rightly emphasizes the irreversibility of the sequence of actions, which occur through risk taking and the combination of the past (experiences) with the future (goals) as derived in the present (i.e., the moment in which action is accomplished). But in his work it is hard to find descriptions of actions and processes placed within the real time of their unfolding, i.e., starts, stops, re-starts, changes in pace, changes affecting goals, protagonists, and directions. What is missing is descriptions of processes that include all of their contradictions, their bricolages, their shared white lies, and the many things that must be conveniently forgotten for action to appear coherent.[19]

It is not always possible to be present when processes or actions occur. The point is that to attend to such moments gives the ethnographer a better sense of the time of action and the action of time in the unfolding of meanings. Seen from this angle, narratives of events and biographies become crucial elements of ethnographic work. And chronicles, historiographies, and archives—all involving temporality because of their chronological character and because they are narratives—become part and parcel of the ethnographer's interest. This is not to say that the anthropologist should also be a historian. Rather it is to insist that by witnessing important courses of action as they happen she/he acquires a capability to imagine processes and motives when dealing with reported events she/he did not witness directly.

In the contemporary world—unlike in the past—the anthropologist is faced not with a scarcity of documents reporting situations and events, but, on the contrary, with their excess, given the unprecedented development of mass media archives. And in any case, it is possible to combine the witnessed and the reported in order to describe gestations and evolutions of processes toward consensus or, inversely, toward dispersals and schisms, for both ritualized and nonritualized procedures. This, it would seem, permits us to see the work of chance, invention, as well as moves and tactics well honed by cumulative practice. Such an approach—unlike the one Bourdieu adopted in his "Kabyle ethnology" studies—could have made it possible to make a more valuable and lasting transposition of the paths opened by the existential phenomenology of Merleau-Ponty into a research program.

Does the notion of temporality I suggest here, as an alternative to Bourdieu's, respond well enough to the current predicament of our world—a "world in pieces" (Geertz 2000) characterized by radically intensified circulations of people, goods, and images, in which the future—not the past—seems to shape an elusive present? At first glance, a negative answer appears to be in order, and many anthropologists insist on the confusing and contradictory paths of time in order to deconstruct notions of "culture" and "habitus." Indeed such questioning is all the more warranted given the new global situation of disarray and its massive, disorienting forms of violence. Such a move would have permitted Bourdieu to explore in more depth his well-known notion of "tradition of despair" (tradition du désespoir); instead of equating it with a survivor's will or magic, he would have also glimpsed in it something of a protest (see Colonna, this volume).

Despite the merit of this argument, however, the intense and massive circulation of people, goods, and images itself produces meetings and collisions in which people come together and argue, among other things, in the terms of tradition, culture, lifeworlds, and pasts to which they attach value. In this regard, constructivist approaches cannot do away with the influence of the past on present situations and processes of human encounters. And, indeed, associative collages—the bundling of verbal and iconographic elements—seem to work simply like another illusory device for the mastery of time, by excluding time itself.

For an approach to action as a temporal process, only sustained presence and prolonged interlocution with people can help us produce—in discussion and argument with them—a claim to truthful knowledge, knowledge on which we can rely for an understanding of the current transformation of cultures and societies. The anthropologist may choose to stay in a village or to follow individuals or groups on the move. What is crucial is that within either setting she/he cannot fail to experience the new intensities and unprecedented disorientations at work everywhere. These disorientations destabilize habit and *habitus* and do so for everyone (including the anthropologist); all now scramble to find a handle on things by inventing new lives. Henceforward, it is not only the implicit, the unconscious, or the taken-for-granted-which-eludes-consciousness that best characterize practice, as Bourdieu emphasizes. For even in times of relative stability, the relationship between what remains implicit and what constitutes an explicit norm (for example, regarding the feel for the game) can erupt into discussion, and often enough into conflict between protagonists. These discussions and conflicts evolve toward something that does not fit the two opposed categories of the conscious and the unconscious. In the same manner, this elastic horizon of expectations also imperils Bourdieu's claims regarding congruence and elective affinities, particularly when we consider what Bourdieu took to be a congruence between religion (here Islam) and the social structuring of the environment as perceived by Kabyles and other North African groups. Here again, Bourdieu's excessive schematization plagues his approach to the construction of the conscious and the unconscious and the synthesis he thought he found between them. And, finally, when we consider situations of radical change, it becomes clear that the horizons of expectations are much less easy to circumscribe. The constant reworking of habits results in ephemeral and unstable configurations of relations that are difficult to decipher. It also forces people into contradictory and unstable positions, which extend from retreats into self and identity, through case-by-case accommodations, all the way to violence.

It is quite telling that the ethnography of discourses, which Bourdieu presents in order to illustrate the work of *habitus*, remains essentially an ethnography of repetition and not (for obvious reasons) an ethnography of discussion, dispute, *quid pro quo*, or accommodations. Witnessing so radical and costly a situation as Algeria under colonialism and war, Bourdieu should have privileged the second type of ethnography. I am not suggesting that anthropologists should ignore the repetitive or the processes of "making virtue of necessity" that Bourdieu made famous. However, it would be more appropriate to speak of plural necessities and virtues. And we should not exclude from *practice* such practices as intellection and contemplation, nor bets and investments that do not provide a return, as Bourdieu does.

The ethnographic encounter would thus again become what it has been for a number of innovative anthropologists interested in transformative dynamics. Without necessarily positing the possibility or the impossibility of synthesis as a matter of principle, the researcher would focus on the inconsistent, contradictory, and difficult-to-organize situations that come her way, in her relationships with

PHENOMENOLOGY AND ETHNOGRAPHY

her interlocutors. Avoiding nonoperative dialectics, the success of which has often proven to be an illusion, it would become possible to revisit spaces of heuristic tension between subjectivity and objectivity. Through a rapprochement of the two, the anthropologist would describe how the one participates in the other, rather than invoke, as Bourdieu does, an interiorized scheme like *habitus*, which functions only as a miraculous *Aufhebung*, and is in no way amenable to description. Anthropology would rediscover the rich and exciting inspirational space of ambiguities and paradoxes. And the anthropologist would develop a sensitive organ for detecting counterfeits that pass as certainties. It would make our work more difficult but probably more rewarding. Such a prospect, instead of being feared, should be wished for. It would authorize a continual reconsideration of our knowledge as a palimpsest and transform forgotten ideas into the means for innovation.

Notes

I greatly thank Mohamed Cherkaoui both for having brought François Héran's excellent article to my attention and for his valuable remarks. I would also like to thank Francis Afergan for his advice and encouragement. Paul Silverstein's help with the translation was gracious and crucial. I want to thank them for it. I owe a special debt of gratitude to Leo Coleman for his several remarks, which greatly helped clarify my ideas, and for his very attentive editing of the text. I would like to thank Gabriela Drinovan for her help in bringing this text to completion.

1. Pierre Bourdieu's theories have been the subject of many discussions among anthropologists, sociologists, and specialists in other disciplines. However, his anthropological work in Algeria, and particularly on Kabylia, has been relatively little discussed.

Camille Lacoste-Dujardin writes about *habitus* and of "the nature of anthropological description" in Bourdieu's work (Lacoste-Dujardin 1976a: 108), noting that Bourdieu "questions the nature of an anthropological description which must account for the way in which a [cultural] model is lived." One can interpret this passage in two ways: either in reference to the level at which anthropological reflection on action and agent operates, which is the level at which the question of "praxological knowledge" relates to "phenomenological knowledge" and "objectivist knowledge"; or, conversely, one could interpret Lacoste-Dujardin's statement as referring to phenomena to be observed and communication among members of the group to be approached, in which case one is dealing with phenomenological knowledge proper to that group—that is, the spontaneous ways of acting (*manières de faire*), the order in which such actions occur, and group members' views on these actions and their order. The two levels of analysis distinguished here are of course related, but the lack of distinction in the formula used by Lacoste-Dujardin renders the discussion awkward to the point that, in her article, the theory of ethnography itself (which would have been adequate to Bourdieu's project) is not truly discussed—and neither (from an ethnographic point of view yet again) is the theory of "fields" as it relates to that of "*habitus.*" In this article, as elsewhere (1976a and 1976c), Lacoste-Dujardin notes the contradiction between, on the one hand, an ethnography that is static and inadequate and, on the other hand, Bourdieu's studies of social transformation. However, when she writes of Bourdieu's exigency to break with presuppositions (with reference to *Outline of a Theory of Practice,* Lacoste-Dujardin 1976a: 105–6) and when she discusses this in relation to concepts emerging from the colonial period, she speaks only of their inadequacy for a new, postcolonial period, forgetting their inadequacy for colonial situations. In addition, according to her, an anthropologist needs to account for such questions of reflexivity and historical rupture "after having accumulated the data" (105)—a rather perplexing proposition.

Alain Mahé essentially worked with secondary sources in colonial archives (Mahé 2001). He claims to reconstruct a sort of "blueprint of village organization" such as it existed before colonial occupation. He also often refers to what he calls "our observations" without elaborating.

Mahé discusses *habitus* in a section of his book dealing with the protection accorded to men by women in certain cases where a man is engaged in conflict by another man. He presents this custom of protection as a transgression of the norms of virility, honor, and *horma* (shame), and thus of *habitus* itself, all the while affirming that this practice "verifies, on the contrary, and somewhat *a contrario* the validity of the model elaborated by Bourdieu" (113). Subsequently, the author contends that the case of protection given by a woman signals a rift (*division*) that the society must confront, a rift that cannot be accounted for or overcome by mythico-ritual practices. In light of this, he concludes with several rather vague propositions on the incompleteness (*inachèvement*) of societies and on their phantasms, before returning to the well-known trope of woman as an intrusion of nature into culture (113–14).

Putting aside the relative paucity of ethnographic data on this custom, the argument fails to mention that the valence of the gendered terms varies according to situational changes (for example, when one either enters or leaves a house, as Bourdieu notes in describing the Kabyle house). Mahé, following Bourdieu in failing to note the diversity and radical transformation of habitat in Kabylia, writes of "*the* Kabyle house." Most importantly, he fails to mention that, since the social hierarchy includes the feminine universe within a more general masculine order, everything still resides within the bounds of culture. Furthermore, the author draws no conclusion from the fact that, in this particular practice of protection, it is the men who are actually fighting. Finally, nothing is said of what happens to the protected man's subsequent status in the community.

Lahouari Addi, for his part, writes relatively briefly of the concept of *habitus* (Addi 2002: 121). He does not discuss Bourdieu's ethnographic practice and its consequence on the image of Kabylia. He quickly calls into question the limited attention Bourdieu accords to Islam, but without drawing any conclusions from this.

Habitus has also been widely discussed by American anthropologists (cf. Ortner 1984: 126–66). Sherry Ortner's critiques of *habitus* are echoed in the works of others who fault Bourdieu for ignoring the difficult-to-define category of "human agency" (autonomy, initiative, liberty, etc.). One example is Jean Comaroff's discussion of reappropriation (1985: 5, 54, 125, 263, and 200, in a way close to de Certeau [1990]). For a reflection on *habitus* as it relates to the process of change in a Moroccan community, see Ilahiane (2001: 380–94).

2. In a photo-essay on Algeria from the time, there are photos of cities and villages and of men and women engaged in different activities.

In his posthumously published *Esquisse pour une auto-analyse* (2004), Bourdieu reflects on his trajectory. He notes, at the start, that "this is not an autobiography," a remark that sounds rather like a Freudian "rebus." Bourdieu gives some details about his career, beginning with his joining the army after he succeeded the difficult final exam of French *aggregation*. Called to military service around 1955–56, he joined the second class of soldiers, refusing the officer rank. Bourdieu writes that he was sent to serve at the colonial *Gouvernement Général d'Algérie* (Algiers). He mentions that it is there where he wrote his *Sociologie de l'Algérie* (published in 1958).

Bourdieu claims he was trying to inform the intellectual French world about a situation that he confronted as a "powerless witness of an atrocious war" (2004: 57). After military service Bourdieu accepted a job as assistant professor at the University of Algiers. From there he conducted his fieldwork "taking photographs, conducting systematic observations and *stolen* [my emphasis] recordings of conversations in public spaces, administering tests in schools, conducting discussions in social centers" (64). Bourdieu also writes that he collected narratives of torture (66) in a monk's cell (among the Pères Blancs) and at the tip of the Algiers jetty.

3. In a very enlightening and detailed article, François Héran (1987: 403) notes that for Bourdieu, phenomenology is "always present in the background and nonetheless regularly singled out as a target"; he also states that Bourdieu follows the path of phenomenology only to doubly "reject mechanism and intellectualism" and install a third, mediating term, "the theory of practice," against objectivist (which is to say, structuralist) and subjectivist (which is to say, phenomenological) modes of knowledge.

Héran (1987: 403–5) also devotes a section of his article to Merleau-Ponty. He shows that the latter's attempts at going beyond the idealism/empiricism opposition, his analyses of *habitudes*, and the expressive and projective powers of the body all prefigure the work of Bourdieu.

I agree with Héran on these points, although in the present article I am limiting myself to examining the transformation of Merleau-Ponty's phenomenology by the type of ethnography that informs Bourdieu's writings.

4. On the theory of segmentarity, see Evans-Pritchard (1940). For its applications to the Maghreb, see in particular Favret-Saada (1966, 1968), Gellner (1969, 1970, 1981), and Jamous (1981). For a critique of the theory of segmentarity and notably of its application by Gellner, see Hammoudi (1974, 1980). On the views of Favret-Saada, see Mahé (2001: 121). Durkheim's use of the work of Masqueray and data on Kabylia collected by Hanoteau and Letourneux is well known. See Lucas and Vatin (1975: 47) and Valensi (1984: 234–36).

5. On "the recurring use of *habitus* as it originates in schemes of *mediation* and *substitution*" see Héran (1987: 393, 403).

6. The concept of *habitus*, as well as the word itself, had already appeared in Bourdieu's article, "Célibat et condition paysanne" (Bachelorhood and the Peasant Condition), reprinted in Bourdieu 2002. Contrary to what Talal Asad affirms (Asad 1993: 75n20), Bourdieu used the terms *habitus* and *hexis* with reference to the famous article of Marcel Mauss on "body techniques."

7. See also Bourdieu and Sayad (1964: 154, 159) where the authors speak of the "language of the body" and of the destruction of spatial and temporal coordinates, respectively.

8. On this dichotomy, see Bourdieu (1990: 280–83) or the text on the Kabyle house in Bourdieu (1972).

9. The first point of view is affirmed by Louis Pinto (1998: 28–29); the

second point of view had been affirmed several years earlier by Loïc Wacquant (Bourdieu and Wacquant 1992: 20–21).

10. The study of the Kabyle house was published for the first time in 1970 in a volume dedicated to Lévi-Strauss. It reappeared in the French edition of the *Outline*. Bourdieu, however, actually wrote it in 1963–64 (Bourdieu 1972: 59).

11. All of this is now well known, and corporeality is Merleau-Ponty's central theme in his *Phénoménologie de la perception* (1942: chapters 4–6, esp. 235–39). On practical intentions—the "I can" (*je peux*), etc.—see Merleau-Ponty (1942: 160, 452).

12. Merleau-Ponty is obviously describing soccer.

13. Bourdieu only later recognized the particular role that Merleau-Ponty played in the development of his ideas (Bourdieu 1987: 15); he cites the latter's work parsimoniously in the *Esquisse* (1972: 246n.24) and *The Logic of Practice*. Bourdieu did not cite the fragment on the football match.

14. On the diversification of academic institutions, see Pinto (1998: chapter 1), and on Bourdieu and his sense of enterprise, see the work of his former professor, Raymond Aron (1993).

15. In addition to supporting the election of Lévi-Strauss to the Collège de France, Merleau-Ponty wrote favorably about *The Elementary Forms of Kinship* (cf. Merleau-Ponty 1964). Note also that Lévi-Strauss's *The Savage Mind* (1966: v) is dedicated to Merleau-Ponty.

At one point, Merleau-Ponty was interested in the structuralist linguistics of Saussure. See the 1964 volume cited above and Eddie (1971, 1981). The question is well studied, although the direction of the whole enterprise is not always convincing.

16. On Taourirt Mimoun and its school, see Arkoun (1990, 1998: 40). On the poem in question, the *Livre de la Rahmaniya*, interpreted by *Livre des dons de Dieu*, see El-Qostantini (1946).

17. In his studies of the "religious field" (*le champ religieux*), Bourdieu, as elsewhere, draws upon the work of Max Weber. See Bourdieu (1971a, 1971b).

18. I am of course not implying that ethnographers must learn all the languages which circulate in the "field" (*terrain*). Bourdieu and others were indeed right to privilege Kabyle, Shawiqa, and other varieties of Tamazight (Berber). However, one must also account for writings in Arabic; to do this, it would have been possible to work with literate bilingual or trilingual interlocutors (with, for example, someone who spoke Kabyle, Arabic, and French). One must also be attentive to situations of oral bilingualism, where, for example, people pass from Tamazight to spoken Arabic and vice versa.

19. I have tried this approach in my *Victim and Its Masks* (1997).

Works Cited

Addi, Lahouari. 2002. *Sociologie et anthropologie chez P. Bourdieu. Le Paradigme anthropologique kabyle et ses conséquences théoriques*. Paris: La Découverte.

Arkoun, Mohammed. 1990. Hommage à Mouloud Mammeri. *Awal* 6–7.

———. 1998. Le message de Mouloud Mammeri. *Awal* 18.

Aron, Raymond. 1993. *Mémoires*. Paris: Juillard.

Asad, Talal. 1993. *Genealogies of Religion*. Baltimore: Johns Hopkins University Press.

Berque, Jacques. 1954. Qu'est-ce qu'une tribu nord africaine. In *Eventail d'histoire vivante. Hommage à Lucien Elbure*. Paris: A. Colin.

———. 1955. *Structures sociales du Haut Atlas*. Paris: PUF.

———. 1962. *Le Maghreb entre deux guerres*. Paris: Seuil.

———. 1978. *L'Intérieur du Maghreb*. Paris: Gallimard.

Bourdieu, Pierre. 1958. *Sociologie de l'Algérie*. Paris: PUF.

———. 1961. Révolution dans la révolution. *Esprit* (January): 27–40.

———. 1962. *The Algerians*, trans. Alan C. M. Ross. Boston: Beacon Press.

———. 1971a. Genèse et structure du champ religieux. *Revue Française de Sociologie* 12 (3): 294–334.

———. 1971b. Une interpretation de la théorie de la religion selon Max Weber. *Archives Européennes de Sociologie* 12: 3–21.

———. 1972. *Esquisse d'une théorie de la pratique*. Geneva: Droz.

———. 1976. Les conditions générales de la production sociologique: Sociologie coloniale et décolonisation de la sociologie. In *Le Mal de voir*, ed. Henri Moniot. Paris: Union Générale d'Edition.

———. 1977. *Outline of a Theory of Practice*, trans. Richard Nice. Cambridge: Cambridge University Press.

———. 1979. *Algeria 1960*. Cambridge: Cambridge University Press.

———. 1987. *Choses dites*. Paris: Minuit.

———. 1990. *The Logic of Practice*, trans. Richard Nice. Cambridge: Polity Press.

———. 2002. *Le bal des célibataires. Crise de la société paysanne en Béarn*. Paris: Seuil.

———. 2004. *Esquisse pour une auto-analyse*. Paris: Raisons d'Agir.

Bourdieu, Pierre, Alain Darbel, Jean-Pierre Rivet, and Claude Seibel. 1963. *Travail et travailleurs en Algérie*. Paris: Mouton.

Bourdieu, Pierre and Abdelmalek Sayad. 1964. *Le Déracinement. La Crise de l'agriculture traditionnelle en Algérie*. Paris: Minuit.

Bourdieu, Pierre and Loïc D. Wacquant. 1992. *An Invitation to Reflexive Sociology*. Chicago: University of Chicago Press.

Cherkaoui, Mohamed. 2006. *Le Paradoxe des conséquences*. Paris: Presses Universitaires de France.

Comaroff, Jean. 1985. *Body of Power, Spirit of Resistance*. Chicago: University of Chicago Press.

de Certeau, Michel. 1990. *L'Invention du quotidien, I Arts de faire*. Paris: Gallimard.

de Neveu, Edouard. 1845. *Les Ordres religieux chez les Musulmans d'Algérie*. Algiers: Jourdan.

Dortier, Jean-François. 2002. Les idées pures n'existent pas. *Sciences Humaines* numéro spécial (1).

Eddie, James. 1971. Was Merleau-Ponty a Structuralist? *Semiotica* 4: 297–323.

———. 1981. The Meaning and Development of Merleau-Ponty's Structuralism. In *Merleau-Ponty: Perception, Structure, Language*, ed. John Sallis. pp. 39–57. Atlantic Highlands: Humanities Press.

El-Qostantini, Sheikh Mustapha Bakhtarzi. 1946. *Livre de la Rahmaniya, traduit par le Livre des dons de Dieu*, trans. Reverend Father Antoine Giacobetti des Pères Blancs. Algiers: Maison Carrée.

Evans-Pritchard, E. E. 1940. *The Nuer*. Oxford: Clarendon Press.

Favret-Saada, Jeanne. 1966. La segmentarité au Maghreb. *L'Homme* 6 (2).

———. 1968. Relation de dépendance et manipulation de la violence en Kabylie. *L'Homme* 8 (4).

Geertz, Clifford. 2000. The World in Pieces: Culture and Politics at the End of the Century. In *Available Light: Anthropological Reflections on Philosophical Topics*. pp. 218–64. Princeton: Princeton University Press.

Gellner, Ernest. 1969. *Saints of the Atlas*. London: Weidenfeld and Nicholson.

———. 1970. Pouvoir politique et fonction religieuse dans l'Islam marocain. *Annales* 25 (3): 699–713.

———. 1981. *Muslim Society*. Cambridge: Cambridge University Press.

Hammoudi, Abdellah. 1974. Segmentarité, stratification sociale, pouvoir politique et sainteté. *Hesperis Tamuda*.

———. 1980. Sainteté, pouvoir et société. *Annales E.S.C.* 35 (3–4).

———. 1997. *The Victim and Its Masks*. Chicago: University of Chicago Press.

———. 2000a. Pierre Bourdieu et l'anthropologie du Maghreb. *Prologues* 19 (reprinted in *Awal* 21, 2001).

———. 2000b. La construction de l'ordre et l'usage de la science coloniale, Robert Montagne penseur de la tribu et de la civilisation. In *La Sociologie musulmane de Robert Montagne*, ed. F. Pouillon and D. Rivet. Paris: Maisonneuve.

Hanoteau, Adolphe, and Aristide Letourneux. 1872–73. *La Kabylie et les coutumes kabyles*. Paris: Imprimerie Nationale.

Héran, François. 1987. La seconde nature de l'habitus. *Revue Française de Sociologie* 28 (3): 385–416.

Ilahiane, Hsain. 2001. The Social Mobility of the Haratin and the Reworking of Bourdieu's Habitus on the Saharan Frontier of Morocco. *American Anthropologist* 103 (2): 380–94.

Jamous, Raymond. 1981. *Honneur et Baraka*. Paris: Presses de la Maison des Sciences de l'Homme.

Lacoste-Dujardin, Camille. 1976a. A propos de P. Bourdieu et de *l'Esquisse d'une théorie de la pratique*. *Hérodote* 2 (2): 103–16.

———. 1976b. Changement et mutation à travers quelques rites paysans de l'Algérie nouvelle. In *L'Autre et l'ailleurs. Recueil d'études offertes à Roger Bastide*. Paris: Berger-Levrault.

———. 1976c. *Un Village algérien*. Alger: SNED.

———. 1995. Rôles féminins et rôles masculins en changement à travers l'observation de deux rituels sacrificiels en Kabylie. *Annuaire de l'Afrique du Nord* 33.

Lévi-Strauss, Claude. 1966. *The Savage Mind*. Chicago: University of Chicago Press.

Lucas, Phillipe, and Jean-Claude Vatin. 1975. *L'Algérie des anthropologues*. Paris: Maspero.

Mahé, Alain. 2001. *Histoire de la Grande Kabylie XIXe–XXe siècles*. Paris: Bouchène.

Mérad, Ali. 1967. *Le Réformisme musulman en Algérie de 1925 à 1940*. Paris: Mouton.

Merleau-Ponty, Maurice. 1942. *Phénoménologie de la perception*. Paris: Gallimard.

———. 1963. *The Structure of Comportment*, trans. Alden L. Fisher. Boston: Beacon Press.

———. 1964. *Éloge de la philosophie et autres essais*. Paris: Gallimard.

Ortner, Sherry. 1984. Theory in Anthropology Since the Sixties. *Comparative Studies in Society and History* 26 (1): 126–66.

Panofsky, Erwin. 1967. *Architecture gothique et pensée scolastique*, trans. Pierre Bourdieu. Paris: Minuit.

Pinto, Louis. 1998. *Pierre Bourdieu et la théorie du monde social*. Paris: Albin Michel.

Poster, Marc. 1975. *Existential Marxism in Postwar France: From Sartre to Althusser*. Princeton: Princeton University Press.

Rinn, Louis. 1884. *Marabouts et khouan. Etude linguistique et ethnologique*. Algiers: Jourdan.

Robin, Colonel. 1901. *L'insurrection de la Grande Kabylie en 1871*. Paris: H. Charles-Lavauzelle.

Valensi, Lucette. 1984. Le Maghreb vu du centre, sa place dans l'école sociologique française. In *Connaissances de Maghreb*, ed. Jean-Claude Vatin. Paris: CNRS.

Afterword

Re-reading Bourdieu on Kabylia in
the Twenty-first Century

DALE F. EICKELMAN

Bourdieu's *Esquisse*, when it first appeared in French in 1972, appealed to many as more conceptually compelling and ethnographically specific than the social theory then offered by Talcott Parsons, Anthony Giddens, and Alain Touraine—although its major impact had to await its translation into English (see Eickelman 1979). Bourdieu's essays on time and space, kinship and genealogical knowledge, and strategies of reciprocity in Algeria's Kabyle region evoked the main currents of sociological thought as embedded in such distinguished predecessors as Emile Durkheim and Marcel Mauss.

Bourdieu, North Africa, and *Habitus*

At the same time, Bourdieu offered the promise of social theory grounded in ethnographic and historical specificity, explaining the dynamics of rapid and massive social and cultural change as effectively as the seemingly stable and enduring elements of culture and society that still formed the core of mainstream social anthropology. Together with Ernest Gellner's *Saints of the Atlas* (1969) and Clifford Geertz's *Islam Observed* (1968), *Outline* reintroduced ethnographic examples from North Africa to anthropology's conceptual map. In retrospect the North African ethnography of the 1960s and 1970s did not become as central to social anthropology as did the ethnography of the Nuer, Tikopia, and the Trobriands for an earlier generation, but it contributed significantly to bringing North African ethnography into the anthropological mainstream.

All of the contributions to this volume explore the ways in which Bourdieu's key concepts, including *habitus*, have been points of reference for subsequent social research. *Habitus* designates for Bourdieu "a system of lasting, transposable dispositions which, integrating past experiences, functions at every moment as a *matrix of perceptions, appreciations, and actions* and makes possible the achievement of infinitely diversified tasks" (1977: 83). The concept is hard to pin down and is best seen as an effort to "communicate a certain theoretical stance" (Brubaker 1993: 216–17) using intellectual strategies that varied according to the empirical context in which they were employed. Unlike the ahistorical structuralism dominant in France at the time of his writing, Bourdieu's concept of *habitus* enveloped both structure and historical practice (Eickelman 1979: 387–88) and emphasized both history and "the material practicality of social concerns, even in the realm of culture" (Calhoun 1993: 62–63). The scope of Bourdieu's work, encompassing among many other subjects education, museums, social class, and masculinity, suggests a lifelong intent to apply his concepts of social thought to explain social practice and to relate them to the immediacies of social life.

Another contextual meaning of *habitus* is "the durably installed generated principle of regulated improvisations" (1977: 78) and— somewhat opaquely—"the product of history [which] produces individual and collective practices, and hence history, in accordance with the schemes engendered by history" (1977: 82). *Habitus* provides the link between what Bourdieu considers "objective" structures and the cognitive structures that they produce and that tend to reproduce them. Thus the Kabyle peasant "does not react to 'objective conditions' but to the practical interpretation which he produces of these conditions, and the principle of which [are] the socially constituted schemes of his *habitus*" (1977: 116). *Habitus*, writes Bourdieu, provides "an endless capacity to engender products—thoughts, perceptions, expressions, actions" (1977: 88). It also delineates specific social groups and classes, so that Bourdieu defines class consciousness as "the direct or indirect possession of a discourse capable of securing symbolic mastery of the practically mastered principles of the class *habitus*" (1977: 83). If the earlier use of the term *habitus* by Norbert Elias (1996) pointed to the shared background understandings of a people or a nation in a general sense, Bourdieu shaped it into a strong sociological concept.

One of Bourdieu's last publications, "Participant Objectivation" (2003), returns full circle to a theme implicit in his early work on Kabylia and to reflections on his natal village in Béarn—how an ethnographer immerses oneself in a social activity or ceremony while at the same time taking part, at least as a watcher, in the experience. For all that has been written on Bourdieu, it remains surprising that the present volume is the first to offer sustained reflection on his studies of Algeria—what was included and omitted in his accounts of Kabyle society and the implications of his approach, both for how it represents Algerian society and for how it illuminates Bourdieu's evolving approach to social theory.

Sociology as Contact Sport

In this respect, Fanny Colonna (this volume) makes a vital and unique contribution to this book. If other scholars have offered an overall sense of French sociology in the 1970s (Lemert 1981) and Bourdieu's role in twentieth-century European social thought (Calhoun 1993), Colonna offers a perspective that is simultaneously Algerian and French—sharply attuned to both the French academic and public fields in which Bourdieu primarily situated his work. She studied with Bourdieu in Algeria in the 1950s and later in Paris, and he supervised her dissertation (Colonna 1975). At the time of Algeria's independence she was one of the few French residents to opt for Algerian citizenship, and she remained in Algeria in both research and teaching capacities until the early 1990s when the increasingly hostile political situation made it impossible for her to stay.

Colonna's stunning metaphor—characterizing Bourdieu's approach to the social sciences: like a contact sport—suggests why his work has a highly accidental quality. She is not the only contributor to this volume who points out that Bourdieu's actual use of ethnography, in his case derived largely from statistical surveys and field interviews, was conducted in resettlement centers (*centres de regroupement*) at the height of the Algerian conflict. Bourdieu's earlier writings on topics such as time and the Kabyle household do not make this context clear. The overall image projected in *Outline* is that of a seemingly timeless village and domestic social organization. The result is a sharp disjuncture between theoretical claims and ethnographic reporting, notwithstanding the promise of *habitus*.

Thus Bourdieu's statement in *Le Déracinement* (1964) that Algerian peasants were radically deprived excludes a presentation of peasant cultural resources—both oral and written. It also discounts Kabyle capacity for reflexivity concerning both past and present. Nor does it adequately account for the pervasive European presence in Algeria and the growing impact of relations between Algerians— Berber, Arab, and Jewish—and settlers. Colonna argues that Algerian peasants are portrayed as virtually out of time and uninfluenced culturally either by the European presence or by a savage war that resulted in as many as a million deaths. Colonna's own approach to Algerian society, particularly her study of teacher training from the 1880s until the eve of the Second World War (Colonna 1975), shows how in historical context the French incrementally abandoned the notion of equality of Algerians and French as citizens in favor of a system of de facto separation and subordination, valuing those natives who "knew their place," undervaluing their culture of origin and knowledge of French norms, but not assuming equality or equal competence.

The Written and the Spoken Word

There is a certain parallel between Edmund Leach and Pierre Bourdieu in their use of ethnography. Leach, having lost his field notes in the Second World War, wrote in *Political Systems of Highland Burma* (1964: 1) that his "originality" was not to be found in the facts with which he dealt, "but in the interpretation of the facts," smoothing over the dearth of specificity. Colonna notes that Bourdieu, for his part, kept no field notes, claiming that they were precluded by the "urgency" of the times in which he worked. He emphasized a "structural misrecognition" that, as several contributors note, is situated outside of time, invoking the often dramatically altered historical and political circumstances only in the abstract.

One consequence of Bourdieu's approach has been to pass over the significance of a written religious and secular tradition in Kabylia. To shed light on Bourdieu's approach, Colonna points to a published conversation between him and the Algerian novelist Mouloud Mammeri (1917–89). Mammeri had an advanced degree in Hellenic studies from the University of Algiers and thus strongly represented

French intellectual influence on Algerian society. Yet throughout the interview, Bourdieu emphasized Kabylia's oral tradition at the expense of a written tradition in Arabic and, since the nineteenth century, in French, in spite of the fact that Mammeri repeatedly invoked images of this written tradition and frequent analogies with classical antiquity.

For Bourdieu, Kabyle "culture" was almost mechanically reproduced through *habitus*. Mammeri emphasized how the professional poets in Algeria (as in Morocco's Berber highlands) vividly evoked images of emigration, military conscription, and schooling under the French. Despite the continuing political turmoil in Algeria—the 1970s was as tumultuous a decade as the preceding two—Colonna notes that Bourdieu has an almost Lévi-Straussian disregard for the impact of this political change and how the Kabyles themselves thought of these developments. Although the French translation of Jack Goody's seminal *The Domestication of the Savage Mind* (1977) was published in a series that Bourdieu directed, the implications of Goody's approach to literacy did not lead Bourdieu to rethink his own position beyond referring in a note to how his "Durkheimian" approach led him to underestimate the role of Kabyle poets or religious scholars in "cultural production."

In general Bourdieu hardly broaches the impact of writing on Kabyle society. Bourdieu's work centers on domination, but does not adequately account for the diverse views of Algerian actors themselves. His work from the 1960s onward broke from the formal structuralism of Lévi-Strauss, but its view of the social, heavily focused on relationships of domination, closed the door to exploring how Algerians themselves saw their society and struggled among themselves to interpret and reshape it.

Like Colonna, Hammoudi also emphasizes how Bourdieu's notion

of "traditional" Kabyle society is based on the idea of a homogeneous and unchanging society that leaves little room for ambiguous
or atypical individuals. Moreover, as Bourdieu develops the notion
of *habitus*, it replaces the idea of "tradition" in his thought. *Habitus*
is collectively orchestrated, but without an orchestra conductor in
place. As several contributors underscore, the Kabyle "misrecognition" of their political and economic circumstances as represented by
Bourdieu allows *habitus* to reproduce itself. Individuals are important only in enforcing conformity to expected ways of doing things
and interpreting events. Yet Hammoudi points out that Bourdieu's
Kabylia is a peculiar place: the influence of Islam, so important to
other observers and to many Kabyle intellectuals, is almost entirely
absent, and the only languages present are Tamazight (Berber) and
French, not spoken and written Arabic. As many Kabyle intellectuals indicate, however, both Sufism and religious lodges (*zawiya*s) are
important in Kabyle society and in Kabyle representations of self and
community. It is as if, Hammoudi writes, Edmund Leach were to have
written of the Kachin highlands leaving out any mention of lowland
social organization. Bourdieu's Kabyle society remains within the
philosophical and political debates of the European tradition.

Social Theory and Social Context

Jane Goodman (this volume) deals with a central paradox of Bourdieu's Algerian ethnography. The basic ideas of *Outline*—*habitus*,
doxa, and symbolic capital—have entered the mainstream of social
thought independently of the political and social contexts in which
these notions were originally developed. Thus Bourdieu's discussion
of Kabyle notions of time treats them as if they were a closed, self-
contained peasant society (Eickelman 1977: 40). It is hard to discern
that the ethnographic content of *Outline* derives from interviews in

261

resettlement camps in a war-torn society. The elegant invocation in "Participant Objectivation" of comparisons between Kabylia and Bourdieu's natal Béarn finds no echo in *Outline* or in *The Algerians*. The Kabyle (and sometimes Moroccan) proverbs and sayings that Bourdieu invokes are taken from collections that range over two centuries and that rarely derive from specific contexts, and Kabyle literacy in Arabic is passed over in silence. At its best, Bourdieu's Kabylia resembles nothing so much as an ahistorical cultural present of the sort found in Evans-Pritchard's *The Nuer*. This atemporality accords elegantly with his notion of *habitus* and perhaps with fashion in anthropological theory of an earlier era, but the disjuncture between his theoretical constructs and the ethnographic context on which Kabyle *habitus* is based calls into question the adequacy of this approach to ethnography.

Bourdieu's juxtaposition of his early life and subsequent ethnographic evocations of Béarn, and his more opaque accounts of his Kabyle ethnography at least partially evoke French precedents familiar to those interested in North Africa. One predecessor is Roger Thabault, a former director of native education in French Morocco and the author of *Mazières-en-Gatine* (1971), an account of how the introduction of national education transformed his village of origin. In the preface to his book, Thabault explains how he was inspired by his observations of the impact of French education on indigenous Moroccan society in the 1930s. Another predecessor was the distinguished French Arabist and former colonial official Jacques Berque (1910–95). Although Berque was born in Algeria in 1910, his autobiography, *Mémoire des deux rives* (1989) was written at his family's estate in Saint Julien-en-Born, and his narrative makes frequent shifts in perspective between the northern and southern shores of the Mediterranean. Thabault's book veers closer to Bourdieu's in spirit, in that explicit autobiography is confined strictly to the preface, whereas Berque, almost for the first time in his prolific career, is explicitly autobiographical.

Sociological Apperception

At its best, Bourdieu's "objectivation" brings to mind an image that Marcel Mauss often evoked in his lectures. Sociological apperception, Mauss argued, is training oneself so that one can board a Parisian tram—clearly a dated image from the early twentieth century—and treat as a puzzle, rather than assume that one knows, the relation of the people aboard it.

Sociological apperception is at the core of Bourdieu's notion of *habitus* and his approach to social thought. It marginalizes—except in stylized, timeless, and disembodied proverbs or short statements recorded on file cards—the perspective of villagers themselves. In a rhetorical sense, Reed-Danahay (this volume) argues, Bourdieu used his rural roots in France to "claim a sort of 'insider' status among Kabyle peasants, and to distance himself from others associated with the colonial power of France." Much like Ernest Gellner's writings on the Berbers of Morocco's High Atlas region, however, Bourdieu's Kabyle peasants were basically portrayed as out of time. Even *The Algerians* (1962), originally published in French in the last years of the war of independence and in a revised edition immediately after independence with a preface by Raymond Aron (1905–83)—an endorsement that must have meant a lot to Bourdieu in his early career—deals only peripherally with the displacement of the civil war on Kabyle society. Bourdieu's approach contrasts starkly to subsequent ethnographic accounts of Kabylia that indicate a highly complex war of wits between anthropologists advising the French military and Kabyle villagers, acting as if they supported the French (in order to receive arms and military training) but in practice aligned with the nationalists (Lacoste-Dujardin 1997).

Such complex representations did not fit into the mainstream of Bourdieu's conceptual apparatus. Bourdieu contributed to the issues of Mediterranean studies as they were conceived in the 1960s, focused on peasant societies, kinship, religiosity, honor and shame, and other topics, but as Mediterranean studies moved to other topics, Bourdieu abandoned these early regional concerns. Indeed the contributors to a recent major retrospective on Mediterranean studies (Albera, Blok, and Bromberger 2001) mention Bourdieu only in passing. Like Malinowski's Trobriands, Bourdieu's Kabylia is good to think with, although the substantive base of his Kabylia may be more ephemeral than Malinowski's Trobriands. The Algerian struggle for independence and the displacements of colonial society were certainly a "rupture" with traditional society, but Bourdieu might have gone beyond the claim of "rupture" to describe how the Kabyle reacted to the rapidly changing situations in which they lived.

Paul Silverstein (this volume) argues that "structural change may not be possible within the strictures of *habitus* as described by Bourdieu." Yet Silverstein examines Bourdieu and Sayad's notion of uprooting associated with colonial land expropriation and the resettlement of villagers in the 1950s. If Bourdieu's account of the Berber house offers a highly stylized representation of the past—a "nostalgic" representation—Silverstein points to Bourdieu's support of Berber cultural movements and for Berber intellectuals from the early 1980s onward. Bourdieu's "structural nostalgia" resonated well with the leaders of Kabyle organizations in France. Silverstein's account of the migrant associations (*tajmaat*s) reminds one of the vitality of Palestinian village associations. Villages erased from the map in 1948 still form the basis for strong mutual support groups.

Death notices and notices of dispute settlements in Israeli, Palestinian, and Jordanian newspapers indicate that "tradition," even if invented in the present and projected into the past, has concrete political implications for the present.

Beyond the French Intellectual Field

Bourdieu's response to an edited volume discussing his approach to sociology focused primarily on the French intellectual field, but by the 1970s non-French influences increasingly shaped his growing influence over Anglophone social anthropology. In 1976–77 I was a fellow at the Institute for Advanced Study in Princeton, where Bourdieu had been four years earlier. The staff mentioned how he often telephoned Paris several times daily, presumably to stay abreast of the micro-politics of Parisian academic politics and the *atelier* that he directed. Yet his 1972–73 stay at the Institute appears to have shaped significantly the re-presentation of *Esquisse* as *Outline*, which also recognizes at least briefly some parallel developments in American anthropology at the time (Eickelman 1979: 389).

Bourdieu's self-image was "to break both with theoreticism and with nearsighted empiricism" (Bourdieu 1993: 265). He refers also to the "highly improbable social trajectory that had led me from a remote village in a remote region of southwestern France to what was then the apex of the French educational system," a trajectory that predisposed him "to a particularly sharpened and critical intuition of the intellectual field" (Bourdieu 1993: 269). In shifting his sociological gaze onto different fields—art, museums, academic prestige, television, and gender—he consistently posed questions that engaged both the French intellectual field and an international public. Non-French interpreters of his work, he claims, "have offered a reading of it limited to its purely theoretical dimension," thus ignoring "its properly empirical dimension" as well as the contribution of his research to our knowledge of French society and, *mutatis mutandis*, of all modern societies" (Bourdieu 1993: 270). The present volume, drawing from American, French, and North African contributors, firmly relates Bourdieu's theoretical work to its North African empirical base. The contributors remind us how sensitive our work is to the historical contexts in which it is produced even when, as in Bourdieu's case, there is a concerted effort (in spite of the near-absence of reference to work in Kabylia) to "objectivize" the intellectual and academic fields in which he played such a leading role. Bourdieu may inadvertently reaffirm to us that even the most incisive sociologist can still fall victim to misrecognition of the contexts in which they interpret their own societies and those of others.

Works Cited

Albera, Dionigi, Anton Blok, and Christian Bromberger, eds. 2001. *L'Anthropologie de la Méditerranée*. Paris: Maisonneuve et Larose.

Berque, Jacques. 1989. *Mémoire des deux rives*. Paris: Seuil.

Bourdieu, Pierre. 1962 [1958]. *The Algerians*, trans. Alan C. M. Ross. Boston: Beacon Press.

———. 1972. *Esquisse d'une théorie de la pratique: précédé de trois études d'ethnologie kabyle*. Paris: Seuil.

———. 1977. *Outline of a Theory of Practice*, trans. Richard Nice. New York: Cambridge University Press.

———. 1993. Concluding Remarks: For a Sociogenetic Understanding of Intellectual Works. In *Bourdieu: Critical Perspectives*, ed. Craig Calhoun, Edward LiPuma, and Moishe Postone. pp. 263–75. Chicago: University of Chicago Press.

———. 2003. Participant Objectivation. *Journal of the Royal Anthropological Institute* 9 (2): 281–94.

Bourdieu, Pierre and Abdelmalek Sayad. 1964. *Le Déracinement: La Crise de l'agriculture traditionnelle en Algérie*. Paris: Editions de Minuit.

Brubaker, Rogers. 1993. Social Theory as Habitus. In *Bourdieu: Critical Perspectives*, ed. Craig Calhoun, Edward LiPuma, and Moishe Postone. pp. 212–34. Chicago: University of Chicago Press.

Calhoun, Craig. 1993. Habitus, Field, and Capital: The Question of Historical Specificity. In *Bourdieu: Critical Perspectives*, ed. Craig Calhoun, Edward LiPuma, and Moishe Postone. pp. 61–88. Chicago: University of Chicago Press.

Colonna, Fanny. 1975. *Instituteurs algériens, 1883–1939*. Paris: Presses de la Fondation Nationale des Sciences Politiques.

Eickelman, Dale F. 1977. Time in a Complex Society: A Moroccan Example. *Ethnology* 16 (1): 39–55.

———. 1979. The Political Economy of Meaning. *American Ethnologist* 6 (2): 386–93.

Elias, Norbert. 1996. *The Germans: Power Struggles and the Development of Habitus in the Nineteenth and Twentieth Centuries*, trans. Eric Dunning and Stephen Mennell. Cambridge: Polity Press.

Geertz, Clifford. 1968. *Islam Observed*. New Haven: Yale University Press.

Gellner, Ernest. 1969. *Saints of the Atlas*. London: Weidenfeld and Nicholson.

Goody, Jack. 1977. *The Domestication of the Savage Mind*. Cambridge: Cambridge University Press.

Lacoste-Dujardin, Camille. 1997. *Opération oiseau bleu: Des Kabyles, des ethnologues et la guerre d'Algérie*. Paris: La Découverte.

Leach, E. R. 1954. *Political Systems of Highland Burma: A Study of Kachin Social Structure*. Boston: Beacon Press.

Lemert, Charles C., ed. 1981. *French Sociology: Rupture and Renewal Since 1968*. New York: Columbia University Press.

Silverstein, Paul A. 2004. *Algeria in France: Transpolitics, Race, and Nation*. Bloomington: Indiana University Press.

Thabault, Roger. 1971 [1945]. *Education and Change in a Village Community: Mazières-en-Gâtine, 1848–1914*, trans. Peter Treger. London: Routledge & Kegan Paul.

SOURCE ACKNOWLEDGMENTS

Chapter 1, "The Phantom of Dispossession: From *The Uprooting* to *The Weight of the World*" by Fanny Colonna, originally appeared as "Le spectre de la dépossession, du déracinement à la misère du monde" in *Annuaire de l'Afrique du Nord* 40 (2002).

Chapter 2, "The Proverbial Bourdieu: *Habitus* and the Politics of Representation in the Ethnography of Kabylia" by Jane E. Goodman, originally appeared in *American Anthropologist* 105, no. 4 (2003).

Chapter 4, "Of Rooting and Uprooting: Kabyle *Habitus*, Domesticity, and Structural Nostalgia" by Paul A. Silverstein, originally appeared in *Ethnography* 5, no. 4 (2004).

Chapter 5, "Phenomenology and Ethnography: On Kabyle *Habitus* in the Work of Pierre Bourdieu" by Abdellah Hammoudi, originally appeared as "Phénoménologie et ethnographie: À propos de l'habitus kabyle chez Pierre Bourdieu" in *L'Homme* 184 (2007).

Fanny Colonna is a research director emeritus at the Centre National de la Recherche Scientifique in France and an emeritus affiliate of the Ecole des Hautes Etudes en Sciences Sociales in Paris where she currently directs a program on the traces of the colonial moment in North Africa. She is the author of numerous works on Algeria including *Les Versets de l'invincibilité: Permanences et changements religieux dans l'Algérie contemporaine* (Presses de Sciences Politiques, 1995) and *Savants paysans: Elements d'histoire sociale sur l'Algérie rurale* (Office des Publications Universitaires, Algiers, 1987). She has also published *Récits de la province égyptienne: Une ethnographie sud/sud* (Sindbad, 2004) and *Le Meunier, les moines et le bandit: Un siècle de vie quotidienne dans l'Aurès, XIXeme–XXeme* (Sindbad, 2009).

Dale F. Eickelman is the Ralph and Richard Lazarus Professor of Anthropology and Human Relations at Dartmouth College. He is the author or editor of numerous publications including *Muslim Politics*, 2nd ed., with James Piscatori (Princeton, 2004); *Public Islam and the Common Good*, with Armando Salvatore (Brill, 2004); *New Media in the Muslim World*, 2nd ed., with Jon Anderson (Indiana, 2003); *The Middle East and Central Asia: An Anthropological Approach*, 4th ed. (Prentice Hall, 2002); and *Knowledge and Power in Morocco: The Education of a Twentieth-Century Notable* (Princeton, 1985). He is currently relationship coordinator for the Dartmouth College–American University of Kuwait Project.

Jane E. Goodman is an associate professor of communication and culture at Indiana University. She is the author of *Berber Culture on the World Stage: From Village to Video* (Indiana, 2005). Her work has appeared in journals including *American Anthropologist, American Ethnologist, Journal of Linguistic Anthropology,* and *Journal of North African Studies.* Her current ethnographic research concerns Algerian vernacular theater as a pedagogical vehicle used to model new practices of citizenship and civic engagement.

Abdellah Hammoudi is a professor of anthropology; the Bayard Dodge Professor of Near Eastern Studies; and the director of the Institute for Transregional Study of the Contemporary Middle East, North Africa, and Central Asia at Princeton University. His books include *The Victim and Its Masks: An Essay on Sacrifice and Masquerade in the Maghreb* (Chicago, 1993), *Master and Disciple: The Cultural Foundations of Moroccan Authoritarianism* (Chicago, 1997), and *A Season in Mecca: Narrative of a Pilgrimage* (Hill and Wang, 2006).

Deborah Reed-Danahay is a professor of anthropology at SUNY–Buffalo. She is the author of *Education and Identity in Rural France: The Politics of Schooling* (Cambridge, 1996) and *Locating Bourdieu* (Indiana, 2005). She is the editor of *Auto/Ethnography: Rewriting the Self and the Social* (Berg, 1997) and *Citizenship, Political Engagement, and Belonging: Immigrants in Europe and the United States* (with Caroline Brettell, Rutgers, 2008). She has published numerous articles and book chapters on the ethnography of rural France, education in France and the European Union, autobiography and ethnography, and has written extensively on the work of Pierre Bourdieu. Her current interests, in addition to social theory, include the Vietnamese diaspora in the United States and France.

Paul A. Silverstein is an associate professor of anthropology at Reed College. A 2008 Carnegie Scholar, he is the author of *Algeria in France: Transpolitics, Race, and Nation* (Indiana, 2004) and coeditor of *Memory and Violence in the Middle East and North Africa* (Indiana, 2006). He is also an editor of the journal *Middle East Report*. His recent ethnographic research focuses on the intersection of Amazigh activism, land rights, and racial politics in southeastern Morocco.

The Moroccan Soul: French Education, Colonial Ethnology, and Muslim Resistance, 1912–1956
Spencer D. Segalla

Silence Is Death: The Life and Work of Tahar Djaout
Julija Šukys

The French Colonial Mind, Volume 1: Mental Maps of Empire and Colonial Encounters
Edited and with an introduction by Martin Thomas

The French Colonial Mind, Volume 2: Violence, Military Encounters, and Colonialism
Edited and with an introduction by Martin Thomas

Beyond Papillon: The French Overseas Penal Colonies, 1854–1952
Stephen A. Toth

Madah-Sartre: The Kidnapping, Trial, and Conver(sat/s)ion of Jean-Paul Sartre and Simone de Beauvoir
Written and translated by Alek Baylee Toumi
With an introduction by James D. Le Sueur

To order or obtain more information on these or other University of Nebraska Press titles, visit nebraskapress.unl.edu.

www.ingramcontent.com/pod-product-compliance
Lightning Source LLC
Chambersburg PA
CBHW071843270326
41929CB00013B/2091